HOW TO
HUG A PORCUPINE

Dealing With Toxic
and
Difficult to Love
Personalities

Dr. John Lewis Lund

HOW TO HUG A PORCUPINE
Dealing With Toxic
and Difficult to Love Personalities

Dr. John L. Lund

Copyright © 1999 by Dr. John L. Lund
Published by The Communications Company
Cover Design by Kim Budd of the Paschal Budd Design Group
Photography by Brent Budd
Artwork by Nicole Lund

For permission to reproduce any part of this book contact
Dr. John L. Lund
via e-mail: drlund@drlund.com

Find us on the World Wide Web at
http://www.drlund.com

First Edition 1999
7th printing, May 2004

ISBN 1-891114-34-4

ACKNOWLEDGMENTS

Is it possible to be grateful for toxic people? They are a refiner's fire. One can learn much by way of patience, long-suffering, self-protection, and self-mastery both because of the toxic and in spite of them.

There are those who have helped in significant ways to produce this book. *Pam* and *Alex Martinez* have given financial and moral support. Thank you.

Elen McConnell, I have dubbed an "editing angel." She continues to appear and work her magic in moments of need.

My daughter, *Heidi Savage,* has brilliant and necessary insights.

It is also a wonderful thing that my son, Rob, is married to an English major, *Marie Lund*, who has been exceptionally helpful and patient in correcting and organizing this manuscript.

Donna Root is a counseling intern and has served as a valuable sounding board.

Thank you ladies.

Bonnie, my wife, is an exceptional human being. Because of her loving, unselfish, supportive nature, she has literally reinvented herself as a publishing expert to aid me in this project. Taking college classes in everything from QuarkXpress to Adobe Illustrator, she has become remarkably savvy in the publishing world of Macintosh computers and software. This book would not have happened without her many contributions. Thank you, Bonnie, from the bottom of my heart.

If you were wondering who the creative people were who designed the cover and did the art work, they were *Kim and Brent Budd from Paschal Budd Design Group*. Thanks.

Thank you *Norman Nelson* for the artistic rendering of "The Knight Surrounded By Porcupines."

The views herein expressed are mine, and I alone am responsible for what has been written. Every effort has been made to modify the names, places, and circumstances to avoid identifying the true characters of these real life stories.

Dedicated to those who don't want to be toxic and to those who find themselves surrounded by "emotional porcupines."

HOW TO HUG A PORCUPINE
DEALING WITH TOXIC
AND DIFFICULT TO LOVE PERSONALITIES

TABLE OF CONTENTS

CHAPTER ONE

WHAT IS AN
EMOTIONAL PORCUPINE?

While researching this very book, I was interrupted by an emergency phone call. I heard the frantic voice of a man who pleaded to meet with me for counseling. His was a story of a ten-year marriage and four children. His wife's parents had just arrived from out of state at the wife's request with a rental truck. It was their intent to take their daughter and four grandchildren back with them. In desperation, the husband implored his wife to meet with me as a counselor. In a matter of minutes, they were in my office. The mother and father-in-law were loading the truck while I was counseling with the couple. I met with them first individually and then together.

"Tell me," I said to the wife, "what is so frustrating about your marriage that you are willing to pack up and leave?"

What follows are her exact statements interspersed with tears and soul-rending sobs:

"He is so critical of everything I do, or wear, or cook...He yells at me for the stupidest things...I can't

1

even hold a map right...he is so controlling...he has to comment on everything I'm doing or not doing...he is always mad at me for something...he is so intense...he snaps at me and I can never have an opinion of my own. He is always angry at me...I can't take it anymore...I called my parents and asked them to come and get me. I've tried to talk to him, but he discounts everything I say...he has to be right...he is so domineering...every time I attempt to express myself he shuts me off with rude remarks...Well, I'm not going to take it anymore. It's not just me; he does the same things with the kids...I can't be criticized anymore...I feel no love for him, only resentment. Well, I guess I do feel some love for him or I wouldn't be so hurt,...but not enough to stay in this marriage."

What more could be said as a testimonial of the negative effects of living with an emotional porcupine? This man's criticisms were like the quills on a porcupine's back. They wounded all who came in contact with him. Porcupines represent the perfect metaphor for toxic and difficult-to-love personalities. Their caustic quills make it impossible to embrace them. Much like their cousins, the skunks, porcupines live an unapproachable life.

The relationship described above could not survive the constant barrage of nonacceptance messages. The husband had adopted constant criticism of his wife and children as normal behavior. When normal is also toxic, the relationship falls apart. Tragically, not everyone that is exposed to the lessons of life learns from them. Many toxic people just go on afflicting the next relationship with the same old toxic pattern. This man could have learned a lesson from the school of hard knocks. He could have learned that unabated and improperly given criticism is a forerunner to divorce. As with all toxins, it is only a matter of the amount and time until the immune system of the receiver is overcome. Acceptance, affection, and appreciation were poisoned by continued exposure to the toxic quills of his constant criticism.

WHAT IS A TOXIC BEHAVIOR?

A toxic behavior is any word, deed, or action which detracts from you being your best self or hinders others from becoming their best selves.

Ironically, many toxic personalities are well-meaning. They sincerely believe they are acting in a loving *way* and that the end justifies the *means.* Frequently these people send the message, "I am doing this for your own good," or "some day you will thank me for this."

Compounding the issue is that there are times when people are required to criticize, reprove, or punish. *The difference between toxic and nontoxic behavior is in the APPROACH. HOW they deal with the negative is the issue. The MANNER in which they treat others is what defines them as toxic.* These people either minimize the detrimental effects of their negative approach upon the other person or justify it as necessary. They fail to recognize the magnitude of their negativity. It not only attacks the issue or behavior, but the very essence of the person. In their minds, the intensity of their negativity is appropriate. They lack a fundamental sense of proportionality. They use a twenty pound hammer when a five pound hammer would do. Most of them lack the knowledge and the skills of positive reinforcement. They assume the negative is the only viable approach open to them.

TOXICITY COMES IN DEGREES

There is a fine line between toxic behaviors and a toxic personality. Everyone may recognize a toxic characteristic in themselves. Even a "good relationship" has times when unkind and hurtful things are said or done. However, there is a difference between a good relationship and an unhealthy one. There are two factors to examine when considering toxicity. The first is the magnitude of the behaviors. The second, is the frequency with which they are used. Imagine that the severity of the toxic behavior could be compared to porcupine quills with varying degrees of poison in them. Contradicting a single statement made by a loved one would be a less significant toxic behavior. However, physically slugging someone, even once, qualifies the hitter as a toxic person. The frequency of these behaviors, can be compared to a bee's sting. Normal bees sting once. An occasional sting is survivable. Killer bees inflict multiple stings which can be lethal. There are killer bees who sting repeatedly until the victim is incapacitated or dead. It is the same with toxic personalities. They repeat toxic behaviors until they immobilize others around them.

Most toxic people view themselves as helpful. They refuse to admit they are toxic. In other words, they live in denial. *They* are not hypercritical; *others* are hypersensitive. *Their* behavior is normal in their eyes and *other people* are just overreacting. Even when confronted with the truth of their blatant excesses of toxic behavior, they will persist in viewing the "real problem" as the inability of others to handle the truth. The irony is that these people feel they should be appreciated, and not resented, for their toxic insights. After all, they are "just being honest," or "truthful," or "observant."

4

WHAT IS A TOXIC PERSONALITY?

The fine line between a toxic behavior and a toxic personality is crossed when these behaviors become part of an individual's daily interaction. Toxic personalities come in many varieties. Some are gruff. Some are pleasant. Some seem indifferent. They can appear affable, but you still walk away emotionally wounded.

A toxic personality is anyone who adopts manipulative behaviors and attempts to control others in selfish ways. These people use caustic methods to obtain conformity to their expectations. They criticize, nag, complain, or withhold love and acceptance as a reward or punishment. They threaten, coerce, and use force to get their way. Toxic people are emotional blackmailers. They are not above using guilt or fear to accomplish their purposes. They hold others hostage to their selfish whims and wishes.

A toxic personality is one you *cannot* please. He or she is incapable of giving total acceptance. YOU WILL NEVER BE GOOD ENOUGH. They dangle acceptance like a carrot on a string. The person who wants to be accepted and appreciated can never quite reach the carrot because toxic people only give partial acceptance. They promise a reward which is often denied and earned privileges are never secure.

Frequently toxic people send the message, "I am unhappy. If you would do this 'certain thing,' or behave in this 'certain way,' then I will no longer be unhappy." However the true message is, "I *won't* be happy. I'll probably find something else which will make me unhappy, and I will have to criticize you about that also." Their mantra is,

> "I will be happy when everyone does everything I want them to do in the way I want it done. My way is the best way or the right way."

Remember, you cannot please a toxic person. You cannot make him or her happy and you cannot even keep him or her from being unhappy.

There are many toxic traits. Not truly being able to give full acceptance, however, is the most common thread running through the fabric of all those who wear the cloak of toxic personality. They do not seem to be able to give a complete compliment and let it stand alone. Even when someone else pays them a compliment it cannot be accepted. Instead, they find a critical thing to say in the name of balance, or fairness, or of being honest.

In addition, they have a very difficult time accepting blame. This is why they always have to be right or have others agree with them. There is often a preoccupation with finding out who is responsible. Of course, nothing is ever *their* fault.

Another trait of many toxic personalities is to change the rules. It is consistent with the toxic personality to be inconsistent. Just when it appears that acceptance is within reach, they jerk it away. They have endless lists of expectations. Just as you seem to meet all of the requirements, they change the items on the list. They tend to be controlling, very judgmental of others, highly critical, and manipulative. They are constantly creating a crisis. They feed on other people's faults and shortcomings.

It is not uncommon for the toxic person to pick out a "favored one." This keeps hope alive in the hearts of others that some day they may be a "favored one." Some day they may be "enough." The most devastating trait of the toxic personality is the ability, consciously or unconsciously, to keep hope for love and acceptance alive. At times toxic people can be very wonderful and even loving. However, their capacity to turn on a dime, to change from Dr. Jekyll to Mr. Hyde, keeps them emotionally unsafe.

Toxic people seem to be aware of their power to keep others seeking for their approval. When someone stops trying to please them, that person becomes the object of rejection. Why? Because the person who stopped trying to "please" took away their power. This is frightening to those who crave control. Often, under the guise of perfectionism, they justify their control of others. Additionally, they sincerely believe it is in other's best interest to do things their way.

On one hand, the toxic person holds out acceptance as a bribe, while on the other hand he uses rejection as a method of control. This sends a message to others, "Beware, or you could be the next person put on the black list of rejection." They also have a difficult time forgiving others. Why? Because withholding forgiveness is one more means of control. Along with guilt, forgiveness can be pulled out of the closet and used as a club to bring conformity to the wishes of the toxic.

OTHER EXAMPLES OF TOXIC BEHAVIORS AND ATTITUDES

1. Constant criticism, fault finding, questioning, inappropriate and improperly given criticism
2. Perfectionism; unrealistic and unreasonable expectations of self or others
3. Manipulating others by guilt, ridicule, and rejection
4. Being judgmental
5. An inclination to reject solutions without adequately evaluating them
6. Failure to respect the personal space of others
7. Mocking, scorning, and belittling others
8. Attacking the worth of another by name-calling, i.e., "dumb," or "stupid," etc.
9. Embarrassing others in front of friends, family or strangers

10. Sending persistent messages of incompetence or inadequacy
11. Constant direction giving to others
12. Ceaseless preaching
13. An unwillingness to acknowledge the legitimate progress of self or of others
14. An inability to show understanding, empathy, or compassion for other people's feelings and views
15. When acknowledging an accomplishment of another, frequently adding "but" to the end of the compliment (known as a "Trailing Barb")
16. Not seeing or recognizing what *has* been done, only what *remains* undone
17. Habitually playing the devil's advocate; defending the opposite point of view
18. Easily offended by others
19. Making others feel obligated by guilt to please them
20. An unwillingness to negotiate
21. An inability or unwillingness to truly be grateful
22. Hypersensitivity to being criticized themselves
23. An inability or unwillingness to send messages of adequacy
24. Incessantly contradicting and correcting others
25. Constantly interrupting and correcting the conversation of others:
    a. their grammar, choice of words, ability to explain
    b. the accuracy of their story-telling
    c. dates, times, and contents of events
26. Consistently being argumentative
27. Sending a preponderance of nonacceptance messages
28. A pattern of constant complaining
29. Frequent reference to the past failings of others
30. Regretting; a persistent pattern of focusing on lost opportunities in the past
31. Martyr; no one truly appreciates their efforts
32. Consistently pointing out the "unfairness" of life
33. Mad, angry, and upset most of the time

34. Being rude, insensitive, curt and abrupt
35. Sarcasm
36. "Parenting" equals (spouses or co-workers), telling them what they "should," "need," and "ought" to do
37. Blatant disrespect for the opinions and attitudes of others
38. Feeling the need to control others
39. Feeling justified in hurting the feelings of others
40 Withholding love, acceptance, affection, or appreciation
41. Fomenting a crisis to keep people stirred up and on guard
42. An unwillingness to forgive self or others
43. A consistent negative attitude toward life
44. A pattern of yelling, screaming, swearing, cursing, or verbal abuse
45. Physical abuse
46. Sexual abuse
47. Constantly threatening divorce or abandonment
48. Making threats of killing self or others
49. Preoccupied with evil, wrong, and negative behaviors
50. False praise or an inability to give a sincere compliment
51. Self-righteous, "holier-than-thou" attitude
52. Others are always worried about hurting their feelings
53. Others are always "walking on eggs" around them
54. Co-dependency

Everyone exhibits toxic behavior at times. However, being able to apologize and accept responsibility for one's behavior is a healthy reaction. Not being willing to apologize and transferring responsibility for behavior to others is one of the signs of a toxic personality. The fundamental attitude of giving oneself permission to continuously act in toxic ways distinguishes a toxic personality from a singular toxic event. The idea that one is justified in acting in inappropriate ways is the core belief of most toxic people. They believe the other person deserves this type of treatment.

WHAT EMPOWERS EMOTIONAL PORCUPINES?

The answer is the desire and efforts of others to please them. All toxic people share a narcissistic characteristic of being exploitive. This means they take advantage of others to achieve their own selfish ends, regardless of the best interest of others. All of their actions are predicated on other people pleasing them. Often it is a grandiose sense of self-importance and a lack of empathy that blinds them to the needs of others to be well treated. The best word to describe a toxic person is selfish. He or she is at the center of a universe that exists to please them. There is a difference between appropriate and inappropriate selfishness. Seeking to become your healthiest and best self is an appropriate form of selfishness. Wanton disregard for others becoming their best selves and exploiting them for selfish purposes is by definition an inappropriate selfishness. It is toxic to others.

SEEKING FOR OTHERS TO BE THEIR BEST SELVES, BUT DOING SO IN UNHEALTHY WAYS, IS ALSO TOXIC. The issue is HOW they go about helping other people. Whether noble goals and toxic ways or ignoble goals and toxic ways, they are bound and determined to retain the unhealthy approach regardless of how if affects others emotionally.

In dealing with a toxic person, remember their rules are

> *"Please me and do it my way, which is the right way,"* or *"my way is really in your best interest, whether you agree with me or not."*

Their rules are usually more important than the quality of the relationship. Others will be partially rewarded if they do what is expected or they will be punished if they don't. It doesn't matter that the expectations of toxic people are unreasonable or unrealistic. Their expectation is that you will do it their way, PERIOD!

Once someone agrees that pleasing toxic people is the governing value of their lives, they are hooked. They are in a difficult situation. They cannot possibly do everything to please a toxic person. It would require them to become mind readers. It means they would have to think and act precisely the way the toxic person would want them to in every circumstance. They would have to possess a perfect memory of everything that makes the toxic happy or unhappy and then control situations and people over whom they have no control. It can't be done. No one can control the circumstances and situations completely enough to please the toxic person.

All frustration comes from unmet expectations. There is no such thing as someone who is frustrated who did not have an expectation. To try to please the toxic person is to live in constant frustration. It is the expectation to please the toxic person that causes the frustration since they can never be pleased.

Toxic personalities are fearful of losing power. They are afraid people will stop trying to do things their way. Once toxic people recognize, consciously or not, that another is committed to pleasing them, the pattern is set in cement. They cannot let others be "pleasing enough." If others are "pleasing enough" it may remove the motivation to chase the carrot of acceptance.

Toxic people cannot fully give you love. When they give love, it is a reward. It is a means of controlling people. They fear that unconditional love will result in the loss of control. This is not always a conscious fear, nonetheless, it is a consistent one. They cannot let the other person be adequate. Most toxic people believe they themselves are not sufficient, so how could anyone else be enough?

The "seekers of approval" believe that with a little more effort, they can achieve acceptance. But no, the carrot is always pulled away. Anything short of perfection is unacceptable. With a toxic person, the agenda is constantly changing in order to keep other people off balance. The focus is always on what *hasn't* been done, not on appreciating what has been accomplished.

Some toxic people manifest their need to control by becoming "overpleasers." They knock themselves out in a desperate attempt to OBLIGATE other people to them.

"It took me three days to recover from preparing Thanksgiving dinner for the family,"

This particular approach to control manifests itself through providing things or services. It is the workaholic who can say, "You owe me," or "Look at everything I've done for you," or "...given you." This type of toxic personality becomes the martyr, the one that no one ever appreciates. In their mind, if they were appreciated other people would be willing to do things the way the toxic person wanted them done.

When the inappropriate behaviors of toxic people are pointed out, they quickly move to an emotional crisis in order to divert attention from themselves. If a crisis does not exist, they will create one. They always seem to be offended. Therefore, the family or associates of toxic people live in fear of antagonizing them.

Toxic people are experts in transferring responsibility and blame for all problems to others. In addition to your not being "enough," not doing the job well enough, not rich enough, not thin enough, not good-looking enough, not a good enough provider, nor housekeeper, nor parent, nor human being, the toxic person feels the need, or divine right, to point out your flaws, shortcomings, weaknesses, errors, mistakes, or lack of perfection. *By definition a toxic person is one who cannot or will not give you the validation that you want.*

CHAPTER TWO

IS IT A PORCUPINE OR A MUSKRAT?

HEALTHY VERSUS UNHEALTHY BEHAVIORS

That which defines a porcupine is its quills. Muskrats, on the other hand, have no quills. Muskrat fur was once highly prized for its softness. Women of high social status would wear the furs around their necks. To date, no one has spotted a socialite wearing a porcupine "pelt." Ironically, both muskrats and porcupines are rodents. One is toxic, the other is not. Toxic behaviors are quills which wound; nontoxic behaviors don't.

Toxic behaviors have to do with "how" things are done. It is the "way" one sets about to accomplish the objective that defines it as healthy versus unhealthy. The issue is not just motive or intent, but application. Emotional porcupines try to achieve healthy outcomes in unhealthy ways.

How would you know if you had picked up a muskrat or a porcupine? There is a simple pragmatic test. If you got hurt, you would know that you had picked up the porcupine and not a muskrat. It is the extended quills of the porcupine that are the problem. They don't seem to be a problem for the porcupine, only for those who want to embrace them.

AN EMOTIONALLY HEALTHY PERSON

How many times do you have to be wounded by a porcupine's quills before you take action to protect yourself? How do you live with a porcupine? It starts with recognizing what constitutes a toxic porcupine personality. Perhaps this is best accomplished through contrast with what comprises an emotionally *healthy* person.

I.   ACCEPTING RESPONSIBILITY

An emotionally healthy person accepts responsibility for his own happiness and unhappiness and owns his expectations and behaviors. He or she is able to say "I was wrong," "It was my fault," or "I'm sorry," and be sincere about it. This does not mean that emotionally healthy people never get upset, frustrated, or annoyed. It means that when they are at fault for overreacting they can own it.

Unhealthy people don't own their behavior. Toxic people are constantly blaming others for their unhappiness. The world they live in is an "if only," and "it could have been" world. They are experts in transferring blame. If they are wrong, they claim it is because someone else gave them false information or they will define their behavior in such a way as to justify it. They weren't really wrong. It only appeared that way.

OWNING YOUR ATTITUDES

Charles was under the pressure of a deadline. JoAnn was chewing her fingernails.

Charles snapped, "You know that irritates me! Are you doing that on purpose to upset me? Do you know how many germs live under your fingernails?"

"I'm sorry," JoAnn responded.

"No you're not," Charles said, "If you were you wouldn't have done it."

The conversation left JoAnn feeling she had disappointed Charles one more time. In her mind, this was further evidence that she was inadequate. Charles had succeeded in making JoAnn feel as if she were responsible for his unhappiness.

The emotionally healthy response for Charles would have been for him to say, "I'm sorry, JoAnn. Chewing your fingernails does bother me, but I have no right to be upset with you. I am under pressure right now and I'm not fit to deal with anyone. This is not about you, your fingernails, or anything else. The truth is that when I get under pressure, I have no tolerance. I'll have to work on that."

II. FORGIVING SELF AND OTHERS

Another characteristic of an emotionally healthy person is the ability to forgive self and others. He or she does not hold grudges nor withhold loving behaviors.

In contrast, the emotionally *unhealthy* person is a radio station constantly broadcasting messages of nonacceptance and inadequacy to others. Since all humans make mistakes, toxic people want to use the reality of mistakes as an emotional club, constantly beating others up. By not forgiving, they can call upon that emotional club at will. They want to "brow-beat" others into submission. They want others to admit they are "less-than" or "not-as-good-as" they think they are.

Toxic people are oppressive. They are constantly putting people down. Not forgiving others is a form of "you owe me." It's a way of keeping a person in emotional debt. The toxic fear they won't be loved just as they are. They are not always conscious of their motives. They believe the only way to be loved is for them to be in a position of power or control. Holding a grudge falsely empowers unhealthy people who callously justify withholding love, affection, or approval to remain in control.

NEVER FORGIVEN

This is an amazing story of an eighty-nine-year old mother and her sixty-nine-year old daughter, Elaine. Of the eight children, only Elaine was willing to care for the mother. As a teenager she was wild and headstrong and the mother systematically began to withhold love from her. Those turbulent teenage years ended with the daughter getting pregnant and running away. Now at sixty-nine she was married to a wealthy man. They had a wonderful marriage of nearly fifty years and they had raised a healthy family of successful children who were well established. Elaine, however, was never able to obtain her mother's forgiveness. All the apologies, all the letters, were never able to heal the wound in the mother's heart.

The eighty-nine-year old mother consented to live with Elaine instead of going to a rest home. The daughter had high hopes of finally atoning for the sins of her youth and of receiving her mother's love, acceptance, and forgiveness. But such was not to be. When Elaine offered to take her mother to the store, or to have her hair done, or to just go for a ride to visit the other children, the mother refused to go. The moment Elaine committed to go with her husband or children, the mother would assert her need to go somewhere else. Elaine would then change everyone's schedule to accommodate the unreasonable and unrealistic mother. This was done to the great irritation of the husband and grandchildren.

When Elaine would go with her husband or children, the mother would call her other children and complain she was being held a prisoner or abandoned. This would be followed by a myriad of phone calls to the husband. They would ask him why the mother wasn't being well treated and why wouldn't they take her where she wanted to go?

When Elaine offered to fix a special meal daily just for the mother with her peculiar eating needs, the mother refused to eat and then called some of her grandchildren and complained she was being denied proper food. She felt she was being starved to death and intimated that Elaine was after the inheritance. Nothing could have been further from the truth because of the substantial wealth of the daughter and her husband. Phone calls would ensue and accusations would be repeated. Finally the husband had endured enough and declared to his wife that either the eighty-nine-year old mother would need to leave the home or he would. The wife was torn between her husband of nearly fifty years and her desire for her mother's approval.

As the counselor, I helped the family work out an acceptable schedule which involved the other children taking turns being responsible for food and transportation on different days of the week. I also convinced Elaine that she would *never* receive her mother's forgiveness or approval. She should let go of trying to please her. I counseled her to define for herself what a reasonable person would do and then to live up to her *own* set of expectations which did not require the approval of her mother.

The eighty-nine-year old mother died about six years later and never did forgive, love, accept, or appreciate Elaine. However, the daughter had the peace of mind that she had done all that she could to be a loving person. It is the expectation for approval that empowers toxic people to continue abusing the seekers of approval. The eighty-nine-year old could never forgive the daughter for running away as a teenager and the humiliation she felt because her daughter had a child out of wedlock. Once Elaine recognized her mother's toxic personality and truly let go of the expectation to please the unpleasable, she had peace restored to her life.

III. Making A Plan

An emotionally healthy person makes a plan to move ahead in becoming his or her highest and best self in spite of difficult circumstances.

By not having a plan, toxic people can keep themselves and others from succeeding. If they were to lay out a realistic plan there would be the possibility it could be achieved. By not having a realistic plan, unhealthy people guarantee their right to remain critical and negative. It preserves the status quo and allows them to stay in control of the world around them.

JANE HAD NO PLAN AND NO APPRECIATION

Jane was divorced and had three children. Her husband ran off with another woman and didn't pay child support. She had real problems. She was constantly complaining to anyone who would listen about what a "rat" she had for a husband. She had an attitude that was negative, envious, and "poor me." She felt that life was over. She was the victim. She controlled others by making it impossible to fix her life. No matter what anyone did, it was not enough. Her parents helped her financially. Her brothers and sisters provided care for her children. Her grandmother cleaned the house and ran errands for her. It was never enough.

Jane traded happiness for sympathy. She believed there could be no true happiness for her. Therefore, she lived in a state of regret and complaint. There is a proverb which states, "Pain in life is inevitable, but misery is a choice." She preferred misery because it allowed her to live in self-pity. It is a truism that "misery enjoys company."

When Jane met with a counselor, all she wanted to do was to complain about how unfair society was and bemoan her circumstances. When the counselor suggested that she stop complaining, she broke into tears and shouted, "That's easy for you to say! You don't have my life!" She did not want solutions. She wanted sympathy. She did not want responsibility for her life. She wanted others to take over and make it right.

The counselor persisted. "Jane, there are only two constructive things you can do with the past. First, you can learn from it; second, you can forgive yourself and others. Everything else you do with the past takes you in a negative direction and an emotionally unhealthy condition. Your frustration in being unfairly treated, abandoned, and victimized is understandable. *You were wronged!* But complaining about it, being endlessly depressed about it, doesn't change the past. We cannot change the past. The real tragedy is that you were a victim in the past, but now you are letting the past rob you of your todays and your tomorrows. Yes, life is hard. But, you are refusing to take control of your life as it is now. Let's make a plan, to go from where you are to a better place. Stop complaining. Stop being offended and envious. It takes a tremendous amount of emotional energy to maintain a negative attitude. I'm sure it is part of the reason you are tired all the time.

"For this next week, I want you to focus on being positive. Your parents love you. Go to them this week and tell them how much you appreciate their financial support. Don't apologize and don't complain; just be appreciative. Go to your brothers and sisters and tell them how much their help means to you and how much you love them for helping you. Go to your Grandmother and give her a big hug. Tell her of your appreciation. Don't apologize for your circumstances; they understand.

"Make a plan to take charge of your life, to go from where you are to a better state. Currently your children have been abandoned by a father whose selfishness knows no bounds. He has failed to provide and to protect them, both emotionally and financially. Don't join him. Don't abandon your children just because you have failed to make a plan. Don't make them suffer the loss of both parents. Take charge of your life. There is a great deal of love in you, Jane. Find a way to let it out. Focus on loving the children and of making the best of a bad circumstance. There is so much good in you and in your children. Make a plan to go from where you are to a better place."

Jane did just that. She made a plan. She returned to college and has taken control of her life. Those who love Jane are also relieved. Her willingness to face life with a better attitude supports a more positive interaction for all the members of the family.

Most toxic people cannot make a personal progress plan for their own individual lives short of perfection. They have no problem making a plan for everyone else, however. In order for them to be happy, everyone in their circle of influence must live in accordance with their expectations. Not only do they require that "everyone" live a certain way in order for them to profess happiness, but "everything" needs to be right. They crave perfect order or nigh unto it. When this happens they are pleased; everyone rejoices. But, alas, it doesn't last long. Someone, somewhere will do something to displease them. Because people and things are generally out of order most of the time, toxic people are constantly unhappy. The temporary acceptance they grant is withdrawn and will not be restored until everything is done "how" and "when" they want it done. Because peace is a high value for most people, those who are toxic use the lack of peace to manipulate others. Peace can only exist when everything and everyone is under the control of the toxic. Putting themselves in the center of everyone's universe is about an unhealthy form of control.

TOXIC PEOPLE ARE EMOTIONALLY UNHEALTHY

Toxic people want freedom to criticize anyone, anywhere because of their special insights. They may assume a role of superior position, wisdom, knowledge, power, or authority. They see themselves as being more responsible than others yet the very reasons they give for criticizing others, they will not apply to themselves. There is a big-time double standard. They are highly critical of others, but resist any negative feedback directed toward them.

There is a fundamental negativity associated with the toxic. It is as if they were suffering from the "ailment of

21

pessimism." They feel victimized and grant themselves the right to be dependent on others for their happiness instead of making a realistic plan for self-improvement. They cast a spirit of negativism upon the plans of others. Fleeting periods of peace are shattered by their fault finding, sarcasm, and character assassinations. As nice, as pleasant, as wonderful, and as good as they may be at times, their negativity erases the positive feelings that others want to have toward them. The toxics want the good they do to compensate for their negativity. It doesn't and it won't. Regarding emotional porcupines, BEWARE! Porcupines come in many shapes and sizes.

CHAPTER THREE

PORCUPINES COME
IN ALL SHAPES AND SIZES

Porcupines are found in nearly every part of the world. There are emotional porcupines in nearly every family, school, and workplace. They may be your boss, your neighbors, or your in-laws. Everyone will encounter a few emotional porcupines during their lifetime. You will know you are involved in a porcupine relationship if there is a consistent pattern of unkind words and behaviors directed toward you.

Some species of porcupines are more aggressive than others. Some are blatantly obvious. Others are extremely well camouflaged. The same is true of toxic personalities. There are those who are universally toxic and some who are only selectively toxic. In addition, there are those that are dangerous only in specific situations. Knowing which variety you are dealing with is an important key to protecting yourself.

SITUATIONAL TOXICITY

There are many people who are situationally toxic. Their negative behavior is predictable whenever they have to face stress or an uncomfortable situation. It may be driving on the freeway, holidays, visiting the in-laws, a trip to the dentist, spending any money even on necessary things, etc. These situations are perceived as stress inducers. Normally upbeat or positive people can become a complaining mass of negative feelings. The "situationally challenged" give themselves permission to vent at unembodied difficult situations. In so doing their emotional negativity takes center stage. Everyone else must act well-behaved in order to reduce the toxic person's anxiety. Once again, others must act in certain "appropriate ways" to make the porcupine happy. This ability to ruin the party, the vacation, or "whatever," for everyone else, is an attempt to maintain control. He or she uses being disagreeable to manipulate others. The hope is unpleasantness will motivate others to conform to the wishes of the toxic. Consider the resultant frustration created by toxic personalities in the following situations at the dinner table and in the car:

EVERYONE HATED DINNER

Kathleen wanted a civilized family who knew how to act in the most culturally correct environment. Every night dinner was a practice run for the big event. Someday, sitting in the presence of queens and presidents, she believed these eating skills would be essential. Manners, manners, and more manners were constantly the focus. One child or another was always sent away from the dinner table for unbecoming conduct.

"No, no, Billy, use the outside fork first when eating a salad."

"Why," asked five-year-old Billy. "A fork is a fork. Besides, it all goes to my belly."

"Because that is the right way to do it," Kathleen retorted.

One of the other children laughed and was sent away from the table. The rest ate dinner in silence with an occasional, "Don't cut more than three bites from your meat."

"Don't place your silverware on the table."

"Sip your milk, don't drink it all at once."

"Bring your food to your mouth, not your mouth to the food."

Dad was equally as guilty as the children in not being well-mannered. Everyone hated dinner.

The question that Kathleen asked was, "When *can* I teach manners?"

As the counselor, I pointed out to her that the issue was not "when" as much as "how." It was the way she was doing it. Kathleen wanted her very toxic approach to teaching manners accepted in the name of the end justifying the means. When I suggested that she could invite, entice, encourage, inspire, reward, praise, etc., she was frustrated. Why couldn't everyone just do what she wanted them to do in the way she wanted them to do it? I told her that it was her expectation for good manners and not theirs that was the issue. Since it was her expectation and not theirs it was her responsibility to figure out a way to "win them over."

"But, I'm the mother and they should do it out of respect for my position," she responded.

I pointed out to Kathleen that appealing to her authority as the mother was the weakest and least effective motivator. "You do it because I said" is the forerunner to rebellion. Threat of physical or emotional punishment does not change behavior even though it might temporarily bring conformity.

In desperation, Kathleen had resorted to a tactic which backfired on her. She had constructed a simple six foot trough wherein she dumped the entire four-course dinner, including salad and dessert, and announced to the family if they were going to eat like pigs they should be served like pigs. The family loved it! They welcomed the unusual opportunity to relax and have fun. Their manners were despicable. Kathleen left in tears. She was angry, hurt, and frustrated.

I introduced Kathleen to the "Art of Giving and Receiving Criticism," which information will be given later in this book. She learned the age-old adage is true, "A spoonful of sugar helps the medicine go down."

"TRAPPED"

Whenever Boyd was in a car with Anna, she used it as an opportunity to criticize him. In spite of repeated requests not to use the situation as an opportunity for venting, it was to no avail. Short trips to the store were survivable. The longer trips were intolerable. Anna was not always a toxic person. She was usually loving and respectful and this behavior seemed out of character. She was afraid to be perceived as a "witch" by others. Therefore she held her tongue until she was confident she could not be overheard. She felt safe when they were alone in the car. In this situation she felt free to unleash all of her nonacceptance messages. Her attacks were vicious and unrelenting. On one occasion Boyd reached over and slapped her face. This event is what brought them to counseling.

In order to deal with and prevent Anna's situational toxicity, we set up a time every night for fifteen minutes where she could deal with her negative issues. Boyd had seven and one-half minutes and Anna had seven and one-half minutes. The timer was set on the stove. After the fifteen minute sessions, which Boyd described as a "root canal without novocaine," they were to have twenty three hours and forty-five minutes of emotionally safe time. This included no negativity of any kind, especially in the car.

In spite of her best efforts, Anna could not control herself. She would consistently violate the agreement. Boyd agreed never to strike her again, regardless of what she said. However, an exit strategy was developed. If Anna began to be critical of Boyd outside of the fifteen minute window, Boyd was free to excuse himself by saying, "I'm leaving the room; I'm not leaving the relationship," or "I'm leaving the house; I'm not leaving the relationship."

Once, on a trip of several hours, Anna could not contain herself and began a tirade. Boyd pulled the car to the side of the road and got out. He said, "Anna, I'm leaving the car; I'm not leaving the relationship." Anna promised she would stop. Boyd, however, crossed the street and hitch hiked home. This happened three different times over a period of months before Anna was able to understand that this particular situational toxicity would lead to her being abandoned.

UNIVERSAL TOXICITY

Another interesting characteristic of toxic behavior, whether physical or verbal, is to whom it is applied. There are those who are simply universally toxic to everyone in all circumstances. It doesn't matter whether they are on the freeway, in a cafe, at home, or at work. They are always toxic. The universally toxic person is easy to identify, but very difficult, if not impossible, to live with. He or she lives in a world of constantly strained relationships.

TOXIC HENRI

Henri is a universally toxic person. Waitresses, clerks, and tellers all tremble when Henri comes in. Some will leave in tears and all will be offended at Henri's abusive language, his constant complaining, and his unending litany of what is wrong.

Henri is seventy-two. He has been married four times. His children do not tolerate him. Henri is a classic Scrooge, Grinch, and Naysayer all wrapped up in a bundle of toxic behaviors. He is always right. His state is the best state. His car is the best car, until he goes to the dealership where he can offend the service manager. Two of Henri's three children will have nothing to do with him. They have confronted him directly and told him to never come to their homes again. He went one time uninvited and was physically assaulted in the front yard and left a heap upon the ground by one of his sons. One adult child tries every year at Thanksgiving or Christmas to have some kind of positive interaction with Henri, but it always turns out the same negative way. At least Henri is predictable. He is a known quantity.

SELECTIVE TOXICITY

There is another type of toxic behavior which is much more difficult to recognize because it is selective. This is revealed in the following story:

RACHEL'S TOXIC MOTHER

Rachel was the first of two daughters. The mother began to be jealous of her daughter the very moment she was brought into the hospital recovery room. The father made a big deal about his new "little princess." The

28

mother resented the affection the father lavished upon the newborn. By the time Nancy, the second daughter, was born there was a well established pattern of selective toxicity for Rachel. Around the father Rachel was treated normally. Once the father was gone Rachel would be treated in cruel and unkind ways. Nancy also came to resent Rachel, who was not only older, but prettier and brighter than herself.

The father loved both of his daughters and told Rachel she was only imagining that her mother had a double standard. She was made to deny her own feelings and her own reality. She was convinced that what she saw was not the way it really was and what she felt was not what she really felt. Therefore, Rachel grew up not being able to trust her feelings or her knowledge.

As the girls grew up and married and began to have children, their mother's selective toxicity passed on to the children of Rachel. Nancy's children would get expensive gifts and presents from the grandmother, while Rachel's children were lucky to get a card. Nancy and Rachel lived a few blocks from each other. The mother would manipulate the circumstances so that there would be time for a nice long visit with Nancy and her children, while Rachel would get a phone call just as the parents were leaving Nancy's house. The mother and father lived in another state. They would drive eight hours one way to visit both daughters, but never made it over to Rachel's home time and time again.

For years Rachel believed the lie because after all when you have been raised with a double standard it is difficult to recognize. Remember, she could not trust her feelings or her experience. Rachel was treated as if she were the "other woman" in her father's life, not a daughter, but the same as a mistress. Never at any time was there any inappropriateness between Rachel and her father.

Eventually, however, Nancy and the mother convinced the father that Rachel hated them when the truth was the opposite. Rachel longed for a normal, healthy relationship with her mother and sister.

To this day the father remains in denial and the two women are quite content excluding Rachel from their lives. Occasionally the mother or sister will call her and feign a desire for a relationship so they can claim to the father their willingness, while blaming Rachel for not being willing. This kind of selective toxicity is the most damaging to the self-worth and the mental health of another. The mother disguised herself as a teddy bear around the father, but was a porcupine around Rachel.

MOST COMMONLY ENCOUNTERED PORCUPINES

Three of the most common toxic personalities involve "The Perfectionist," "The Control Freak," and "The Critiholic." Examine the next three stories and imagine yourself in the role of a counselor. How would you counsel those who have to deal with them?

THE PERFECTIONIST

AMY'S AURA OF NEGATIVISM

Amy was the mother of five children, two from a previous marriage and three with Phil, her current husband. Amy was a perfectionist. She took a great deal of pride in being a person of high expectations. Her first two children were girls. They never came to accept Phil. The relationship between Phil and the girls was strained at best, and not close. Amy blamed Phil and resented him for not connecting with her daughters. However, every time Phil attempted to assert himself as a father, Amy would rush to the defense of her daughters. Phil quit trying. This was one more reason Amy was frustrated with Phil. He wasn't involved enough in their lives and when he did involve himself he over-reacted, according to Amy.

The first daughter ran away from home at sixteen and never returned. The second daughter married at seventeen. The premature exodus of these two daughters was blamed on Phil. When the third child, a boy, also left home at sixteen, Amy was perplexed. She wanted to blame Phil but could not quite settle on a reason. When the fourth daughter ran away at sixteen, they wound up in a counselor's office.

Amy came to the realization that although Phil had his problems, she did too. It was a revelation to her that she was the major reason for her children leaving. Her perfectionism had translated into constant criticism. Phil, with all of his shortcomings, had not driven off her oldest two daughters. She had. Her smug attitude about her perfectionism was shattered. Amy worked hard to keep her house looking good. In her mind it was her job to criticize others into helping. However, the more she criticized, the less they did. When they became lazy, rebellious, and unwilling, her criticisms were backed by punishments. The privileges they enjoyed, such as having their friends over for a night, driving the car, going out on weekends, etc. were restricted. All of their freedoms were being curtailed. Being grounded was the norm.

Some of Amy's children were verbally abusive to her. Others were passively aggressive. They dragged around. They were always late. They left most jobs incomplete. Even when the children did what they thought was a good job, Amy's perfectionism would find something that could have been done better. They were never quite good enough. The result of Amy's constant carping was hopeless alienation. She was emotionally unsafe. Her true feelings of love were never able to break through her aura of negativism. Her habit of criticizing had become a self-defeating behavior. In her mind she was right. They were wrong. It was her duty to point out the flaws. She had the truth on her side.

Amy was toxic. What counsel would you give her? What counsel would you give someone who had to deal with Amy?

Criticizing Amy for being toxic will not solve the problem. No one is going to change Amy but herself. If the Amys of the world recognize they have a problem and are willing to change, there is hope. Otherwise it is up to those who have to interact with the toxic to protect themselves.

In the spirit of becoming his best self, Phil needed to define what a good person would do and fulfill his own agenda. By definition, you will never measure up to the expectations of a perfectionist. However, Phil gave up on doing anything. What he needed to do was to let go of pleasing Amy, but not let go of being a good person. Phil would be criticized by Amy no matter what he did. The healthiest thing for Phil to do was to be responsible in each relationship to which he was a party. He might as well be criticized for doing his best.

THE CONTROL FREAK

There is an axiom in psychology which says the more insecure you are on the inside, the greater the need you have to control the outside. In order for the control freak to feel good about his or her world, he or she must stay in control of it. This means controlling others. Being a control freak is a form of toxic behavior. The message it sends is, "I must control you because you are not smart enough to control yourself. You are incompetent. You must do as I say because you are not capable on your own."

THE KINGDOM OF LESTER THE CONTROLLER

Lester was an accountant. He was of one religious faith, and his wife was of another. They had four daughters. There was no television in their home and only classical music was allowed. There was a very strict dress code enforced. Each of the daughters had a serious list of chores to perform each day. Music lessons were mandatory. One half hour of free time was granted if the day's homework from school had been completed. School let out at 2:20 p.m. and the girls were expected to be home by 2:45. The daily vacuuming, yard work, cleaning and laundry would take an hour and fifteen minutes. At 4:00 p.m. all five women would begin to prepare for the evening meal. Dinner was always formal. There were always cloth napkins and fresh flowers except for a couple of months during the winter when an appropriate potted plant, like a poinsettia, would do. A display of poor manners or laughter at the table would result in one or more of the girls being sent to their rooms without dinner. A mandatory apology was required. Following dinner the girls were sure to be quiet while they cleaned up after the meal. Excessive noise was forbidden. Shoes were not worn in the house but neither were they allowed to go barefoot. Slippers were the preferred standard and stockings were tolerated.

A large part of the evening was spent practicing the musical instrument chosen by the parents. Lester was adamant that each daughter learn the piano and one stringed instrument. Guitars were not an option. After music practice it was time for homework. The parents met regularly with the teachers and knew precisely how each girl was doing. At 8:30 p.m. the girls prepared for bed. They were expected to be in their rooms by 9:00 p.m. All lights were out at 9:15 p.m. The father made a personal bed check on each daughter. Each girl had her own room. However, it was made clear that the room was on loan to them. The beds had to be made immediately after arising.

This routine was followed religiously from Monday to Friday. A music lesson after school or a pre-approved school activity would be the only exception. Friends were not permitted in the house except on Saturday afternoons between 12:00 and 4:00 p.m. The girls were not permitted to sleep over at someone else's house and of course, they were not allowed to have friends sleep at their place. The truth is the girls were afraid to have their friends over. They were embarrassed by the strictness of their life style. Even minimum exposure to others at school made them aware of their limited freedom.

Trouble started when the girls began to be teenagers. Ironically, the oldest was outwardly conforming. However, behind her parent's back she was living a double life. She smoked. She sneaked out of her window at night and was sexually active contrary to her parent's values. She had earphones and listened to acid rock when her parents thought she was listening to classical music. She had cleverly exchanged the inside of her personal classical cassettes by opening up the plastic and by super-gluing it back. On the outside it read Mozart; on the inside was the obscene music of "Black Sabbath." Much like her own life, on the outside she was the perfect daughter, on the inside she was a "wild thing."

It all came to a point of crisis when Lester heard a noise in the house about midnight. He opened the daughter's bedroom door. There he found his daughter and a young man. He went into a rage and ran for his 45 caliber gun. The youth fled from the house. The home was in an exclusive wooded area with a long serpentine driveway. The police report stated as the youth fled, the father pursued, firing his gun as he ran. Large pieces of bark flew as bullets ripped through them. The second daughter had an abortion at fifteen and was sent away by the father to live with one of his sisters.

Lester, was a CPA and operated his own business. He had a rigid schedule and few employees would work for him for any length of time. He experienced a high turnover. Everything was black or white for Lester. There were few grey areas. Things were right or wrong. Anything that was different from what Lester thought, was wrong! Life was absolute. Everything needed to be done a certain way. It was wrong to paint with simple up and down brush strokes. Lester's way was the right way. It wasn't just a "different" way, but the "right way." "King" Lester could control his world. He had power at home and at work. It was "his way" or "the highway."

What counsel would you give Lester? What counsel would you give to someone who had to deal with Lester?

People like Lester have a hard time learning that the art of parenting is not the art of hanging on, but the art of letting go. When a baby is born, it is helpless. Abandoned, it will die. A parent or caring adult must assume full responsibility for the life of the infant. True parenting involves gradually transferring the responsibility for life to the shoulders of the child. Lester could never let go. His need to control everything extended to the lives of those around him. His control style of parenting did not allow for personal growth. Obedience, conformity, and outward performance replaced individual value judgements. The girls had no personal values. They were not allowed to have their own opinions. Therefore, they rebelled. Even in rebellion, they had not yet come to their own values. They were only reacting to their father's control of their world.

Ironically, the father died in his mid-forties. The mother immediately changed her hair style. Lester had liked it only one way. She redecorated the house and started to discover who she was. She loosened up considerably and found out she had a sense of humor. Her marriage to Lester was an exercise in fear. She was constantly afraid of his disappointment or disapproval. She had enabled him as a "control freak" out of her own fear. She was equally responsible for supporting this unhealthy environment which tried to force change from the outside.

The principle that Lester did not understand was that criticism is external. Change is internal. Much like a sponge, Lester could force his family to conform by external pressure. The question is, "Has the sponge truly changed?" No, it has only temporarily altered its shape. As soon as the hands which hold it let go, it will return to its natural state. Threats, intimidation, and criticism are external forces. They may cause short term conformity in the presence of toxic people. However, free of control they revert to their original behaviors.

What most toxic people fail to recognize is the real issue. Those being criticized seldom lack knowledge of their weaknesses and flaws. What they lack is a commitment to the toxic person's values. No one can change a person who is unwilling to change. Not even fear of death by cancer will stop the smoker who is unwilling to change. *Other people don't change you. You change yourself.*

The term "education" comes from the word "educe," meaning to draw forth. True education is that which is drawn from within the person. Change can be encouraged. It can be brought forth by enticing, by inspiring, by rewarding, and by loving. Remember, most people do not lack knowledge of their need to change, they lack motivation.

Continued criticism leads to rebellion and stubbornness. It breeds contempt for the critic. Defiance, justification, and excuses will abound, but behavior will not change. It engages the giver and receiver of criticism into an adversarial relationship with no winner and two losers. Only when the alcoholic decides for himself on the inside that change is worthwhile, will change take place. All of the external criticism, job loss, or family humiliation will not substitute for a decision which can only be made on the inside.

THE CRITIHOLIC

BELINDA WAS ADDICTED TO CRITICISM

Belinda was a very hard worker. She gave one hundred and ten percent all the time. She had high expectations of herself and others. She had no time for soap operas or anything unproductive. Her whole value system revolved around the work ethic. Few could match her stride for stride. She was generous and dependable. She received great praise at work from her employers. She had been advanced several times on merit alone. When she was advanced, her replacements were not able to accomplish as much work as she had accomplished. Extra workers were hired. Belinda took her work home and would come in nights, work weekends or whatever the job would require. She was a workaholic. From her perspective she was a hard worker, dependable, and reliable. To her family, husband, and friends, she was out of balance.

Belinda gave much of herself and expected others to do the same. All of her relationships were strained. Few wanted her help if it obligated them to her high expectations to return in kind. She was not sought out and yet she worked hard to please.

The problem with Belinda was her tongue. She had no tolerance for the lazy. The slow were only endured. Belinda honestly felt she was entitled to be critical of others. Her hard working efforts gave her the right to be judgmental of others who were less committed. She felt she did not need their permission to be critical. As a mother and as a wife and as a sister in her own family she found herself alienated and isolated. Not one wanted to be around her. She was devastated and deeply hurt. Not only was she frustrated by their lack of commitment to the work ethic, their rejection of her seemed totality unwarranted. She felt unappreciated. After all she had done and continued to do, why would she be treated with such aversion? Belinda was truly dumfounded.

What counsel would you give Belinda? What counsel would you give someone who had to live with Belinda?

Assuming that Belinda was honestly searching for help and was teachable, the following information would be helpful to her:

> "Belinda, the reason you have alienated everyone is your caustic tongue. People don't feel emotionally safe around you. You are judgmental, condemning, and critical. These are not attractive traits. You must eliminate them from your life in two stages. First, stop being critical. Second, before you speak, ask yourself if what you are about to say is positive. Will it make a difference for good? If life has taught you anything, Belinda, it is that your negative and critical approach doesn't work.
>
> "Insanity has been defined as repeating the same behavior over and over again and expecting a different outcome. Replace your negative approach to your loved ones with a positive one. Wait until your husband, your children, or your family does something right and comment upon it with sincere appreciation. Set up a time once a week for just five to ten minutes to deal with what you believe is 'essential criticism.' Allot no more than ten minutes per relationship. Write down your criticisms and bring them to the meeting. If you can't cover all of

your criticisms in ten minutes you will have to wait for the next week's meetings. Then you must honor this commitment. No criticism outside of the designated time. If you honestly work hard at this, your loved ones and friends will begin to trust you as you demonstrate restraint and consideration."

For those who interface with the "critical buzz saws" like Belinda, there is only one healthy choice. It is to protect yourself. Further on in this book you will encounter the tools and the skills necessary for survival. There is one fundamental principle to which you must commit. It is to define for yourself what a good person would do and then do it.

ANOTHER TRIO OF EMOTIONAL PORCUPINES: THE ABUSER, THE MARTYR, THE VICTIM

THE ABUSER MENTALITY

A man hit his wife because she had not done something he had asked her to do. The abusive man felt justified. He tried to explain he would not have done it had she only accomplished his expectations. This of course, negates individual accountability. Each person is responsible for his or her own behavior regardless of the actions of others. Each has a right and opportunity to act and to react. We cannot always choose the circumstances, but we can always choose our response.

When we say that someone else made us do it, we are not accepting responsibility for our own behavior. This is the abuser mentality. We violate the first principle of emotionally healthy people, i.e., to accept responsibility for our own happiness, unhappiness, and behavior and to respect the boundaries of others. Abuse is never justified.

THE ABUSER

SUE AND HER FATHER

Sue is a runaway. Her father had caught her breaking curfew, not doing her chores, and lying to him. He began yelling at her, grabbed her arm, and pulled her downstairs. Sue tripped and broke her arm in the fall. Child Protective Services was called and the father was mandated to take an anger management class by the court. He was also required to report for regular counseling. As the counselor talked with Sue and her father, it was obvious the hostility that each had. Sue confessed she was wrong. She fully expected to lose the privilege to use the phone and to be grounded for the weekend, which were the punishments prescribed by the father. With child-like wisdom she said, "But I didn't deserve to be treated that way. Certainly I would not have broken my arm if you had not pulled me down the stairs." The father was in bewilderment that somehow he had become the focus. He felt that Sue's misconduct justified his behavior. It was explained to them what it means to be emotionally healthy. It is important that each accepts responsibility for his or her behavior. They role played the situation over again as to what should have happened. Sue accepted reluctantly the responsibility for each poor judgment decision she had made.

Then it was the father's turn. He had a very difficult time accepting responsibility for getting angry. He chose to act out his aggressive behavior. It took several sessions before he could admit that her behavior did not justify his reaction. Other people don't make us do anything. The "abuser mentality" was hard for him to own.

40

THE MARTYR CYCLE

MARVIN THE MARTYR

Marvin was a tease and was easily offended when people criticized his behavior. He would sulk. He would go from normal to martyr in a manner of seconds. His pouting was obvious. Attempts to include him were in vain. His wife or children would hear him muttering, "Everyone would be better off without me."

Marvin worked hard but tried to make the rest of the family feel guilty. He was an expert in making statements like, "You go on without me, you'll have a better time anyway."

"No thanks, I'll just get in the way."

"Don't worry about me, I'll be fine alone."

Finally his wife and children got tired of asking him.

Marvin didn't want to get better. He had learned to substitute sympathy and self-pity for happiness.

THE VICTIM SYNDROME

VICKIE THE VICTIM

Vickie had a unique way of defeating all of the solutions to her problems. "I've tried that, and it didn't work," she would say.

Vickie only wanted to complain, to gripe, and to bemoan her circumstances. Life was a dirty trick played upon her. Each new crisis was fuel to feed her negativity. Vickie craved sympathy, and of course sympathy could only come if she were the victim. Her husband leaving her was a self-fulfilling prophecy. He became sick and tired of her complaints. His divorcing her just gave her one more reason to play the victim card.

Vickie wore people out. Friends, family, neighbors, relief agencies, social workers, counselors, religious leaders, all of them tried to help Vickie take control of her life and function in healthy ways. They all failed because Vickie did not want to be healthy. She wanted to be a victim and complain about life.

THE CONFESSOR

It is not uncommon for a guilt ridden spouse to dump their guilt and all the garbage of their inappropriate past upon their mate. I seriously counsel against this selfish behavior. It only serves as brain clutter for the spouse. Well meaning people, in quest for total acceptance, do not consider the ability of their mate to process the information. The person who "dumps" usually feels a great sense of relief and a burden lifted from off their shoulders. However the burden is now brain clutter for the spouse and often creates doubt, fear, and insecurity for the one who is the receiver of the guilt and garbage. Unless it is absolutely essential for the well-being of the relationship, these are truths which never need repeating. Being brutally honest in the name of truth is still brutality.

SURROUNDED BY PORCUPINES

What if the toxic person is a parent, a spouse, a child, or all of the above? What if you are surrounded by porcupines? How can you survive a such a negative environment? Is the only answer, "If you can't beat them, join them?" What does it do to your self-concept when you notice toxic behaviors, like porcupine quills, beginning to emerge as a part of your own personality? How do you avoid adopting the same behavior you abhor in a toxic person? How do you hug a porcupine and not come away from the encounter wounded by its sharp quills? Porcupines need love too. Is it possible for you to maintain a healthy self-concept and still relate to a toxic loved one? *Yes!!*

However, relating to a porcupine does not mean that you are expected to tolerate abusive behavior. In a relationship where both parties are willing to change, the sense of mutual efforts encourages both to keep trying. Even if one party is willing to change there is hope for improvement in the relationship. But, what about a relationship where one party has no intent to change?

CHRIS AND DAYNA

Dayna's step-father was a demanding, unkind, and domineering man. In today's society he would be arrested for abusive behavior, and the children would be taken by Child Protective Services. Dayna's mother was an appeaser. Her fears of being alone were greater than her willingness to take her children and leave the relationship. She was an enabler. His inappropriate and abusive behavior was excused. "He was tired," the mother would say, or "He is under a lot of pressure." The entire family walked on pins and needles.

Dayna had learned well the art of "appeasing." She married at eighteen and thought she was fleeing the prison and influence of her intolerable step-father. Dayna wanted a relationship with her mother independent from him. His control of Dayna's mother would not allow for it.

Chris was the new son-in-law. His early efforts to accommodate his father-in-law's demanding nature were interpreted as signs of weakness. Schedules and activities were always altered around the father-in-law's whims and wishes.

When Chris stood up to his father-in-law and announced he would no longer play by the rules of "let's appease Dad," the trouble began. The step-father went to Chris' place of work and physically assaulted him. Chris called the police, filed a report, and obtained a protective order. After the begging and pleading of his mother-in-law and wife, he dropped the assault charges, but maintained the Protective Order. The step-father was even more enraged. He forbade his wife from any further contact with Dayna or Chris. The women were crushed. Dayna wanted her husband to apologize to her step-father so she could have a relationship with her mother.

When they came to me it was a classic case of how to define a relationship with a "porcupine." This would be a *one-sided* effort. Dayna's step-father would not change. He was a sick human being. So was Dayna's mother for tolerating his behavior. The couple wanted to know how to have a healthy relationship with unhealthy people.

My counsel was straight forward. "You can't ! You must protect yourself and your future children from this unhealthy environment. The two of you must define what efforts you are willing to make which will keep you physically and emotionally safe."

Dayna and her mother could have phone contacts without the step-father's knowledge. An occasional lunch might also be worked in at a safe place. Cards and letters were risky because they might inflame the anger of the step-father if discovered. Chris and Dayna decided to move away to another state and establish a safe home environment. In a year Dayna's younger brother would be joining the military and Dayna's mother would be free to leave her toxic spouse. Chris said she was more than welcome to come and live with them until she could get on her own two feet.

In this situation there was no compromise or approach that would have been safe for Dayna, Chris, or the mother. The step-father was not just verbally abusive; he was physically and emotionally abusive and capable of serious physical harm. He would only respond to the legal restraints of society. If he crossed those bounds, Chris was to have him arrested and prosecuted to the full extent of the law. The reason this very real life story is included is to make the point that some porcupines are so toxic the best thing to do is to leave them and then leave them alone.

It is not necessary to abandon most relationships with toxic people. There is a safe way to deal with them. That is what this book is all about. It is about being in control of your life. It is about learning safe and appropriate ways to relate to toxic people.

CHAPTER FOUR

HELP!
I MARRIED A PORCUPINE

Some people are painfully aware they have married a porcupine. Others have a feeling things are not quite right but do not know what the problem is. It is a rude awakening when one discovers he or she has been living with a porcupine and didn't recognize it.

GRANT THE ENABLER

Grant said:

"I live for my wife, Amanda's, love and so do the children. We crave it. When she is happy, our world is wonderful. We laugh and visit the mountain tops of joy. I would do anything to keep her in that mood. Life is good. I'm not talking phony or illusional. Things are exceptional. We hug and kiss; there is an outpouring of warm communication. Physical intimacy is passionate and intense. Our friends and our children's friends envy our relationship. People hold us out as an ideal.

47

"Then in an instant, if Amanda feels unappreciated, she turns cold. I mean really cold. Anyone who offends her gets the silent treatment and she completely withdraws her love from them. This can last for days at a time. It's just like a switch that turns on and off. When Amanda is in her 'off mode,' life is hell. I've never been so depressed in my whole life as when she withdraws her love. And it's not just the one who offends her who suffers. We all suffer! We long for the good times and the happy moments. When Amanda is on, life is beautiful and when she is off, it is ugly.

"It's worth doing things her way. Believe me, the rewards far out weigh the negatives. She feels the need to control every aspect of our lives. The children resent it. The two older children are now out of the home. Amanda still feels the need to control their lives and is highly critical of them. They have come to me and asked me why I put up with it. I told them I didn't get married so I could get divorced. The good times are worth it. The problem is the good times are becoming fewer and far between. I crave those times. I have this fear in my gut that they may never return. I don't care anymore about being right or being equal. I just want the love, joy, and passion of the good times. I want the sunshine back in my life."

It is easy to see that Grant did not recognize Amanda as an emotional porcupine. He needed help to identify her toxic behaviors. He was abundantly aware of Amanda's rejection and need to control. However, he had not labeled these behaviors as dysfunctional, only as hurtful. I explained to Grant that he needed to acknowledge her toxic behaviors for what they were. He felt the need to keep pointing out the good traits in his wife. His searching for the positive kept him in denial about the negative. He said, "After all, nobody is perfect and isn't it a small price to pay for the good times?"

GRANT'S RUDE AWAKENING

I responded by saying,

"Grant, you are an enabler. Amanda has become more and more unhappy because as the children have grown up and taken identities of their own, she has had less and less control. Her control worked when the children were small and she could manipulate everyone's world.

"You said Amanda is blaming you for not supporting her with the older children. She believes she would still be able to control the lives of the children if only you had been and were now, more supportive. Amanda sees support as agreement and having you force the children to do things her way. That is how Amanda interprets support. As time has gone by you have become the focus of her blame. She does not recognize her need to control as a toxic behavior. Her need to control is not the problem in her mind. The problem is you and your lack of support.

"The question I have for you is how can you fix Amanda's world and give her the support she needs to be in control of the universe as she sees it? When your children were little you could do it. How are you going to fix it? Amanda doesn't like her son-in-law, because he has an opinion different from her own. Are you going to go to the son-in-law and fix him? She also doesn't approve of the son-in-law's family. Are you going to fix that as well? Her own children resent her. How can you fix a relationship between two other people when one party is unreasonable, demanding, and uncompromising? Her attitude is 'my way or the highway.' Well now she has the 'highway' and she doesn't like it. If you truly want to help her, you are going to have to accept reality. There are some things you can't fix.

"There are some things you *can* do. One of them is

to protect yourself from the barrage of hurt which is being hurled upon you. Another thing you can do is to accept the reality that she may not change. The third thing you can do is to recognize what is and isn't a toxic behavior. Next, you need to learn the skills to deal with damaging behaviors. Currently, as long as you are of a mind to either change the whole world to please her or to fix her, you are on a guaranteed pathway to failure. My point is that there is a way to improve the situation. It requires that you take control of the healthy options which are available to you."

In Grant's life there are several issues. The first thing that needed to change was his set of expectations. As long as he expected to change what he could *not* change or to fix what he could *not* fix, he would remain in frustration. After years of having your focus on "pleasing" another person, it is hard to let go of what has become a way of life. In the present reality, Grant needs to redefine his role as a good person. Currently, his definition of a good person is pleasing Amanda. The problem is Amanda cannot be pleased. Amanda refuses to accept the reality that the world is not going to be the way she wants it to be.

The term "enabler" refers to Grant's unhealthy behavior of contributing to his wife's "delinquency." Her behavior of controlling others was and is toxic. Recognizing a toxic behavior and not supporting it means that he will have to define for himself what healthy behavior is.

Another challenge that faces Grant, after he defines for himself "what a good person would do," is facing his wife. Her rejection of him is predictable. What Grant needs to accept is that he is gong to be "darned if he does" or "darned if he doesn't." Since all current efforts on his part, short of changing his wife's universe, have failed, he is condemned.

Since condemnation is inevitable for Grant, he might as well be condemned for being a healthy person. Grant's focus should not be on pleasing his toxic wife. His focus needs to be on becoming his best self. The key is who gets to define Grant's best self? If the definition is left to Amanda, Grant will never be good enough. He must define what a good person would do and live to his own definition. Only then does he have an opportunity to succeed. If he truly lets go of trying to please his wife and focuses on being a good person, her negative behaviors will escalate in an attempt to bring him back to his enabling position.

Amanda increased the negative messages, the brutal attacks, the nonacceptance, the silence, the withdrawal of love, all in an attempt to bring him back on board the old program of "fix my world" and "I'll be happy when everyone I love does everything I want them to do, in the way I want it done." When her coercion didn't work on Grant, she threatened divorce as a way to increase the "ante."

ARE YOU HELD HOSTAGE?

I shared with Grant a truism:

"The person who cares the most is held hostage by the one who cares the least."

Until Grant cared more about being healthy than being pleasing in an unhealthy way, he would be held prisoner to his craving for his wife's very conditional approval. Grant finally had the courage to commit to be healthy. Only then was his wife willing to come to counseling, which she did. It could have been different. She might have demanded a divorce. Grant had to be prepared for that option. In this case there was

51

improvement in the relationship. Grant focused on loving his wife and loving his children. He stopped trying to fix "her world." He decided that if she wanted to have lousy relationships with her children, she was entitled to them. Her world and her relationships would be her sole responsibility. Grant was released from any expectation to fix her relationships. He was cautioned not to undermine his wife with the children. Amanda's relationship with her husband has improved one hundred percent. Although she is still inclined to go back to the old standards, Grant does not respond. She gets over it more quickly now, but she is still struggling with wanting to control everyone's life. Things are better for Grant.

One woman, in a situation similar to Grant's, said, "I knew the way my husband was treating me didn't feel right, but I had not identified him as a toxic personality." Awareness and recognition are the forerunners to changing how you live with an emotional porcupine.

The following questions will help you determine the degree and seriousness of toxic behaviors in a spouse.

DO I HAVE A TOXIC MATE?

		TRUE	FALSE
1.	I seldom feel as though I measure up to my mate's expectations.	_____	_____
2.	I feel constantly criticized about my approach to life.	_____	_____
3.	My mate consistently interrupts me in the middle of a conversation.	_____	_____
4.	My mate uses anger to manipulate me.	_____	_____
5.	I feel blamed for my mate's unhappiness.	_____	_____

		TRUE	FALSE
6.	My mate seems to be upset with me over one issue or another most of the time.	____	____
7.	My mate does not react well to being criticized.	____	____
8.	I receive persistent messages about being incompetent or inadequate.	____	____
9.	I feel discounted and unappreciated in this relationship.	____	____
10.	I live in fear of doing or saying the wrong thing around my mate.	____	____
11.	I feel treated like a child. My mate is constantly telling me what I "should," "need," and "ought," to do.	____	____
12.	I feel emotionally and/or verbally abused.	____	____
13.	My mate projects an attitude of superiority.	____	____
14.	The good times are few and far between.	____	____
15.	We are always arguing about something (sex, money, children).	____	____
16.	My mate is constantly bringing up the past.	____	____

TOTAL "TRUE" ANSWERS ____

EXPLANATION FOR NUMBER OF "TRUE" ANSWERS:

0 — 4	Normal, but not necessarily healthy.
5 — 9	Serious problems, defensive skills needed
10 — 13	Definitely Toxic, counseling recommended
14 — 16	Emotionally unhealthy and probably living in denial; protective gloves are essential.

WHAT IS NORMAL ?

Let's address the term "normal." Normal is a term used in statistics to describe a given population. It is a relative term based on the group being dealt with. For example, normal behavior for a group of inmates at a State Prison is different from the normal behavior of the general population. Likewise, normal behavior at a hockey game and normal behavior at an opera will be different.

The bell curve is designed to measure any given population with 2/3 being in the middle and 1/6 being on either side. "Subnormal" represents the 1/6 of the population who are less than normal. "Normal" is the middle 2/3 and "Abnormal" is the 1/6 who exceed the norm.

NORMAL CURVE

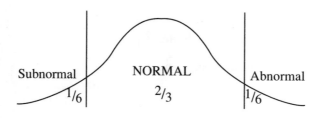

Subnormal   NORMAL   Abnormal
1/6   2/3   1/6

Being normal is not good when one is talking about toxic behaviors which have become generally accepted. In our current society there are many toxic behaviors which are in the normal 2/3 range and at the same time are destructive. There are numerous studies in Sociology which show that the very poor and the very wealthy are more physically abusive than the middle class. The point is "normal" depends upon the group that is being measured. Just because someone scores normal on this test does not necessarily mean they are emotionally healthy. *Remember, a toxic behavior is any word, deed, or action which detracts from you being your best self or hinders others from becoming their best selves.*

PORCUPINE MARRIAGES
VERSUS HEALTHY RELATIONSHIPS

There are people who have as their greatest need the expectation to have their toxic behaviors accepted as normal. The problem, of course, is that everybody comes to a marriage with a set of "areas of needed improvement." How this area of needed improvement is dealt with is the issue. The WAY we approach our weaknesses and the weaknesses of others is at the very core of what is healthy versus what is unhealthy in a marriage. The MEANS we use to address shortcomings in ourselves and others is what defines toxic from nontoxic behavior. In healthy relationships the quality of the relationship is never sacrificed at the expense of inappropriate or uninvited criticism.

Problems arise in marriage when spouses want the inappropriate HOWS, the unhealthy WAYS, and the very unacceptable MEANS to be justified. There are respectful and proper ways to ask a person who is your equal for permission to criticize. No one should be asking all the time. However, when they do ask it should always be in an appropriate manner consistent with respect.

STEWARDSHIPS

A stewardship is the authority or responsibility to act within certain appropriate limits and boundaries. Using the paradigm of the family, we could say that all stewardships fall into one of three relationships: Father-Mother, Brother-Sister, or Son-Daughter. The nature of the stewardship defines what is appropriate in the relationship. In other words, you are either a parent, a brother/sister, or a child. Each role carries with it certain prerogatives. There is appropriate and inappropriate conduct for each responsibility.

Continuing to use this model, pursue the question, "What is the Husband-Wife relationship?" The answer is a relationship of equals; it is a Brother-Sister relationship. There seem to be few who understand and accept this as true. Many husbands act as if they are "Fathers" to their wives and not co-equals. They treat their spouses as if they were children. In all fairness, there are many women who parent their husbands. They assume a "Mother" role over their husband without the slightest regard for co-equality.

More than thirty years of watching and observing healthy and unhealthy marriages have confirmed the following point: most marriages have partners who take turns parenting each other. They give themselves permission based on supposed greater insight, superior wisdom, or special knowledge. The problem is the arrogance implied by assuming the parent role. Regardless of superior knowledge, wisdom, or power, we are not justified in parenting a spouse. A marriage of unequals is not a marriage. It may be a benevolent dictatorship. It may be a well-meaning tyranny, but it is not a relationship of equals.

At some point a marriage which lacks the respect of equality will face the crisis of disunity. The longevity of a marriage, is not a sign of either happiness or unity. People stay in unhealthy marriages for many different reasons. Some are economic, some are religious, and some have to do with staying together for the sake of the children. In unhealthy marriages the spouses take turns parenting each other. Consider the following diagram:

INAPPROPRIATE HUSBAND-WIFE STEWARDSHIP

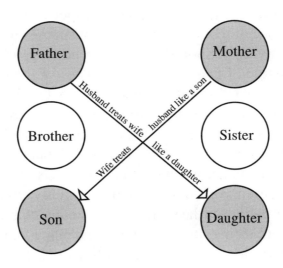

Each stewardship has language which is appropriate for that relationship. Toxic people generally have respect for authority figures. However, they do not speak to equals or subordinates with the same civility.

1) The Father-Mother Language is **"Directive."** It is appropriate for the parent to use the words, "should," "need," or "ought" in addressing a child.

2) The Brother-Sister, or Marriage Language, is the language of **"Request and Respect."** "It would mean a lot to me if you would..." or "I would appreciate it if..."

3) The Child or Employee Language is that of **"Permission."** "May I..." or "Can I...?"

THREE TYPES OF LANGUAGE

It is clear that the stewardship of a spouse is not the same as the stewardship of a parent. So when spouses or equals are using the words "should," "need," and "ought" they are acting outside of their stewardship. These are parent words and when directed toward a spouse show disrespect. People generally avoid those who disrespect them. They resent the inappropriate parent figure. They develop a double life. Just like many teenagers, they act one way around the "Parent Spouse" and another when the toxic spouse is out of sight.

This defensive "double-standard" only confuses the relationship. It gives the toxic spouse another reason to attack and "parent" their mate. It is one of the many vicious cycles that emerges in a relationship with a toxic spouse where language is not appropriate to the stewardship and disrespect abounds.

WHO IS RESPONSIBLE FOR CHANGE?

We are responsible to change ourselves. This is the natural law of accountability. Change is the exclusive stewardship of the individual. Spouses are not charged with the responsibility of changing their mates. It is the duty of a spouse to love, forgive, respect and be supportive. This does not mean they have to tolerate the inappropriate or abusive behavior of their companion. It also means they do not take over and "parent" the spouse. The answer to the question "How do I respond to inappropriate behavior in a spouse?" will be discussed in detail in coming chapters. For now, understand that the responsibility for change belongs to the one who needs to change. This is essential to achieving a healthy marriage of equals.

LANGUAGE APPROPRIATE TO THE HUSBAND-WIFE RELATIONSHIP

Language appropriate to the stewardship of a spouse is the language of respect. It is the language of "request." It is the use of words "if," "would," "could," "will," or "can."

"It would mean a lot to me if you. . ."
"Could we talk later tonight?"
"I would appreciate it if you . . ."
"Will you take a turn with the baby?"
"If you could take that call, I . . ."

Generally the language of request doesn't begin with "You…" but with "I…, It…, If…, Would…, Could…, Can…, or Will…." It is a language of equals. Parent talk of "Should, Need, and Ought" is not appropriate to the relationship of equals. There is a thin line between Permission Language of a child and Respect Language of equals. It has more to do with feeling equal in the relationship than the words. How a husband speaks to his wife and how a wife speaks to her husband reveals their true perception of their relationship. It communicates either a "respect for an equal" or whether they perceive marriage as a Parent-Child interaction. When a couple takes turns parenting one another, it not only displays a misunderstanding of stewardship, it perpetuates a lack of mutual respect for an equal.

RESPECT: GIFTED OR EARNED?

Respect in marriage is a gift. It is not earned. It says more about the giver than the receiver. Spouses who do not treat their mates with respect, are toxic. They are using their respect as a weapon of control. Withholding respect is a form of manipulation and coercion. The toxic mate will discount the entire notion of respect being a gift. The common saying is that respect must be earned. This is a great example of how "normal" is unhealthy. Justifying unhealthy behavior as normal is the excuse the toxic personality uses to continue disrespecting their spouse. The truth is simple. Everyone deserves to be treated with respect.

Trust, however, is different from respect. Trust is the function of responsible behavior. No one is suggesting that you should trust the untrustworthy. However, treating an untrustworthy person with respect says more about who you are than who they are.

One of the great messages from the Broadway play *My Fair Lady*, is how people respond to being treated with respect. What is it about that drama which lifts the human heart? Why do tears come into the eyes as someone triumphs over a difficult background? What is it about the human spirit that calls you to a higher and better self? Why do people cheer when common men act in an uncommon manner and rise to the occasion in heroic ways? In this presentation the defining characteristic was the gifting of respect.

THE "POSSIBLE" DREAM

In Man of La Mancha, Don Quixote possesses an impossible dream. He treats people with respect and sees in them a higher and better self. Surrounded by the mirrors of reality which bespeak of filth and wretchedness and of man's lowest nature, he encounters a bar maid, known by many men. Her name is Aldonsa, literally a "dunce," a slow minded dullard.

There was a time when children were humiliated by being required to sit in a corner of a school room upon a dunce stool. Some were required to wear a "dunce cap," a tall cone-shaped hat. Its intent was to punish the child who was slow in learning his lessons in school. In like manner, Aldonsa bore a similar stigma through her name. However, Don Quixote refused to call the bar maid the "dumb one." Instead, he called her, "The sweet one," or Dulcinea. A "dulce" in Spanish is a sweet or candy.

"No," she responded. This was a case of mistaken identity. She had been confused with someone else. She was toxic in her own eyes, a dumb one, a dunce. And as long as self-perception was reinforced by those around her, she continued to act the wench. She concluded Don Quixote was nothing but a crazy old man, deluded by his impossible dream. Yet he refused to see her in any other light. There, in the darkened heart of Dulcinea, he saw sweetness. Finally she became convinced that in his eyes she was "sweet." His perception became hers.

Don Quixote was much like an obsessed miner panning for gold. He continued to search in the mud of humanity for the gold nugget. He swirled the water about his pan again and again. He washed away the dirt until the precious gold was freed from its earth bound prison. So it was that Don Quixote, undaunted, continued to see the best in Dulcinea. He treated her with respect and was mocked and scorned for it. Even Dulcinea at first mocked the old fool. However, time passed and with unrelenting respect he treated her as "a fair lady." She could not resist imagining even for a moment what it felt like to be respected by someone, even a crazy old fool. As judged by everyone else, her reality rejected all rights to be respected. Ah, but it was his reality to respect her.

Don Quixote saw the good within Dulcinea. He saw the sweetness of her, and he gifted to her respect. He treated her with respect, because it was *his* standard. He chose to respect her independent of all others, independent of her own perceptions, and independent of all circumstances. His respect for her was a gift. There were many willing to condemn, but few who loved and gifted respect because it was *their* standard.

As the play continued, a marvelous transformation occurred. Aldonsa became Dulcinea. Self-respect was born because someone gifted respect. The bar-tending wench, a woman bought for any price, was now offered a new price, i.e., respect, and she liked it. She liked how it made her feel inside. It felt better than anything else.

At the very end of his life, Don Quixote questioned for a moment if he had just been a fool after all. His friends assured him that he had not been a fool. He died firm in the faith of his "possible dream." As the wench left the death bed of Don Quixote, a former acquaintance called out to her, "Aldonsa, Aldonsa." Her eyes flashed. She fixed her gaze upon the supplicant and announced with conviction that her name was Dulcinea. And so ended the movie, but not the message: *Respect was a gift, and perhaps the ultimate gift was self-respect.*

JOHNNY LINGO

There is another great story told of one Johnny Lingo, a Polynesian who was considered a wonderful catch by both the island maidens and their fathers. In their culture women were compensated for by paying the father in cows. As totally disgusting as that appears today, and as politically incorrect as it could be as judged by current societal standards, it was nonetheless the accepted practice.

Johnny Lingo was wealthy; he was also handsome and owned many cows. The father of Mahana held his daughter in lowest regard and complained to the intermediary he would only be able to bargain one cow for Mahana, as she was ugly and shy and hid in the trees so as not to be seen of others. She let her long hair hang in front of her face in shame so that others could not see her. However, one day Johnny Lingo saw her face and remembered her as his childhood friend. He knew of her goodness and true beauty.

As was the custom and tradition, the father of Mahana sat across from Johnny Lingo with the mediator at the side of the father. The women in the village were in the background. They were recalling the days when their husbands met with their fathers and bargained for their hand in marriage.

"I was a 'two cow' wife," proudly boasted one. She was quieted by another who had been a "three cow" wife. Sometimes a cow would be sacrificed and divided as a part of the bargaining.

The father whispered to the mediator, "I'll be lucky if I get the ears and a tail for Mahana." Then the father spoke up and told of all of Mahana's virtues. He said she was strong, and a good worker, and how much he would miss her.

Johnny Lingo listened very carefully and agreed with the father that his loss would be great, and he truly needed to be compensated for such a great sacrifice. All were listening, the unmarried, the one-, two-, and three-cow wives; all were waiting for Johnny Lingo to offer a cow for Mahana. Even Mahana, hidden by a tree, awaited the outcome.

"I offer you eight cows, but no more," Johnny said.

The father was stupefied. The women were agape; their mouths were open, but no one spoke. No one had *ever* offered eight cows before, not on this nor any other island. It was unheard of! Many thought Johnny Lingo was a fool, for he could have had her for one cow, but he offered eight cows. Johnny Lingo was any thing but a fool. He knew that Mahana's self-esteem would mean more than all of his cows and wealth.

Johnny Lingo treated Mahana with respect and continued to do so. Everyone knew Mahana was an "eight cow" wife. As her confidence grew, her natural beauty began to show forth. Her hair no longer drooped in front of her face. Her self-confident smile radiated an inner worth. After awhile, the father came to see Johnny Lingo and Mahana. He could not believe his eyes. Her beauty was unsurpassed; her grace and charm were abundant.

The father left by saying to Johnny Lingo, "You cheated me, Johnny Lingo, she was worth more." Perhaps respect, like beauty, lies first in the eye of the beholder.

Some will discount the entire notion of respect being given as a gift. Nevertheless, we appeal to the Supreme Court of the Conscience of husbands and wives to find the truth within their own minds; i.e., respect emanates from the giver and should be gifted to all. Those who believe that respect must be earned will discover that eventually no one can be respected except the "perfect." The toxic mate is simply using earned respect as an excuse for treating his or her spouse poorly.

In regard to human relationships, it is important to allow

people their own lousy (or good) interactions. Any form of abuse is the exception. However, if a father and son have a poor relationship because neither of them is willing to make the effort to improve, they need to accept responsibility for what they have. It is an illusion for a third party, like the mother, to try to compensate for their lack by being a "go-between." This type of mediator is eventually blamed by one or both for contributing to the poor relationship. She winds up being a judge or umpire. The real damage done by the third party interventionist is to take away the responsibility which the father and the son have to make the relationship work. Also, it creates the illusion that the relationship is somehow better than it truly is.

On occasion, a counselor will ask this question to the well-meaning and well-intentioned meddler, "Where would this relationship be if you were killed in a traffic accident tomorrow?" The answer is the relationship would be where it was before the meddler got involved. Assume the father stopped communicating with his son when the boy was a teenager. All messages were carried between them by the mother who served as a mediator, negotiator, and arbitrator. The father and the son were more than willing to let her carry the messages. Although she was frustrated, it gave her a sense of being needed.

In this case, the mother did die when the boy was eighteen. The father and his son had to go back to the point where the relationship was abandoned. From that point they had to communicate to make it better. They were willing to do so. If one or both of them had been unwilling to communicate, it would have revealed the true nature of their dysfunctional relationship. They needed to face reality. The basic truth has always been a third party cannot have a relationship for two other people who need to have their own relationship.

MOM AS A "TRAFFIC COP"

In the previous example, the mother was acting out of her stewardship. She was simply trying to compensate for the "lousy" relationship of the father and the son. The mother should have felt free to communicate with her husband and to communicate with her son as two separate relationships. In a situation like this, the best alternative for the mother would have been to become a "traffic cop." This means she should have directed the negative, verbal traffic to its proper destination. When approached by her husband with a complaint about the son, a more appropriate response would have been, "You are so right, dear. May I suggest that you go to him and tell him what you have just told me." The mother would offer understanding, but she would not accept responsibility to communicate for her husband.

In like manner, when the son brought his concerns to the mother, she should have directed him to his father. This could have been done by her sympathizing with the son. "It must be very hard for you, son, not to feel like you can communicate with your father. However, I think you have a point. It's important that your father hear from you. Perhaps you may want to write him a note." This way the mother would have been free to love her husband and to love her son independent from feeling the responsibility to make the relationship better.

EXCEPTIONS TO THE RULE

Sometimes the question is asked, "What about verbal or emotional abuse? Would I not be justified in intervening in a dysfunctional relationship if my husband were verbally or emotionally abusing my son or daughter?" In the case of a child, the mother does have a stewardship to protect her offspring. This, however, does not give her license to act inappropriately. It does not authorize her to take responsibility to communicate for the husband or the son. Each situation is unique. All of the circumstances need to be considered carefully. There will be times when intervention in a situation of serious verbal and emotional battering is an appropriate response.

If someone is so emotionally unhealthy as to be constantly assaulting their spouse or children with verbal and emotional abuse, the questions should be asked, "What is being done to protect the child? What is being done to obtain help for the abusing spouse?" Most want to run off and get a divorce. The nonabusing spouse has to be willing to put his or her relationship with the abusing spouse on the line and say, "You cannot verbally or emotionally abuse these children anymore. If you do not go and get professional counseling help, I am leaving you for a week, a month, etc.," and then do it. This is a proper response to someone who is out of control with verbal or emotional abuse.

People will say they can't leave because they have no where to go, they can't afford it, they fear for their safety, etc., etc., etc. Seldom are these valid reasons. There are women's shelters in every major city, and anyone with determination will find religious and charitable groups willing to help. The purpose of this entire explanation is to give permission to leave when necessary. The reason for leaving is to protect yourself or minor children.

CHAPTER FIVE

LITTLE PORCUPINES

"Little porcupines" may be more difficult to identify because it is normal for a child to be selfish, self-centered, and demanding. Being toxic as a child goes to a different level. Besides feelings of "entitlement," "you owe me," and "I didn't ask to be born," a toxic child transfers responsibility for their own personal happiness to the parents. *There are adult children who have these same attitudes.* The following test also applies to them.

DO I HAVE A TOXIC CHILD?

Toxic children believe their problems are caused by the inadequacy and insufficiency of their parents. They believe life is miserable because the parents do not give them what they want.

MY CHILD DOES THE FOLLOWING:

		TRUE	FALSE
1.	Complains that life is unfair.	_____	_____
2.	Accuses me of unfair treatment.	_____	_____

	TRUE	FALSE
3. Yells, screams, swears, name calls, or throws a tantrum on a weekly basis (or more often).	_____	_____
4. Threatens injury to self or others if he doesn't get his way.	_____	_____
5. Has an inability or unwillingness to be truly grateful.	_____	_____
6. Rejects responsibility for his own behavior. Blames other circumstances for his inappropriate behavior.	_____	_____
7. Expects me to "bail him or her out" of poor judgement decisions.	_____	_____
8. Tries to make me feel guilty for being less than perfect as a parent.	_____	_____
9. Projects a feeling that I "owe him" and that he is entitled to special treatment because of my inadequacies.	_____	_____
10. Reacts dramatically to any criticism.	_____	_____
11. Projects an attitude of never being satisfied.	_____	_____
12. Hurts others in the name of "teasing."	_____	_____
13. Seems to be angry or sullen most of the time.	_____	_____

TOTAL "TRUE" ANSWERS: _____

EXPLANATION FOR NUMBER OF "TRUE" ANSWERS:

0 - 3	Normal, but not necessarily healthy
4 - 6	Child is testing boundaries
7 - 9	Has a serious problem
10 - 11	This kid thinks he/she is the parent
12 - 13	This kid thinks he/she is a god.

"I'M BORED!"

Manny came to his mother and said, "I'm bored." He was not looking for ideas to explore. He expected his mother to do something so he wouldn't be bored. She suggested several options, i.e., watching TV, going to a friend's house, playing computer games, etc. He defeated all attempts to please him. He stood there defiantly glaring at his mother, expecting her to come up with an acceptable alternative. He left the room furious at his mother.

Later, Manny cut his arm with a small piece of broken glass until he bled all over a towel. In Manny's mind he was punishing his mother. He believed that in hurting himself he was punishing her.

When the two of them came into my office, I asked Manny how old he was. He responded that he was twelve. After an hour, it was evident that both Manny and his mother felt as though it was the mother's job to please Manny. After several visits it was clear what the mother needed to do. First, stop calling him Manny and call him Manuel. This was the first step in beginning to treat him more as an adult. The second step was to follow Dr. Lund's rules of good parenting. I reviewed with the mother a very basic parenting philosophy.

THE RULES OF GOOD PARENTING

1. The Art of Parenting is the art of transferring responsibility from the parent's shoulders to the shoulders of the child as he or she demonstrates an ability to manage it.

2. The Art of Parenting is the art of "letting go," not the art of "hanging on."

3. Life is a gift that the parents give to the child. What the child does with his life is his gift to his parents.

4. The *loving* thing to do as a parent is the *responsible* thing. When in doubt as to whether you should or shouldn't permit something, answer the question, "What is the responsible thing to do?" It will also be the loving thing to do. Not to hold someone accountable for their behavior is not loving.

5. There are only three ways children learn:
    a. By what they see in the examples around them
    b. By what they hear
    c. By what they experience

6. "Natural Consequences" are the best teachers. If you don't brush your teeth you wind up with the natural consequences, i.e. cavities.

7. "Imposed consequences" are the next best teachers. If you get cavities because you didn't brush your teeth, there will be no candy and you can help pay for your cavities.

8. *Loving* a child and *trusting* a child are two totally different concepts and they are not connected. It is possible to love a child and not trust him. Trust is the function of responsible behavior. To be trusted children must be where they say they will be and doing what they say they will be doing. Trust is earned as credibility is established.

9. Do not deny children their reasonable requests just to show you have the power as a parent. Don't say "no" just to demonstrate you are in control.

10. Follow Dr. Lund's Parent Creed:

   "Because I love you, I will assist you in becoming your highest and best self. But, I will not enable you to self-destruct, nor will I help you one inch to hell."

LOVE AND TRUST

Maybe the most profound way to effect change in others is to love them, to strengthen them and their self-worth in such a way they come to believe in themselves. The power of unconditional love has yet to be measured. This much is known: It is difficult to resist forever the unconditional love of another. There is so much to say about the power of love, of acceptance, affection, and appreciation. However, there are some cautions. Once again love and trust are two different things. You can love someone and not trust them. Also, you can trust someone and not love them. You can both love and trust or you can both not love and not trust. TRUST is the function of freedom and responsibility.

> *"I will give you as much freedom as you demonstrate responsibility to handle."*

Unconditional love, on the other hand, does not mean you have to be stupid or be taken advantage of, or made to feel a fool. Unconditional love is something one does because he is a good person, not because the loved one *deserves* it. However, the loving thing is almost always the responsible thing. The loving thing is to help a person become their highest and best self. It is not love to enable someone in poor judgment decisions. "I will not help you one inch to hell," is a loving stance. Irresponsible people want to play upon the love others have for them in order to escape the consequences of their poor judgment decisions. People who are constantly rescuing their loved ones from the consequences of their poor choices, create a loved one who begins to believe he or she does not have to obey the rules.

SAM'S STORY

Sam was a responsible seventeen-year-old in everything but driving fast. In a single month he received three speeding tickets. There was an important prom dance coming up. Sam asked his father if he could borrow his Dad's expensive car. The father responded, "No."

Sam was disappointed and naively asked, "Why?"

Dad's reply was straightforward, "I love you, son, but I don't trust you once you get behind the steering wheel of a car."

Sam pleaded, "How can I ever prove to you that I can be responsible if you never trust me?"

The father replied, "When you have paid back the money I loaned you to pay the speeding tickets, and if you receive no more traffic violations for three months,

74

I'll be willing to extend trust once again and loan you my car."

Sam said, "But Dad, the dance is this Friday night. In three months it will be too late. I promise I'll drive responsibly."

Sam's mother would have let him take the car. In her heart she thought it would be the loving thing to do. She looked at her husband with pleading eyes.

The father stood firm, "I'm sorry son, the answer is no."

Sam stomped off angry and mad and slammed the door to his room. The mother was also upset with the father. She felt that mercy was needed. The dad explained that doing the responsible thing is almost always the truly loving thing to do.

Remember trust and love are two separate issues. The mother would have caved in to the disappointment she saw in her son. She would have given trust in the name of love. Trust, however is unlike love, respect, and forgiveness which can be gifted. But to forgive doesn't mean you have to trust the untrustworthy. A child molester can be forgiven, but never trusted again with children. An alcoholic can be forgiven, but not hired as a bartender. Trust must be earned by responsible behavior. However, there are some behaviors, like molestation, that are so abhorrent trust should never be reinvested even though forgiveness is granted.

Sam would agree with the statement, "If you love me, trust me." So would his mother. The problem is the mother winds up being an enabler. Sam wanted his freedom without responsibility for the past. The father's decision was a correct one, a loving one, but a very unpopular one. Sam could be forgiven for the past, but had to earn trust.

You can quickly see that in each relationship you need to

have two programs: one is an "I Love You" program, and the other is an "I Trust You" program. This is especially true when dealing with toxic personalities. The two programs should be kept separate. When love and trust become mixed up, people begin to act in bizarre ways. They set themselves up to be taken advantage of and then are hurt and wounded. In the name of love, they trust the untrustworthy. Unconditional love does not mean unconditional trust.

People have a responsibility to protect themselves from the untrustworthy. To allow another to take advantage of you in the name of love is to be foolish.

> *"Fooled once, shame on you; fooled twice, shame on me."*

It is to be an enabler in the worst way. It reinforces manipulation as a reward for the untrustworthy. The untrustworthy party decides to withhold love as a punishment for not being trusted. When the "I Love You" program is separated from the "I Trust You" program, clear-headed decisions can be made. Indeed, love and trust need not be related at all. Remember the "I Love You" program has a simple governing creed:

"I LOVE YOU" CREED

> *Because I love you, I will assist you in becoming your highest and best self. But I will not enable you to self destruct, nor will I help you one inch to hell!*

This in a nutshell is the affirmative statement which declares your position of loving. There is also an "I Trust You" program with the following governing creed:

"I TRUST YOU" CREED

I will trust you as you demonstrate responsible behavior. I will trust you when your words and behavior are consistent. I will trust you when you are doing what you say you will be doing and you are where you say you will be.

Children frequently demand trust as a sign of being loved. Only the naive parent will be convinced by this faulty reasoning. Those who are unable to separate love and trust often wind up enabling unhealthy behaviors to continue in the name of love.

Remember, it is normal for children to be selfish, demanding, and unreasonable. This is where the art of parenting comes in. It is the parent's role to transfer the responsibility for the child's happiness or boredom to the child's shoulders. The "you owe me" attitude only works when both parties buy into it. Children are pragmatists. They do what works. If throwing a tantrum gets a child what he wants, why not throw a tantrum?

There are two serious questions regarding children acting out. The first question deals with the parent. "Is the parent behaving responsibly and reasonably toward the child?" An abused child has a right to act out. It must be established that the behavior of the parent is appropriate?"

Assuming that the parent behavior *is* appropriate, the second question deals with the child's physical and mental health. "Is the child's condition a result of physiological or medical causes?" Only a qualified medical professional is empowered to answer that question. A good rule of thumb is "when in doubt, check it out." However, most children engaging in toxic behaviors are just testing boundaries. Socialization is the process of learning to respect the space and property of others. Many children learn they can manipulate their parents by dysfunctional behaviors.

"SPOILED BRAT"

Christmas was not a good experience for the father. He was expected to go into debt to buy extraordinary gifts for his wife and children. Over the years all of the children came to expect bigger and more expensive gifts. This year the sixteen-year-old daughter, Pam, was expecting a car. Dozens of hints and tremendous pressure were placed upon the father to provide a car. Careful shopping and looking around on the part of the father produced a clean, sharp, and nice looking used car. It was a ten-year-old Opel. It had low mileage and a new paint job. With new brakes and seat belts it was not only safe but attractive and serviceable.

On Christmas morning an elaborate effort was made to make finding the car a fun experience. However, Pam was not only disappointed in the car, but burst into tears and ran into her bedroom and slammed the door. She had expected a new car. Once again Christmas was ruined. Over the next few days the parents became more and more concerned. She would not come out of her room. She would not eat and she would not even talk to her parents.

"Go away, go away!" she would say, "You don't love me. You never have. You always have money for what you want , but never for me. I hate you! I hate you!"

By New Year's the father broke down and went to the new car dealer. He went into a deeper debt than he could possibly afford. Pam was ecstatic. She hugged and kissed her Dad and told him he was the best Dad in the whole world. This same behavioral pattern repeated itself for the "prom dress" and other very expensive clothes.

What this "spoiled brat" lacked, of course, was perspective. She had no appreciation of the effort required to provide for a family. She also lacked the confidence that comes from self-reliance. The parents failed in two areas. The first area was in transferring the responsibility for happiness to the sixteen-year-old's shoulders. As long as the parents felt responsible to please the child, make the child happy, and fix her world, so did the child. In her mind, when she was unhappy it was the parent's fault. The parents were manipulated by their child's disappointment and unhappiness. The second area of parent failure was in teaching self-reliance. Obviously, the parents could not turn back the clock. They could, however, begin to act responsibly.

Pam had expressed her desire to attend a very expensive university. The parents had already explained they could not afford it. But, the parents had no credibility. Why should the daughter believe them? In her mind, a few days of crying, not eating, and isolating herself in the bedroom should bring the desired results. It had always worked before.

The father explained that staying home where she could have free room and board and attend a local community college for the first two years was what the family could afford. This was not acceptable to Pam. When the beleaguered parents came to my office, they did not want to hear what common sense had told them all along they should do. *Let go of trying to please this "toxic child."*

"Yes," they were told, "You created this selfish, demanding child by acting as if it were your responsibility to make her world happy. You as parents must be prepared to accept the 'wrath of your daughter.' You cannot be manipulated by her disappointment. You must be firm in asserting what it is you can reasonably do. Remember, you have no credibility. She is not going to believe you. She may even escalate her threats to self destruct. In her mind, if a five pound hammer won't work maybe a ten pound hammer will. Your responsibility is to remain steadfast in your position."

"Offer her some options where she has control. For example, because of your income and the size of your family, she can qualify for student loans. You can figure out how much you could contribute to her going away to school and offer to help that much . She could go to work and save her money for college. Any alternative you offer will be rejected. You will be perceived as 'not loving,' 'not caring,' and as 'selfish.' Letting go of being well thought of is your first challenge; holding firm is your second. Once your daughter is convinced that resenting you doesn't work, she may begin to flatter, tease, and plead. You must ignore her pleadings. Only when she accepts responsibility for making her dreams come true can she become an appreciative daughter."

This story has a happy ending. The daughter stayed home and attended the community college. She worked and saved her money. However, she was rude, resentful, and unkind to her parents. She was punishing them and hoped they would recant and make her wishes come true. After that first year was over she was finally convinced she could not persuade her parents to change, she underwent an attitude change on her own. She accepted responsibility for her life. Achieving her objectives on her own brought with it a new found sense of confidence and independence. Appreciation for her parents eventually came as she realized the great sacrifices they made for her.

WHEN LITTLE PORCUPINES GET BIG

There are toxic children who never abandon toxic behaviors and simply get older. These adult-children still feel their parents owe them. No matter how much money, time, or energy the parents continue to pour into the adult-child, it is never enough. The parent is held hostage by the guilt of a

80

divorce, or lack of opportunity the child may have had, or that indeed the child may have been abused and mistreated. In all cases of the toxic adult-child, the parents are held responsible for the adult-child's lack of happiness or success.

POOR POOR PAULINE

As a child, Pauline grew up in poverty. She always resented her lack of new clothes and her lack of music lessons. She especially hated the fact she couldn't even try out for the drill team because her single-parent mother couldn't afford to pay for the outfits. Later, when her mother married a successful lawyer, they moved to an upper middle class neighborhood. Now she had a nice car, new clothes, and even a maid to clean her room.

The more Pauline received, the more she demanded. When she went away to college, she failed three straight quarters. She expected to be sponsored without taking responsibility for her failures. To compound the issue, the mother felt that all of Pauline's failures were the result of poor mothering skills on her part. Pauline believed it too. As long as she and her mother were tied into this unhealthy codependency, the situation would not change. Pauline got pregnant, married, divorced, and dropped off the baby with her mother for days at a time. She didn't want to work and lost several jobs just to prove it. The mother was being held hostage by fear of what would happen to her grandchild.

When I suggested that this cycle of insanity be broken by holding Pauline responsible for her current behavior, the mother freaked out. "What if...," "what if...," and "what if...," worst case scenarios were her concerns.

I asked the mother my own "what if" questions: "What if you were killed in a traffic accident tomorrow? What would happen to the grandchild? What would happen to Pauline? The answer is, she will either take responsibility for her life and child or she will not."

Pauline's toxic behavior continued because the mother's guilt sustained it. Three more times she asked for money. She went to a computer school, but she dropped out after two weeks. It was too hard. The beauty school and real estate school were too boring.

Pauline was right. The mother was responsible for her failures. Once again I had to convince a parent that until the adult-child cared more about being a mother and a responsible human being than the parents did, they would be held hostage. I suggested no more money and no more sponsorship of her irresponsible life style. If Pauline did not get and keep a job, she would be kicked out of the house and Child Protective Services would be called to take the child away. If she wanted to go to school, she would have to earn the money or qualify for student loans. Her stepfather agreed to pay off her student loans if she successfully completed school with "C" grades or better.

The hardest call the mother ever made was to Child Protective Services. It was also the end of codependency. Six months with supervised visitations of her own child convinced Pauline to take charge of her life. She hated her mother and refused to talk to her during that time. With the help of a woman's shelter and a job as a waitress, Pauline eventually was able to afford an apartment. Night school and weekend study finally paid off in a real estate license. Pauline became successful and now has a reasonable relationship with her mother. This story illustrates how one cannot change a toxic person. Pauline was the only one who could change herself. Only when she cared more about her life than her parents did, was she willing to make the needed life adjustments.

HAPLESS HAROLD

Harold seldom finished anything. Graduation from high school was not an earned achievement. It was a gift. He was pushed, shoved, and cajoled by his parents and teachers to graduate. Piano lessons, his Eagle Scout Award, and a number of abandoned opportunities were left incomplete. They were always more important to others than to Harold. Unfinished projects by the dozens marked Harold's life. He was always looking for the easy way, the fast buck. He left college. It was too hard. He has been married three times. Marriage was also too hard. His true job resume included fifteen to twenty jobs. He had joined every multilevel marketing organization that he had encountered, hoping to strike it rich. But when Harold had to perform he left it to chase the next rainbow.

People were drawn to Harold. He was pleasant, easy going, and a social butterfly. He possessed great verbal skills. However, his ex-wives described him as "all talk and no work." Harold was a toxic person in a passive aggressive way. His inaction drove other people crazy. In trying to "make him" responsible, and not being able to do so, they became toxic in the process

Harold's parents constantly bailed him out financially. As he got older they shifted from trying to make Harold responsible to making excuses for his behavior. Feeling guilty as parents, they assumed that Harold was still their responsibility.

Harold is fifty-five years old now. His father has passed away. Harold is still borrowing money, which he never pays back, from his aging mother.

Regardless of the age of spoiled children, whether five or fifty-five, their toxic behavior will be tolerated until the parent gets serious about transferring to them the responsibility for governing their own lives. Until and unless that happens, an unhealthy relationship will exist. It is one thing to help a child who is really trying. It is an unhealthy parent who pours in time, money, and effort to compensate for a child who is unwilling to accept responsibility for his or her own life and happiness. Children or adult-children who are toxic will act helpless. They will cling to the status of dependent. They lack confidence in their ability to care for themselves. They look to be rescued while resenting the rescuer for not doing more.

KICKED OUT OF THE NEST AT 27, 37, AND 47

Like the proverbial "bad penny," Smitty kept showing up on his parent's doorstep. The first time his parents asked him to leave he was twenty-seven. He had a job and had all his toys parked around his parent's place. There was a snowmobile, a jeep, a boat, and a couple of cars that had stopped running. The mother enjoyed his company, but not his messes. He left, but not really. His stuff was still all around. At thirty he came home to live just to save some money. It wasn't long until his clutter became overwhelming and he left again at thirty-seven.

After a failed marriage and two children, he returned to live with his parents at forty-four. The parents had finally cleaned up their place from all of Smitty's clutter. Now he was back and the parents were fearful of history repeating itself.

They came to see me when Smitty was forty-seven. The parents were concerned that Smitty was ready to retire and have them sponsor him the rest of his life. The parents had saved and sacrificed to own a motor home. Now they wanted to travel, but were not comfortable leaving Smitty at home. Neither were they excited about taking him with them.

It was time for the final boot. I suggested that Smitty's parents help him find a place to live, pay for the first three months rent, and tell him only to come to the house when invited to do so. There would be no more living at home. Holidays and an occasional Sunday dinner would be it. No more loans and no more borrowing of the parent's things. Until the parents had the courage to set the boundaries, Smitty would continue to take advantage of them. The truth is, Smitty adjusted quickly to the new rules. In this case the parents did not fear losing Smitty; they feared he would return and never leave.

THE BURNING QUESTION

Porcupines, whether big or little, have a way of making us feel responsible for their life's choices. Somehow, we are the bad guys if we don't rescue them from the consequences of their poor judgment decisions. We are expected to feel guilty for allowing them to remain in difficult situations of their own making. They resent it when we require them to act responsibly. They would have us feel guilty for not doing more. The emphasis is always on their current needs, not on what has already been done for them. Their failure to prepare for the future leads them from one crisis to another constantly looking to us to save them. Usually this means our time or our money. They are cooperative only if they get their way. Their willingness to act responsibly lasts for a short time until their next crisis. This type of relationship only works if we as parents buy into it. We are faced with the burning question, "Can we change them?" "Can we pluck the quills from these little porcupines who don't quite grow up?"

CHAPTER SIX

CAN I PLUCK THE
QUILLS FROM A PORCUPINE?

After every seminar and each lecture on dealing with toxic personalities, someone will say, "I have a toxic person in my life. What can I do to change them? There must be something I can do."

A difficult truth to accept is that no one can change toxic people. They can only change themselves. "Can toxic people change?" is a different question. Yes, absolutely; but the desire to replace unhealthy behaviors with healthy ones has to be the decision of the toxic person.

A better question to ask for the person who has to live with the porcupine is "What can I do to coexist with these 'spiked ones'? I accept that I cannot change them. I understand that the willingness to alter their lives must come from them. I get it!! No matter what I do toxic people *may not* change. I realize that my energies are best spent on developing my skills to *coexist* with emotional porcupines and *not on changing* them."

A WISH OR A GOAL?

There are two kinds of expectations, i.e., those that depend upon what you do and expectations that depend upon what others do. For the purpose of our discussion, we are going to redefine the words "goal" and "wish." Independent expectations which depend solely upon *you* carrying them out will be called "goals." Dependent expectations which require *other people* to perform in certain ways will be called "wishes." These definitions help us understand our relationship to the toxic and why we can not change them. Changing yourself is an independent goal. Trying to change someone else is a wish. Even if the expectation we have for another is reasonable, it is a wish. In spite of our love and our intense desire for their well being, our expectations for our loved ones to change are still wishes because they depend upon someone else for their fulfillment.

It becomes painfully clear the more our lives depend upon wishes, the more frustrated we become. The more our lives depend upon self-fulfilling goals, the more control we have over our lives. Remember *all frustration is based on unmet expectations*. If we did not expect anything we would not be frustrated.

> "I expect my older children to keep their rooms clean..."
> "I expect my children *not* to argue and quarrel..."
> "I expect my spouse to know how I feel because of our past history together..."
> "I expect my mate *not* to criticize me..."
> "I expect to please my loved ones and be appreciated for it."

As reasonable as these expectations may seem, they become unrealistic wishes if the other party upon whom they depend is unwilling to fulfill them. Self-confidence and a greater sense of self-mastery are obtained by setting goals consistent with the personal time, energy, and will of the individual goal setter.

"I will define for myself what a *good* person would do in
my circumstances."
"I expect to exercise today."
"I will call my toxic spouse and ignore his criticism."
"I will not swear today."
"I will focus on loving one child today."

Expectations which are solely dependent upon you for their completion are achievable goals. Because you are in control of a goal, no one can keep you from obtaining it. Relationships are one-half wish and one-half goal. You are only one-half of any relationship to which you are a party. You can make the goal to become the best "half" of that relationship you are capable of becoming. If you are in a relationship with a toxic person, the only person you have power to change is yourself. Regardless of the intensity of your heartfelt wish, you cannot change the toxic person.

TOXIC PEOPLE MAY ENGENDER
TOXIC BEHAVIOR IN OTHERS

The challenge for those who have reasonable and realistic "wishes" for others is not to become toxic in an attempt to force others to conform. The danger for the frustrated person is in adopting toxic behaviors in order to deal with the one who is causing the frustration. It is like yelling at someone to stop them from yelling. In so doing they instill a pattern of responses that make them as toxic as the person they are criticizing. Dealing with these difficult personalities is like cleaning the old coal stoves. There is no way to do it without getting soot, coal dust, and dirt all over you, unless you have the proper equipment. Without the proper clothing or a wet-dry vacuum cleaner, the result will be the transfer of ashes from the stove to the person. Toxic people tend to engender toxic reactions from others. Both parties become embroiled in dysfunctional behaviors. Both now appear equally guilty. Only when one party determines to act or react in healthy ways can the truly toxic person be revealed.

WILL THE REAL PORCUPINE PLEASE STAND UP?

Eve and Jim fought like cats and dogs. As far as their children were concerned, both of their parents were equally guilty of toxic behaviors. Jim grew up in a very critical home. He was used to criticism, arguments, and contention. His parents yelled, screamed, and swore at one another.

Eve came from a quiet environment. Peace was a highly prized value in her home. Her parents went out of their way to avoid conflict. It was considered a virtue to suffer in silence rather than stand up for yourself. When Eve and Jim first were married, Eve tolerated Jim's criticism and negativity. As time went by she became more and more confrontive. It was destroying Eve. Jim, however, was used to it. He did not know anything different. He didn't enjoy the fights but he considered his relationship normal.

From the outside both parties were acting and reacting in toxic ways. Jim's toxic actions inspired Eve's toxic reactions. Eve said, "I hate who I have become. I don't like myself anymore. He makes me act this way. I have to defend myself all the time. He is so critical. Then he expects me to be intimate with him. He drives me crazy."

I explained to Eve that nobody *makes* you do anything unless they have a gun to your head. "You are choosing to respond to him in unpleasant ways. It's true, you don't like the person you have chosen to become. You could choose a different set of responses." I asked Eve to fill out the following worksheet:

HOW DO YOU GENERALLY RESPOND TO FRUSTRATION?
Circle the responses to frustration you most commonly choose:

EXAMPLES OF NEGATIVE RESPONSES TO FRUSTRATION

pouting	criticism
anger	verbal abuse
crying	spanking
rebellion	preaching
throwing things	fear
being contentious	cursing
being contrary	swearing
despair	resentment
hopelessness	intimidation
resignation	defensiveness
yelling	arguing
physical abuse	threats
blaming others	hitting the wall or door
discouragement	kicking the wall or door
depression	making others miserable
laughing in their face	silence as punishment

Eve marked her current responses to Jim's criticisms as anger, being contentious, defensive, yelling, criticism, arguing and feelings of resentment.

I asked Eve, "Why do you think you choose to react with these negative responses?"

Her candid answer was insightful. "I want him to

91

suffer like I suffer. I'm just giving him some of his own medicine. When we were first married I tolerated it, but it never stopped. Finally I decided to give it right back to him."

Eve cried as she expressed her sorrow that somewhere in the past conflicts she lost her own identity. She stopped living her life and took on a life of reacting to Jim. Her new identity was defined by Jim's negativity and criticism.

I asked Eve if she would like to find herself again. "You will have to stop living your life as a reaction to Jim. You need to take control over yourself and your reactions to him."

She nodded her head.

"The purpose of negative behaviors is to express your frustration. The problem is toxic behaviors are all counterproductive and self-defeating. They do not change Jim for the good, nor do they inspire you to become a higher and better self. They alienate others and demonstrate an immature ability to cope with life. Remember, these are learned behaviors entrenched in your personality by repetition and practice. Negative behaviors are choices you make by habit and by tradition. They can and must be replaced by positive responses to frustration if you are to gain self-respect and establish a healthy identity.

"The list of Negative Responses consist primarily of emotional reactions. They require no real thought because they are emotional and not mental reactions. Positive reactions require time to think and ponder. This means, Eve, you are going to have to give yourself time before you respond. It means developing a different set of reactions to Jim's criticisms. The objective is to give yourself time to think about an appropriate reaction to Jim. The goal is to keep yourself in control of you. As long as you continue to take the bait or to internalize Jim's criticisms, the situation will not change."

I asked Eve to choose from the following list, a reaction which would be most consistent with her comfort level:

EXAMPLES OF POSITIVE RESPONSES TO FRUSTRATION

1. Excuse yourself and go for a walk to ponder responses which keep you in control of yourself and being a caring person.

2. Count to ten *slowly* and remain in emotional control. Sort through your best options.

3. Visualize something absurd, like Jim, dressed in baby clothes, sitting on a block of ice, sucking a pickle.

4. If you are under verbal attack or criticism, simply announce your need to write the criticisms down on paper in order to ponder them. Also announce that you will seriously consider the criticisms and get back to the person later.

5. Request the criticizing person to rub your back while he or she is giving the negative message, or ask the person to hold your hands while he or she criticizes you.

Negative responses to frustration are almost always emotional or feeling level reactions reflecting a lack of control. Positive responses to frustration are primarily thinking or mental reactions arrived at after meditation. Pondering takes time and therefore it is imperative that you develop the character trait of patience by staying in control of yourself as your first response to frustration.

Next, practice the skill of "thinking" by sorting through your options. Write them down and think them through before you act. Without over-analyzing it, just understand that you cannot achieve a loving response without a set of skills that allow you to stay in control of your value system.

The old expression, "think before you act," is apropos. However, it requires that you extricate yourself or leave the situation before you say something you will later regret.

THERE ARE FOUR LEVELS OF RESPONSE IN ANY SITUATION

Level Four	Loving Response
Level Three	Rational Response
Level Two	Emotional Response
Level One	Physical Response

A physical response, like hitting, shoving, or kicking, is an example of a level one reaction. It is intolerable except as a response to life endangering behaviors.

Negative emotional responses may involve verbal abuse. They almost always include anger and criticism. A toxic relationship is defined as mutually unedifying. These kinds of relationships are characterized by a war of hurtful words or by silent resignation to unhappiness. Level One (Physical Responses) and Level Two (Emotional Responses) are frequently joined together in unhealthy ways. If the relationship is to improve, one party or the other has to move up to levels three or four.

Rational responses (Level Three) are thinking responses. By definition, you need time to think about an appropriate reaction. This is why writing things down can help the mind focus on rational behaviors.

Loving responses (Level Four) involve working through the rational options and choosing a reaction which reflects behavior which is in the best interest of both parties. It is nearly impossible to achieve a level four "loving response" without thinking.

As much as Eve wanted to change Jim she could not. Only when she changed herself and her reactions to Jim were Jim's toxic behaviors able to emerge as the real issue. Eve's negativity only enabled Jim to stay where he was. She was contributing to his emotional delinquency. The more Eve focused on being a healthy person the more obvious it became to everyone, including Jim, that he had a serious problem.

HERDING A PORCUPINE

True change comes from within each person. Imagine how difficult it would be to herd a porcupine. Every time a porcupine is threatened, he curls into a round form and stops. So ends the herding. You can not force porcupines in a direction they are unwilling to go.

In dealing with Toxic Behaviors and Toxic Personalities, you cannot join the enemy. You cannot improve a relationship unless you are willing to stand on higher moral ground. If you expect to have any influence whatsoever upon toxic people, it will occur only as you focus upon remaining healthy yourself and staying in control of your own behaviors. If you are in a relationship with a toxic person, the absolute best that you can hope for is to create an environment conducive to change. You may not be able to herd the porcupine, but you can become a catalyst.

A CATALYST

By scientific definition a catalyst is an "agent of change" in chemical reactions which speeds up the process. Becoming like Jim couldn't change him. Becoming healthy made Eve an agent of change, a catalyst. She didn't change Jim; she changed herself. Now Jim had a decision to make. He either had to stop his behavior or lose Eve. As long as Eve cared more about Jim's toxic behavior than he did she was held hostage by it. When Eve let go of gaining Jim's approval or caring about his disapproval, she cut off his power supply. When Eve's focus turned to becoming healthy and believing that it was *more* important to be healthy than to be approved of by him, things quickly began to change.

The irony was in all the wasted effort Eve had put into their twenty-three years of marriage to change Jim. It had not worked. It only disheartened her and made her a person she did not like. Eve became "a catalyst" when her focus was upon changing herself. I asked Eve, "Do you really want to see Jim change? Then change you reactions to him!"

KEEPING THE FOCUS WHERE IT BELONGS

The focus needs to be on preparing yourself to remain emotionally healthy when interacting with the toxic loved one. Parents and others want to speed up the process of change in the life of the one about whom they are concerned. Therefore, they criticize them hoping the truth of what they have to say will speed up a change. It doesn't. It simply increases frustration and leads to more detrimental behavior.

The negative downward spiral continues until one, or both, flee the relationship.

For an outside party to create an environment for change requires a different approach. The challenge faced by most "want-to-be-change-agents" is patience. What they face is a friend or loved one who doesn't want to change. They may even be belligerent about it. They face loved ones who are out of control with their own lives. Because of frustration, both parties are out of control, but for different reasons. The toxic is out of control because of poor behavioral patterns. The catalyst, or the "I-want-you-not-to-be-toxic" person, is out of control because of frustration. The frustration usually leads to equally harmful reactions, making the individual a part of the problem and not a part of the solution.

True change comes from within. Control is not change. Conformity is not change. Submission and acquiescence are not change. The frustrated wonder what more they can do. They try to save the toxic from the consequences of their own poor behavioral patterns. This is especially true of parents. They want to rescue recalcitrant children from themselves. They bail them out of problem after problem, only to find that nothing has changed. The loved ones are still on a course of self-defeating behaviors. They loan them money. They pay for programs to help. They engage the services of counselors. It seems that almost every solution is defeated by the toxic's unwillingness to accept responsibility for making his or her life better. Nothing seems to work.

Most do not start out with a toxic approach, only a loving desire. When their reasonable approach doesn't work they resort to emotional or physical responses. They run the gauntlet of frustration and exhaust all of their personal options. The parents try what they think is love and understanding, but eventually their impatience and frustration reach the breaking point. They abandon love and understanding as one more failed attempt. They resort to improper criticism, force, coercion, punishment and finally abandonment. Hurting and smarting, they give up. They emotionally withdraw to a safe distance and mourn the lost potential of what might have been.

This pattern is being played out daily in the lives of thousands. What a waste of energy, finances, and personal effort. What a tragedy! The healthy approach requires a change of focus. It requires the developing of positive replacement skills when dealing with the difficult. The responsibility for change must be left to the toxic person. It also requires the focus on developing coping skills to deal with them. Patience combined with rational and loving behaviors have a chance of working. Those who think they have tried the healthy approach sometime are frustrated with the results of their failed attempts. They abandon healthy behaviors believing they do not work. However, becoming disagreeable and reacting with unhealthy behaviors doesn't work either. Responding in noxious ways to the toxic only adds *your* name to the list of toxic personalities.

Healthy behaviors are their own reward. Life is better when a person is in emotional control of his or her choices. In the previous story, Eve foolishly invested in the wish to change Jim. Constant disappointments led to reactions which left her equally toxic. She did not receive the immediate response she expected to her sincere efforts. Her frustration with him expanded to include frustration with herself. Many conclude the only answer is to abandon the relationship instead of abandoning the approach.

There does come a time, however, after healthy approaches have been patiently and thoroughly applied, that the next healthy alternative may be separation. The operative words here are "patiently" and "thoroughly" with "healthy approaches." Consider the following story of Jill and her wayward daughter.

JILL AND HER SIXTEEN-YEAR-OLD

Jill had a sixteen-year-old daughter who was out of control. Jill was a single mother of five children and worked full-time out of the home. Brenda was her challenge. The other four children seemed to be on track. They were doing well in school and active in their social lives. Brenda was failing school because of her unexcused absences. The mother had become a screaming banshee. At one point, there was a physical fight between Brenda and her mother. Punishment only led to more rebellion. What Jill was doing wasn't working. She thought she was doing the best she could, but it was not effective. Brenda was dishonest, uncooperative, immoral, and now violent. This is when the counselor was brought in. A very basic contract was drawn up with minimal requirements.

In a private session with the mother, the counselor reviewed her alternatives:

- Things could stay as they were.
- Things could get worse and Brenda would be removed from the home.
- The mother could react in healthy ways to Brenda.

One of the difficult issues Jill had to face was the feeling she was rewarding Brenda for acting poorly. To show love to an abusive child, an immoral and dishonest child, went against Jill's basic values of respect and responsibility. The relationship had degenerated. Now neither of them could be civil one to another. Brenda resented her lack of freedom. She just wanted to have fun and be with friends and live in the moment.

It was agreed that "perfection or nothing" would be

unrealistic for either the mother or the daughter. There would be mistakes and setbacks. In order for Brenda to change, the mother would have to change her approach. It began by Jill stopping her constant messages of disapproval. Jill truly thought criticizing and carping were signs of responsible motherhood. It was difficult for her to keep her mouth shut. Only the fear of losing her daughter altogether motivated Jill to follow the counsel. She began by analyzing her frustrations and not just dumping them on Brenda. Jill was afraid Brenda would think she had won the power struggle if she stopped criticizing her. The mother was concerned that Brenda would become more difficult to manage.

The truth was, Jill wasn't managing Brenda at all. Control was only an illusion. Brenda agreed to five minutes a night where her mother could give her negative feedback. The rest of the day, for twenty-three hours and fifty-five minutes, Brenda would not be criticized. The counselor recommended that Jill write down her criticisms in black and white where Brenda could see them without the mother's facial expression, body language, and tone of voice. This would allow Brenda to focus on the content. With a few major exceptions, it began to be more peaceful in the home. Jill still had absolutely no trust for her daughter, but she still continued to gift unconditional acts of love, one each day.

Brenda didn't lack knowledge of values. She lacked commitment to values. Brenda's selfish need for peer approval had caused her to trade away all values except the acceptance of her friends. Her guilty conscience made her angry with her mother, her family, and society. Just to see her mother was a reminder to Brenda of the values she was rejecting. To see her mother was to feel guilt. Brenda was the black sheep and she knew it.

This story is not over. Brenda is now seventeen and attending an alternative high school. The mother has let go of nearly every expectation she had for Brenda. She continues to do daily deeds of love. Brenda and her mother are talking, not yelling.

In a subsequent counseling session, Brenda confessed she is a disappointment to her mother, but now she knows her mother loves her anyway. Brenda has not come all the way back, but she will participate in family activities. While not perfect, the relationship is much better. It would not be where it is now except for Jill's willingness to change her approach. *Remember that which identifies toxic behavior from non-toxic behavior is the way, the how, and the approach, we take in achieving our expectations.*

NO, YOU CAN'T PLUCK THE QUILLS

No, you can't pluck the quills from a porcupine. They must shed them from themselves. Like the "Prodigal Son," each toxic person must "come to himself" and desire a better way. There is no substitute for coming to oneself. The alcoholic, the criminal, the negative can be led like the proverbial horse to water, but the desire to drink the water cannot be forced upon them. Desire for change is a seed which must grow in the soil of one's own heart. The toxic are often held hostage by self-doubt and by the knowledge of their own inadequacy. They know they are in rebellion against their best self and live in fear of further rejection. If they keep their lives busy enough, they can ignore, for a time, the difficult nature of their lives. The fact that others love them is lost in selfish pursuits. In this dysfunctional state they are hypersensitive to any criticism. They demand freedom without responsibility, acceptance for noncompliance, and trust in the face of being untrustworthy. Even justified criticism is rejected. Dysfunctional behavior is excused. Addictive behaviors are obsessively pursued in a determined effort to escape from responsibility and reality.

It is not just others who are rejecting these difficult personalities. Toxic people do not like their own lives. As frustrating as their lives may be for them, they are the only ones who can make a difference. Others will only wear themselves out trying to change them.

CHAPTER SEVEN

PUTTING ON THE ARMOR

Assume you have come out of denial and have come to accept that you cannot change toxic personalities. You can only change how you choose to relate to them. Suppose you have decided that becoming as toxic as they are is not the way you want to live your life. You have also decided you are unwilling to abandon the relationship. For darn sure, you are not going to let the abusive person control you. These choices leave you with only one healthy option. *You must put on the armor of realistic goals and expectations for your life.*

REALISTIC GOALS AND HEALTHY EXPECTATIONS :

1. CHOOSE HEALTHY RESPONSES TO THE TOXIC PERSON.
2. SET BOUNDARIES TO PROTECT YOURSELF.
3. STAY IN CONTROL OF YOUR VALUES.
4.. SHARE TO THE LEVEL OF THE TOXIC'S WILLINGNESS TO SHARE.

All of the above expectations are achievable goals and depend upon what *you* do. This means you can be successful as a healthy person. It does not guarantee change on the part of the toxic person. These behaviors, however, are conducive to creating the only known environment which has been helpful in encouraging change in the toxic personality.

The healthy person in following an appropriate plan will need to subject his or her frustration to logic. For now the focus is on converting the want-to-be-healthy parent or spouse to a new way of doing things. *Therefore, it is actually the victim of the toxic who must undergo a mind transplant.* By staying focused on healthy behaviors over which we have control, an environment conducive to change is created. However, it does not guarantee the change of anyone but self. Let's review what positive behaviors can help a person feel good about who he or she is. It begins by defining yourself as a healthy person.

HEALTHY EXPECTATION NUMBER ONE:
CHOOSING HEALTHY RESPONSES TO THE TOXIC PERSON

The only effective program for dealing with a toxic person begins with self-preparation.

1.   Let go of all expectations to *change* the toxic person.

2.   Focus on becoming your healthiest and best self.

3.   Define a set of loving behaviors which reflect what you are realistically able to do. Define for yourself what a "good" person would do.

4.   Realize there is some good in the worst of us and some areas of needed improvement in the best of us.

There is wisdom in focusing on the good in a toxic person and building upon it. Truly there is a spark of goodness in the hearts of even the most toxic. However dim the glow of that ember it can be fanned into a fire. It may begin with them believing there is something loveable about themselves. It is an adage in psychology that "behavior rewarded is behavior repeated." By rewarding even the slightest improvement, love can generate love. However, if the expectation is to receive the toxic person's approval, the mission will fail. Remember, to be a loving person is a goal. To be loved in return is a wish. The GOAL is to be a loving person. It is a WISH for the toxic person to change.

Wanting approval from a difficult-to-love person is like wanting gasoline for your car. You need gasoline for your engine. Looking to toxic people to fill your tank is a mistake. The toxic person will not or cannot give you the fuel of true acceptance. The gasoline in your tank must come from a "self-service" pump. If you require them to maintain your fuel supply, neither the car not the relationship will function. Indeed, you will run out of gas.

Most toxic people do not lack knowledge of loving and nonloving responses. They dole out love as a reward for positive performance and withdraw it for negative behavior. Love is held hostage to the ebb and flow of the tides of whim and circumstance. Treating them as they treat you is futile. What they lack is confidence in a positive approach to life. They are frequently harder on themselves than others. The toxic are *self*-toxic. They lack a belief in their own worth and the worth of others. Many toxic people advertise a tough exterior. Underneath is tremendous insecurity, self-doubt, and fear. They cannot be driven from the cave of their insecurities. However, they may be enticed if they can come to believe in themselves.

TAKE YOUR LOVE TO YOUR SON
AND YOUR FRUSTRATION TO AN EMPTY CHAIR

MARTI AND HER TOXIC SON

As a counselor, I asked Marti to go one month without once criticizing her fifteen-year-old son. I challenged her to go talk to an empty chair every time she felt upset or frustrated with her son. "Talk to an empty chair as if your son were in it, but not where he can hear you."

"Lay the responsibility for change upon your son. Become a healthy mother by becoming an 'agent of love.' Every time you are tempted to vent your frustration to your son, talk to the empty chair. Take your love to your son and your frustration to the chair. For one month do at least one loving thing a day for your son with no expectations for appreciation. Do it because you are a good person, not because his behavior merits it. Remember, not one word of criticism."

Marti asked me what she should do with her resentment. I told her to take it to the empty chair or turn it into a loving behavior. "For one month, Marti, just thirty days, don't give one criticism. If you make a mistake start your thirty days over again. Think of this as the loving thing to do. Will you do it, Marti? Will you remember once you leave this office? You have done it your way for fifteen years. Give me one month of doing it this way. Follow your heart, but not your frustration. You and the chair will become very good friends. Your son will make sure of that."

We met once a week for the next month. She reported how hard it was at first to break the old habit of criticizing. She spent several tearful minutes each day talking to the empty chair. No one, not even her husband,

106

was to know of our little secret. After the first week it was easier. She said it was becoming easier for her to go over to her son and put her arms around him and say, "I love you, son."

He was hostile at first and didn't want to be touched. By the end of the third week he began to hug her back. It was during the fourth week he came to his mother and cried. He just wanted to be held. Her words were words of love "It's been hard for you, Son. I'm sorry you're hurting. I know you'll get through this. I love you and I'll always be here for you."

"Mom, I've made such a mess out of my life and I'm only fifteen years old. I've got to stop screwing up!"

Marti was tempted to lecture him, but she did not. Only when the son felt more responsible for his life than Marti did, was he able to take control of his life. Her son did not lack knowledge. He lacked commitment to values. He was so busy rebelling against his mother's values he had not stopped to evaluate where it was taking him. For the first time Marti saw a ray of hope. She was fearful her expectations would run ahead of his willingness. She continued, however, to encourage his slightest improvement at home, at work, and in school. Several years passed and one day the phone rang. I was invited to his college graduation.

RECOGNIZING YOUR LIMITATIONS

Healthy people must come to recognize their limitations. Also, they must come to trust in the power of love. Truly, love is the catalyst, not inappropriate criticism. If criticism worked, we would have changed the world long ago. Love will benefit both the giver and the receiver. Self-love will power the engine of self-change. In a later discussion with Marti, after the son's graduation, we were able to reminisce and review why the program worked. Her son needed love. But Marti's messages of love were drowned in the sounds of her criticisms. Where was he going to seek love? The answer was "in all the wrong places, with the worst of friends, who had all the bad habits." Her toxic son was desperate for acceptance and belonging. Desperate people go to great lengths to avoid the storms of disapproval. They set up barriers which block out their ability to enter healthy harbors. They fear running aground on the reef of disapproval. They avoid self-evaluation. They hate what they do and what they have allowed themselves to become in their quest for acceptance at any price.

Marti could not change her toxic son. She could only change herself. If there was any hope for him to accept the responsibility for changing his negative ways, it would happen because he was able to focus on himself and not on the barrage of nonacceptance messages from his mother. Finding something to love in himself could give him the motivation to change himself.

If the healthy person is in a critical mode and their frustration manifests itself in raging disappointment they cease being a safe harbor. They are neither an "agent of love" nor an "agent of change." Compounding the problem is the healthy person's overwhelming feelings of failure. They are as inclined to give up as the toxic person, but for different reasons. The toxic person gives up on being healthy and the healthy person gives up out of a feeling of failure. For the healthy person to give up on the failed approach is okay. It is important not to give up on a healthy response to the toxic. Nevertheless, there is no healthy alternative, except to love the unlovable. The healthy person must take his or her frustrations to the "empty chair" and nurture the one who is difficult to love. To find the strength to love is ultimately a gift. Every man, woman, and child on earth has the ability and need to love and be loved. Even porcupines need love.

The question is which value will survive as your governing value? Which behaviors will direct your life: the dysfunctional ones or the emotionally healthy ones?

WHICH ONE WILL LIVE ?

Living inside of me are two wolves. Only one can survive as the leader of the pack, the Alpha-wolf. One wolf is a toxic wolf. He is mean, defensive, and unapproachable. The other is a wolf of love. He is noble and nurturing. Which wolf will emerge and dominate? The answer is, *the one I feed !*

If the wolf that emerges is the noble and nurturing one, his first instinct will be to protect. It is understandable that we would rescue a child from an abusive situation. However, as adults we are responsible to protect ourselves. This is best accomplished by establishing appropriate boundaries.

HEALTHY EXPECTATION NUMBER TWO:
SET BOUNDARIES TO PROTECT YOURSELF

Boundaries are behavioral limits we consider acceptable or unacceptable. In declaring a boundary we are identifying what we will or will not tolerate. A border between two countries is a boundary. One does not cross the border without the permission of the host country. Property lines are boundaries and people are expected to respect the rights of their neighbors.

Setting a boundary is always in relation to self. It is what we will do if that boundary is crossed. The truth is we are not really setting boundaries for other people. What we are doing is declaring what *we* will do if our boundary is violated. Toxic people hold others hostage to inappropriate boundaries. Teenagers may threaten to run away unless they have freedom to go to a party. Spouses may threaten emotional, economic, or physical abuse if their will is not adhered to. Some even threaten injury to themselves as a way to manipulate others. All of these forms of blackmail only work because we allow them to continue.

There are healthy boundaries and healthy ways to respond when a boundary is crossed. The principle of protecting ourselves from physical, emotional or mental abuse seems obvious. However, there are well-meaning people who confuse the issues of love and boundaries. It is as if these two issues were put into a blender and mixed together. The resultant effect is a hodge-podge of confusion wherein the victim of abuse is unable to discern between loving behavior and enabling behavior. Nevertheless, it is the responsibility of each individual to set limits on what he or she is willing to tolerate. For example, using illegal drugs in the home, loaning money, or staying in an abusive relationship all have their limits. We must decide for ourselves, according to a healthy value system, what we will or will not tolerate.

For example, if someone were yelling, cursing, or giving uninvited, unauthorized, and improper criticism, to say the following would be appropriate:

> *I'm leaving the room, (or the house, or the car,) because I do not give you permission to treat me in this manner. I am not leaving the relationship. I will be available to talk about this when you are in emotional control. If you cannot handle a calm discussion of your concerns, please write them down and I will read them tonight.*

THE PROBLEM OF CONFLICTING VALUES

GENNA'S HUSBAND IS AN ALCOHOLIC

Genna said, "I believe in marriage, but I don't believe in alcohol. My husband is an alcoholic. He becomes mean and abusive to me and the children when he drinks. He is a wonderful husband and a terrific father when he is sober."

As the counselor, I asked Genna, "Would your problem be solved if your husband would stop drinking?"

"Yes," Genna replied, "but he is drinking more and more."

"Have you encouraged him to go to AA, and have you considered going to Alanon, the support group for families of alcoholics?"

Once again she said, "Yes, but he won't go, and I don't want to if he is unwilling."

"Genna, why haven't you left him?"

She cried, "Because I love him, because I believe in marriage, because he is the father of my children, that's why I haven't left."

I suggested to Genna there was another motivation underlying her not leaving. "Genna, is it also true that you are afraid to leave him?"

She continued crying, "Yes, yes, I'm afraid! I don't know what I would do. I don't have any skills. I couldn't get a decent job. Nobody is going to want me with four kids or even without them."

"So the real issue is your fear. The reason you haven't left your alcoholic husband is your fear of being alone, your fear of not surviving economically, and your fear of the unknown future?"

Genna nodded her head. She had threatened to leave her husband a hundred times. On a couple of occasions she did take the children to her mother's house for a few

111

days. Then Jim would apologize and promise to give up the drinking. She would go back. A few weeks later she would find evidence that his drinking had returned. Whenever the topic came up it would lead to a battle of words.

Genna is "between a rock and a hard place." She is faced with two difficult choices. Does she stay in this relationship with an alcoholic or does she go out on her own into a very scary world? Her life choices are not between easy and hard. They are both hard choices. Genna has a very real boundary problem; she is confused. My responsibility as a counselor was not to make her decisions for her, but to clarify her choices and help her understand the difference between healthy and unhealthy alternatives.

"Genna, let me ask you a few questions in hopes of clarifying the issues. Let's decide that whatever decision you make will be based upon what is healthy and not on fear, doubt, or what is difficult."

Genna was not prepared to set a real boundary until she had dealt with her fears. We discussed an exit plan from her marriage and even explored a "worse case scenario" plan. Next, we explored various employment alternatives and the positives and negatives of being alone. Equally explored were the options of what it would take to stay in the marriage and make it work. Genna was now prepared to set realistic boundaries. However, she would have a problem with credibility. In all likelihood her husband would not believe her. His expectation would be that the past would repeat itself.

Genna decided that her first option was to work on the marriage. However, she would not stay in an unhealthy relationship. She set the following boundaries as conditions for her staying in the relationship:

GENNA'S CONDITIONS FOR STAYING

1. Jim's commitment to stop drinking would include weekly attendance at Alcoholics Anonymous meetings.

2. They would go to counseling individually and together on a weekly basis for the next six months.

3. He would attend a ten-week anger management class.

4. If these boundaries were violated, she would file for divorce, obtain a Protective Order from the court, and have him removed from the home.

5. If he violated the terms of the Protective Order, she would call the police and he would go to jail.

6. If he persisted in drinking she would follow through with the divorce.

The difference between a threat and a boundary lies in the follow through. Genna's credibility was on the line. Truly it no longer mattered what Jim did or didn't do. The issue was what Genna would do if he crossed her boundaries. Would she have the courage to face her fears and act in a responsible way even if he chose a dysfunctional life style?

If someone becomes physically abusive, a call to the police is in order. To stay in a physically, emotionally, or mentally abusive situation only encourages the abusers. It gives them permission to continue and to escalate their abusive actions. Not only does it set a bad example for children, it contributes to a "culture of abuse." It fosters more coercion, intimidation, and manipulative behaviors as acceptable ways of interacting. It is understandable that children who are exposed to a "culture of abuse" have a harder time as adults recognizing abuse. It is also easy to comprehend why abused children have difficulty as adults in drawing healthy boundary lines. Once aware of the healthy boundaries, there is no excuse to permit abusive behavior from friend, family, spouse, or child. Sometimes calling the police is the loving thing to do. As hard as it may be, parents may have to remove a toxic child from the home.

DARLA'S PARENTS FINALLY SET BOUNDARIES

Darla was a fourteen-year-old who was verbally abusive to her mother and father. She learned her parents would tolerate everything. They did not know how to set limits on her abusive behaviors. Darla discovered power in abuse. She found more freedom to be with her friends, to have fun, to enjoy autonomy and to live for the moment by being belligerent, arbitrary, and combative.

The parents, in the mistaken guise of love, tolerated Darla's abuse. They thought it was the loving thing to do. They were fearful of her running away and being in a worse environment. They were concerned about her losing future opportunities. They were, in fact, being held hostage by fear, doubt, and a confused notion of love.

When the counselor outlined a strategy for dealing with Darla, the parents were horrified. They feared it would cause them to lose her entirely. What they failed to recognize was they had *already* lost her.

The counselor's strategy involved setting boundaries for Darla. The new boundaries were based solely upon trust. Her freedom was dependent upon her willingness to be responsible for her behavior. They included more freedom for responsibility. What the parents lacked was credibility. She did not believe her parents would follow through with their stated intentions. The boundaries included being placed in a home for troubled girls. The counselor explained that this final option was to send the message loud and clear that the parents would not tolerate abusive behavior. It was not the first option; it was the last. Because Darla's parents had no credibility, it would be a boundary quickly tested.

The parents held the power, but were not currently exercising common sense. There was room in the new program for Darla to be forgiven and to earn trust by obeying a few simple rules.

DARLA'S TRUST PROGRAM

1. She would be where she said she was going to be.
2. She would be doing what she said she was going to be doing.
3. There would be a curfew. She would be expected to be home at the mutually agreed upon time or the arbitrary time imposed by the parents.
4. She would clean up after herself.
5. She would do her few chores as a member of the family. (It is a good idea not to assign chores that will hold the family hostage if not performed. For example, ask Darla to groom the dog, not to do dishes. If she fails to groom the dog, the family still functions. If she were assigned dishes and didn't do them, the family wouldn't function.)
6. She would get reasonable grades in school.

THE PARENT'S TRUST PROGRAM

1. The parents would grant freedom according to responsible behavior.
2. They would not arbitrarily deny a request without a reasonable explanation.
3. They would follow through with
   a. The "I Love You" program
   b. Rewards
   c. Restrictions
   Darla's freedom to function at school, at home, and

with her friends was conditioned on her behavior. Each violation of a boundary would add one week onto the time she would be permitted to obtain a driver's license. The parents were going to enforce the new rules completely. There were several rewards for positive behavior. If Darla did not respond to the positive reinforcement program, the parents were required to implement the consequences in three stages:

Stage One: Cooperation and Negotiation
Stage Two: Probation and Restriction
Stage Three: Removal from the home to an all
              girl's school

The last stage would be Darla's exit from the home. By following through with their stated objectives, it was hoped that the parent's credibility with Darla would be established.

The counselor warned the parents that unless their resolve was firm and unwavering, Darla would return to her old ways. The parents were told to expect that Darla would try escalating the conflict. They were to exit the room if Darla became verbally abusive or critical. They were to offer her another opportunity to communicate, following the rules of courtesy and respect. Under no conditions were they to allow her to take them out of control of what they would tolerate and not tolerate.

The parents committed to the counselor that they would consistently implement two separate programs, i.e. "I Love You" and "I Trust You." They agreed they would support Darla with all of her positive choices, but they would not help her "one inch to hell." The parents agreed to put her into a Christian girls' school near Orlando, Florida for a minimum of six months if she failed to respond to their few, but reasonable, boundaries. The parents continued to do loving things on a daily basis with Darla. The parents agreed to try this approach for three months. At the same time they held firmly to their stated agenda.

As the counselor predicted, Darla increased her belligerence and escalated the conflict. Soon Darla was looking at over a hundred violations. This meant she could not drive until she was eighteen. Quickly, Darla moved through each of the three levels of strategic retreat the parents had outlined. One day, unannounced to Darla, two huge Samoan security guards, a lady hired as a companion, and a driver entered Darla's room and hauled her off to a girl's "reform school." She was kicking, screaming, swearing, and cursing at her parents. " I'll never forgive you," she shouted, "I hate you! I hate you! I'll run away, you'll never see me again. I'll kill myself !" She yelled "rape" and tried to get someone to rescue her, but she was no match for the Samoans.

The facility was escape-proof. The girls could earn privileges by obedience. There were four levels of freedom. It usually took forty-five to sixty days before the girls realized this was real. Darla was told to make her bed. She refused and found her bed was taken away and she was given a sleeping bag and a pillow. She was informed that if she faithfully rolled up her sleeping bag for a week they would restore her bed.

After a month Darla earned her bed back. She could write only to her parents. All mail that arrived for her other than from her parents was sent back. Darla begged and pleaded with her parents to let her out. She promised obedience. She had learned her lesson and would be a new person. The concerned parents wavered and called the counselor. The father wanted mercy, but the mother held firm. The counselor informed the parents that the real issue was their credibility. They had said six months and they needed to stick to it or they would be right back where they started.

The parents agreed. They wrote to her and told her of their resolve. If she worked her way up to at least the third level of trust and responsibility she would be released at six months. If not, she would be required to stay another six months. Darla was beginning to believe her parents for the first time in her young life. At six months Darla had achieved the fourth level of freedom which permitted her to go with a group to an outside movie. Later she confessed that she thought she would run away while at the movie. What she didn't know was that the Samoans were guarding the exits. Had she run she would have been returned to the first level and a sleeping bag and a six month extension. She finished a year's worth of high school home study in six months.

Her parents met with her at the end of the six months and informed her that if she returned to her old ways they would send her back. She believed them. A contract was drawn up with very specific behavioral objectives. The past was forgiven and Darla would again be able to obtain her driver's license at sixteen. Violations would add one week beyond her sixteenth birthday for each infraction before she would be able to get her driver's license.

After the honeymoon period of a couple of months, Darla tested her parents again and found them absolutely committed to do what they said they would do. The parents continued to love Darla. They remembered trust was a separate issue. Darla went on to drive at sixteen years and one month because of a few infractions. She graduated from high school and attended a local community college. She married a wonderful young man, with her parents crying for joy at the wedding. The parents ended up influencing Darla because they had credibility. They had learned that the loving thing to do was to hold her responsible for her behavior.

Darla's parents learned the value of real boundaries. They also recognized the need to be realistic in their expectations. Their "I Trust You" program was based on responsible behavior, not on perfection. They learned that the art of parenting was the art of gradually transferring responsibility for life from their shoulders to Darla's as she demonstrated an ability to handle it. They found the art of parenting was the art of letting go, not the art of hanging on. By protecting themselves, establishing boundaries, and setting reasonable behavioral objectives, they now enjoy a loving daughter.

THE PROBLEM OF
ARBITRARILY CHANGING BOUNDARIES

It is equally important that children can trust their parents to deliver promised rewards. The arbitrary, the whimsical, and the unreasonable parent or spouse stands to lose more than credibility.

JOAN AND THE DOG "DOO DOO"

For Joan the Prom was everything. A concerned, but misguided, father saw Joan's desire as a great opportunity to motivate her to be responsible. For two months Joan walked the line. Looming over her head was the fear of being grounded on Prom Night.

One of Joan's major responsibilities was to be a super-duper-pooper-scooper. It was her job to clean up after the dog. As distasteful as she found the job, she nevertheless followed through. Unbeknownst to her the dog had left very recent droppings in the garage just before the father came home. As one might predict the father stepped in the dog feces. He was irritated, angry and frustrated.

In less than two hours Joan was to leave for the Prom.

But no longer was that the case! The father called the boy who was coming to pick up Joan and told him Joan was grounded. All pleadings and tears were ignored. Joan ran away that night. She eventually returned only to leave again and never come back.

Hope is a delicate thing. If someone feels they are giving everything and it is not enough, they will soon give nothing, for likewise it is not enough. The father's promise that she could go to the Prom should have been honored based upon two months of responsible behavior. An attitude of "perfection or nothing" left the man without a daughter. This was a case where the daughter could not trust her toxic father.

HEALTHY EXPECTATION NUMBER THREE: STAY IN CONTROL OF YOUR VALUES

In preparing yourself to deal with porcupines it is important to stay in control of your values. In one way, this is setting a boundary. It is a declaration of what is important to you.

"What you do speaks so loudly I can't hear what you are saying," is an old adage.

When people hold firm to their values, it keeps them in control of their lives. A common problem is the belief that sacrificing your values will appease toxic people. It doesn't appease them and it doesn't change them. What is worse, it only empowers them to believe in their own dysfunctional ways. Furthermore, when you abandon a personal value system in order to "relate" to another, it engenders disrespect. It gives the toxic person another reason to discount you.

FRED SR. AND FRED JR.

Fred Jr. wanted very much to please his father. Fred Sr. had divorced Fred Jr.'s mother when he was eleven. Minimal contact through the years created a greater desire for a relationship with the father. However, Fred Sr. was toxic. He was highly critical of everyone including his own son. At eighteen Fred Jr. left home for college. For more than a year he had planned to spend a week with his father. Yet, his expectations for man to man male bonding were unrealistic. Fred Jr. had grown up with strong religious values. His father, on the other hand, shared none of these values.

Fred Sr. invited his son to spend three days with him in Reno, Nevada. With a desire to please his father, the young man agreed knowing that the trip would place him in a compromising position. In the name of getting closer to his father, Fred Jr. sacrificed his core values. Under the chiding of his father, who accused him of being "holier than thou," "self-righteous," and a "religious fanatic," the son compromised his principles. During the three days with his father in Reno, the son drank, smoked, and went to nude bars with his Dad, all in an attempt to draw closer to his father. Even though the father encouraged this behavior, he had no respect for his son.

At the end of their week they were no closer together. The father was critical of his son's choice of college, his field of study, and of his hypocritical life-style. The son's religion was cast into his face. "If you weren't such a hypocrite you wouldn't have gone to the nude bars and had something to drink. Apparently you have no backbone to stand up for what you believe."

The son had made the fatal assumption that he could compromise his principles and it would please his father. The truth is, it would not have mattered whether he compromised his values or not. He still would not have pleased his father. Had he stood firm on his Christian principles, his father would have continued to mock him. With toxic people you are "darned if you do or darned if you don't." It would have been better for the son had he held to his values. At least he would have pleased himself and walked away with self-respect.

The expectation for acceptance is understandable, but unrealistic when dealing with toxic people. No amount of compromise will appease them. Total submission will not do it. They will never be pleased. It will never be "enough." Holding firm to your values is the only way to deal with them. You must decide what a "good" person would do and hold to that value. If you stay true to your own values, you may not have the respect of the toxic person, but you will have something even greater, i.e. self-respect.

HEALTHY EXPECTATION NUMBER FOUR:
SHARE TO THE LEVEL OF THE LOVED
ONE'S WILLINGNESS TO SHARE

A basic truth about human relationships is that they cannot be forced. Each relationship stands on its own merits. It is a wise person who realizes the level of willingness another possesses. Once the level of willingness is recognized, a bridge can be built from where they are to a better place.

A relationship cannot grow beyond the common consent of each to participate. Frequently, one party, or both, do a lot of compromising in order to share the world of a friend, a spouse, or a child. The best relationships are built by sharing. They share time together. Often they share their hopes and dreams. The nature of a relationship will be a function of age difference, varied interest, and mutual respect. Sometimes the best way for a relationship to grow is by taking turns in choosing the shared activity. However, priorities prevail and some relationships have to settle for the best efforts of each.

JACK AND HIS WORKAHOLIC FATHER

Jack was eighteen and the only son in his family. His father was cold and very business-like. Jack desperately wanted a relationship with his father. Jack was a great athlete, but his father was always too busy with work to attend any games. Finally, Jack realized that if he were going to have a relationship with his father it would have to be on different terms.

I suggested to Jack that he show up unannounced at his father's place of business. His dad was shocked and wondered if there was an emergency. Jack told his father that he wanted to understand what his father did for a living. The father was too busy then, but set up a time to meet with Jack. The father was excited that Jack would show an interest in the business. Jack invested many hours learning more about the business than he wanted to know. After six weeks Jack looked up into the stands and saw his father for the first time in his life come to a game.

Finding a common ground and sharing to the level of the other's willingness to share is always a good place to start. However, this story could have ended with Jack making a lot of effort and finding no change on the part of his father. Jack has to settle for what his father is willing to share. It may have been that all Jack received was some shared time with his dad at his father's business. Relationships are limited by what each party is willing to contribute to make it happen.

What a toxic person will choose to do is never certain. The only real control you have is over your own behavior and choices. Protective armor shields you from the unstable world of a toxic individual. Wearing the armor of realistic goals and healthy expectations, you are prepared to examine the tools you will need to deal with emotional porcupines.

CHAPTER EIGHT

ARMORED GLOVES
AND OTHER TOOLS FOR
HANDLING PORCUPINES

For a number of years I have been involved in excursions to the jungles of Mexico and Guatemala. Most of these adventures to study the ruins of the Maya have taken place in the spring and summer. I have been going for nearly four decades. It is a passion. However, the change in diet almost always upsets my stomach. If I take one-half tablet of Imodium daily, I have no problems. In addition, I have been immunized to protect myself from disease. I understand that clothing needs to be appropriate and hammocks are preferable to beds or sleeping on the ground. The jungle is a beautiful place when you are prepared to enjoy it. Not having bug spray or insect repellent can make the entire experience miserable. The important issue is to be prepared and to protect yourself from the negatives of a hostile environment. The same can be said of living with an emotional porcupine.

PICKING UP A PORCUPINE

Knowledge is power. There are tools necessary to deal with the toxic personality. There are attitudes which are essential to acquire and maintain in order to survive living with a toxic parent, mate, child, in-law, boss, or friend. It is like putting on a pair of metal protective gloves to handle or pick up a porcupine.

SELF-PRESERVATION IS YOUR RESPONSIBILITY

Self-preservation begins with one hand up to protect yourself while having the other hand extended to cooperate. Both hands, however, are covered by armored gloves. To approach a porcupine or to have a porcupine approach you requires the mental equivalent of a protective shield. Armored gloves like those worn by knights of old are vital.

The first essential attitude is personal responsibility for self-preservation. Why should others value you when you do not value yourself? Being controlled, manipulated, and defined by a toxic person means you have let go of your own identity. Underlying the need to survive is a commitment to be your best self. It is the individual's responsibility to define who he or she is and what is important in life. Even if toxic people are right about what is "good," they are wrong if the approach is not healthy.

Taking control of life requires a degree of autonomy and independence. Many teenagers and wives are held hostage by a toxic father and husband who enforces his will by economic bondage. It works until the teen flees the oppressive environment, the spouse sues for divorce, or they learn to cope with the toxic person in healthy ways. "Rebelling" for the sake of "rebelling" is behavior which allows the contrary

126

person to control your life. Living life in defiance of a toxic person's values is different than living to become your best self. Defining yourself, and not being defined by others, is a beginning. Once that identity has been defined as becoming your healthiest and best self, protecting and preserving "the healthy you" is the first essential attribute in surviving among porcupines.

LET GO OF THE EXPECTATION TO "PLEASE"!

The second essential attitude requires letting go of the expectation to please toxic people. The key is letting go without becoming as bitter, resentful, and as difficult as they are. Pleasing yourself must replace trying to please *them.* Developing emotional health is a personal journey. Empowering yourself by learning the necessary skills required to live with a porcupine is also a personal quest.

Always remember it is not possible for you to change toxic people. They can only change themselves. Until you accept this fact you will waste a tremendous amount of time and energy. There is an expression that encompasses this thought: "Don't lean your ladder against the wrong wall!"

Your challenge is to develop a healthy self-concept while living with people who want you to exist to please them. They will want all their toxic ways to govern your interactions. Becoming your healthiest and best self should be your primary objective. Cooperation, negotiation, and mutual agreement are all appropriate as long as the outcome does not violate your prime objective of becoming your best self. This quest for a healthy self requires the development of protective skills. It means putting on mental and emotional armor. We will now explore the world of how to co-exist with porcupines without becoming a pin cushion.

TOOLS TO USE WHEN
DEALING WITH A TOXIC PERSONALITY

STAYING IN CONTROL OF SELF

Staying in control of self is the objective when confronted by an emotional porcupine. Listed below are a number of tools which have proved effective when dealing with the toxic personality. Don't be afraid to experiment with these tools to determine which ones work best for you.

THE TOOL OF SELF-PREPARATION:

Remember the objective of life is for you to become your healthiest and best self. Anything that detracts from that goal is detrimental and unacceptable. The real challenge for those who live in a toxic relationship day after day is to survive without becoming toxic themselves. Those who are successful are those who focus on being their healthiest and best selves. They let go of trying to *change* the toxic person and they let go of trying to *please* them. They define their own standard of "what a good person or what a loving person would do." They follow through with their program because the focus is not on pleasing others. The focus is upon being their healthiest and best selves.

THE TOOL OF DEFINING ENOUGH:

Individuals who want to feel they are good enough cannot let toxic people define them. That would be equivalent to letting the "fox guard the chicken coop." Remember, a toxic person is one who will not allow you to be enough. The following story illustrates the need for self-definition:

BOB DEFINES ENOUGH

Bob's mother was a constant complainer. No matter how much Bob did he could not satisfy his mother. According to her, Bob never called her enough, visited her enough, or showed that he truly cared enough. She was a lonely old lady. Her complaints and demands grew worse and worse. Bob felt guilty and depressed because no matter how much he did he could not fix her world.

With some guidance, Bob was able to define the role of a good son. He would phone her once a week. He would visit her once a month at her home. He would spend some time repairing or lifting and carrying things. She would be invited to come to Sunday dinner at his place. He would make sure she was able to spend a part of each holiday with his family. This was Bob's definition of enough for a good son to do.

Each person must define what enough is for each relationship. This would include how much time, money, energy, and resources you are willing to give. It will not be enough for the toxic person, but it doesn't matter. It will be enough for you. Learning to live with your own definition of enough and not being governed by the guilt trips of others is the essence of coping with the unreasonable demands of toxic people.

THE TOOL OF REWARDING SELF:

One way to stay in control is to reward yourself when you are criticized by others. There is a woman who gave herself 25 cents every time she was criticized by her husband or children. Each time she was criticized she just blinked her eyes like an old-time cash register and added on 25 cents more. It wasn't the money that was important. It was her ability to keep the focus on the critic's behavior and not become depressed because she had internalized the criticisms. She was able to avoid depression and discouragement by rewarding herself for handling the criticism in a healthy way.

One day the woman called and left the following message, "Tell Dr. Lund I just bought myself an $80 pair of shoes. He will know what I mean."

Consider how this principle can also be applied to a child's interaction with a toxic person:

TOXIC STEP-GRANDMA

No one could talk about Grandpa's deceased wife at family gatherings without offending his new wife. All pictures and references of the natural grandma were removed and her grandchildren had to pretend she never existed. Adding insult to injury, the step-grandma was toxic. She was highly critical of everyone and everything. The grandchildren dreaded the family gatherings. Step-grandma would criticize the grandchildren in very degrading and caustic ways until they ran off in tears.

One step-daughter-in-law came to me and asked how she could help her children cope with this disagreeable woman. She said she could handle the criticism for herself, but when it came to her children it was altogether intolerable. I suggested that before each family gathering this mother collect her five children together and play a game. It would be a secret game. They were not to provoke step-grandma and if they did they would not be rewarded. However, the grandchild that was criticized the most would be rewarded with a triple-decker ice cream cone. The next most criticized child would receive a double-decker and the rest would get a single scoop on the way home.

The entire mood of the family changed. From a psychological point of view, the focus and negative energy remained with the toxic step-grandma. The children were able to let her caustic remarks roll off their backs. It was all they could do not to smile while she criticized them. Family gatherings became a game. The only argument was who was really criticized the most. Sometimes everyone got a double scoop of ice cream, including Mom and Dad.

The tool of reward can make hugging a porcupine quite a "treat."

THE TOOL OF DIVERSION:

Diverting toxic messages is another way to stay in control. Rather than to internalize the negative message, keep it out of your mind by responding in an unorthodox manner.

OUCH !

By putting a rubber band on his wrist and snapping it every time he was criticized, Bob was able to divert his focus from the criticism to his wrist. He also rewarded himself $1.00 for each criticism

THE TOOL OF WRITING THE CRITICISM DOWN:

The tool of transferring criticism to paper also promotes self-control.

SPOCK, THE COURT REPORTER

Spock, on Star Trek, always placed logic above emotion. I explained to Jake that a court reporter was also to record information without becoming emotionally involved. Jake was to become "Spock, The Court Reporter," He was always to carry a small writing pad in his shirt pocket. Whenever anyone would criticize him,

131

he was to write it down. Transferring the criticism from his head, through his hand, and onto the paper, would take the criticism out of his body. There were several benefits to writing it down. Putting it on paper allowed him to objectively evaluate the criticism. It gave him time to think before he reacted.

Also, writing down a criticism served as a visual reminder to the *critical* person of how often he or she criticized. One highly critical person once said to Jake, "Get your pad and pencil! I have something I need to say." An awkward situation was made a little lighter by keeping the focus on the content of the criticism and not on personalities.

THE TOOL OF FOLLOWING THE COUNSEL YOU WOULD GIVE YOUR BEST FRIEND OR YOUR CHILD:

Imagine your own child comes to you with the identical problem you face. Your child explains to you in precise detail the nature of his or her concerns, which mirror exactly what you face. What counsel would you give your friend or your own child? Do you have the courage to follow your own best counsel? If not, why not?

THE TOOL OF ALWAYS HAVING AN EXIT PLAN:

Limit your exposure and vulnerability. Preplan another overlapping activity that allows you to excuse yourself after you have reached your level of tolerance. Take two cars if possible so your exit does not impose on others and so you are not dependent upon others to rescue you. Prearrange to have others phone you and give you a reason for leaving. The point is to always have an exit strategy in place. It is your responsibility to protect yourself from the toxic person.

THE TOOL OF STRATEGIC RETREAT:

There are alternatives to quitting or giving up on a relationship with a toxic person. Between surrender and desertion, there is an option called "Strategic Retreat." It is a term used in the military referring to a logical and systematic withdrawal to the *next best option*.

The best option is a healthy relationship. A healthy relationship is one in which both parties give and receive love and acceptance. Respect and trust abound. Decisions are made by common consent and each party feels emotionally safe. Likewise, in a healthy relationship, the needs of the other party are valued. There is negotiation so that both parties participate in the decision making process. It is a mutual improvement association. Both parties are enhanced by their interactions and there is a sense of fairness and cooperation.

The next best option to a relationship where *both* parties are healthy is a relationship where *one* party to the relationship is healthy. The healthy party is able to protect himself or herself from the abrasive behaviors of the unhealthy member of the relationship. This requires that the healthy person acquire the necessary skills and *attitudes* to survive the interaction with the toxic person. Among the skills to be developed is the ability to excuse yourself when under attack and the ability to stay in emotional control. Letting go of the expectation to change the toxic person and focusing on changing yourself to more *effectively deal with the toxic personality* is an important attitude to possess.

The third best option in strategic retreat may include significant distance both emotionally and geographically. Being an emotionally healthy person may require a divorce or separation. The decision to separate is not based on the toxic person changing. It is based on the ability of the healthy or want-to-be healthy person to deal with them. Some people are so very toxic that no one can live with constant exposure to their negativity. It would be a tragic mistake to abandon any relationship before you had thoroughly examined your ability to adopt a new attitude which would allow you to flourish in a difficult situation. However, before a decision of this magnitude is reached, it is appropriate to carefully explore the final checklist of skills needed to survive living with a porcupine.

THE TOOL OF GIVING OTHERS THE BENEFIT OF THE DOUBT:

JILL'S ATTITUDE WAS EVERYTHING

Jill was hypersensitive to all criticism. Her father was a critiholic. Because of this, she assumed other people were being critical of her, when they were not. Even normal conversations were reacted to in defensive ways. Non-verbal behaviors were also interpreted as being critical, when they were not meant to be. When her husband Steve came home, he started picking up some clutter in the front room. Jill came in the room and tearfully said, "Leave it alone, I'll get to it just as soon as I can."

Steve was genuinely being helpful. Jill saw and interpreted his behavior as a sign of her inadequacy instead of his helpfulness. There was a presumption of inadequacy in her mind. Steve's behaviors were held hostage to her attitude. When I spoke to the two of them, we agreed that any criticism would be written down or verbalized. Steve was to be given the benefit of her doubts to the contrary. There would be no assumptions of what this meant or that meant. Each was to own his or her criticism. If it were not spoken or written down it didn't exist. Jill was to focus on the content, not the "intent" of what was spoken or written. By changing her attitude, life became much more pleasant for Jill and Steve.

THE TOOL OF LIMITING NEGATIVE INTERACTION:

Many people have appreciated the concept of placing time limits on the amount of negative interaction. This gives them emotionally safe time. For example, Charles and Elsie agreed they would only criticize after dinner, between 7:30 p.m. and 7:45 p.m. Each had seven and one-half minutes. The timer on the stove was set. By limiting the time to only seven and one-half minutes each, it forced them to prioritize their concerns. For some people, listening for seven and one-half minutes is an eternity. However, seven and one-half minutes a day each, leaves one with twenty-three hours and forty-five minutes of time free from criticism. Elsie was much less frustrated knowing she had a time and a place to express her concerns, frustrations, and expectations. It bothered her that Charles frequently would have nothing to say during his seven and one-half minutes. This, however, was his choice. Elsie eventually adjusted and continued to relish using her seven and one-half minutes.

Some people have chosen to limit their criticism to one day a week. Marv and Lexus set aside one hour on Sundays after dinner to deal with their criticisms. They referred to it as "The Red Hour." This gave them six days and twenty-three hours a week of emotionally safe time. They quickly learned to write down their concerns. They eliminated the ones that seemed frivolous by the time they came to the Red Hour. The key was to honor the commitment to stay with the agreed upon time frame. Limiting the time to deal with the negative was a great tool for creating "emotionally safe time."

The Tool Of Zero Tolerance For Abuse:

Appropriate self-respect means you do not tolerate abuse. In most cases where a "culture of abuse" is already firmly established, it requires setting a new standard for personal interaction. This is best accomplished by removing yourself from inappropriate communications. The toxic person cannot be trusted with your emotional, mental, or physical well-being. You must excuse yourself from any interaction with them the moment the conversation or behavior becomes inappropriate or abusive.

Until the victims of toxic personalities care more about being emotionally healthy than they do about approval, they will be held hostage. If divorce, separation, financial hardship, fear of being alone, fear of failure or any issue is greater than concern for becoming their healthiest and best selves, toxic people will use it for control. Armored gloves are imperative in protecting yourself from direct contact with abusive quills.

Before other protective attitudes, skills, and tools are identified and employed, let us return to recognizing a toxic mate or child. Recognizing the problem is the first step in finding a solution to deal with it. All too frequently people are blind-sided. They don't see it; they don't recognize it. This comes from having been raised in a dysfunctional home where various toxic behaviors were a part of everyone's daily interactions. They accept abuse as normal behavior or blame themselves for provoking it.

The following is an excerpt from an actual letter from Linda when she was a teenager:

LINDA'S BLIND SPOT

"I told him about Daddy whipping me and how I have a blue, bruised arm and stripes on my back. I laid

136

down on the bed and cried mostly 'cause Daddy don't understand. I didn't hate him as I usually do when he whips me."

The problem continued when Linda became a parent herself. She had run away from home and had become pregnant. As a mother, she adopted many of her father's toxic attitudes and behaviors. However, because she was "not as bad" as her father she failed to recognize that she too was abusive. Linda did not beat her daughter, like her father beat her, but she slapped her face regularly. In Linda's mind she was not abusive. She felt that screaming, name calling, and slapping were *not really* abusive or toxic behaviors.

This inability to recognize toxic behaviors in oneself comes as a consequence of being raised in the "culture of abuse." The inability to recognize these behaviors in others is a blind spot. It comes from not knowing anything different. Recognizing what "is" and what "is not" a toxic behavior is critical to dealing with it in a healthy way. Far too many people raised in a "culture of abuse" minimize and play down toxic behaviors as "no big deal." *There can be no compromise with abuse.* It must be acknowledged for what it is. Only then can people adequately protect themselves. Ignoring abuse, pretending that it is not that bad, or tolerating it, is to perpetuate the "culture of abuse."

THE TOOL OF LEAVING THE ROOM, NOT LEAVING THE RELATIONSHIP:

There are things worse than divorce, abandonment, and being financially destitute. One of them is being destitute of the emotional courage to become your best self. Nothing you can do or say to the toxic will have a greater impact than asserting your right to be treated with respect. Leaving the room, leaving the house, or leaving the car does not mean you are leaving the relationship. It is a way to set boundaries on what you will or will not tolerate.

Do not be surprised if your statement is ridiculed or challenged. Frequently the toxic person will threaten divorce or abandonment unless you stay and tolerate abuse. This may or may not be a bluff. It would be healthy to respond to any threat by saying,

> *"If that is what you choose to do, I will accept it, but I will not tolerate abuse. If you can talk to me with respect and in a civil manner, I will listen. Otherwise write down your concerns and I will read them, or wait until you are in control. Until then I am leaving the room but I am not leaving the relationship."*

Remember, as long as you can be blackmailed by your fears, doubts, and insecurities, you will be. Most relationships are not all bad or all good. But the good does not justify acceptance of any abuse. Fears, doubts, and insecurities which keep you from acting and reacting in emotionally healthy ways are self-defeating behaviors. The problem is not the toxic person. The problem is your unwillingness to stand up for yourself. The issue is not the toxic behavior, it is your willingness to tolerate it. All the tools, all the solutions, and all the knowledge in the world are of no value until your willingness to become your healthiest and best self reigns supreme as the governing value in your life.

THE TOOL OF LEAVING THE RELATIONSHIP:

It is better to live alone and be emotionally healthy than to live in an unhealthy emotional relationship. You are only one-half of any relationship to which you are a party. You must continually remind yourself that you cannot change the toxic person. You can only change yourself. They will change only when the motivation comes from within themselves or they will not change at all. They will persist in their toxic ways until challenged. When they are faced with someone who will not tolerate their behavior, a crisis is created.

FEARFUL FRANCIS

Francis was afraid of being on her own. She was willing to tolerate abuse. She was held hostage by her insecurities. Whenever she was abused, her husband would threaten to leave her. He was aware of her "fear buttons" and would push them to keep her in line. His verbal abuse of his wife was surpassed by his physical abuse of his children. In Frances' mind the thought of being divorced was petrifying. She had visions of a horribly destitute life. She was convinced that there was no escape.

I said to Frances, "Are you willing to have Child Protective Services take your children away from you?"

She began to cry and admitted her husband had moved the family from two different states because they had been reported to the authorities. Francis lacked knowledge of women's shelters and of the resources which were available to her as a battered wife. I put her in touch with the YWCA and a couple of other support groups for women. Armed with confidence that she had a place to go, she began to focus on her choices. In this case she did not confront her husband alone. She moved to a safe house with her children. Facing an abusive husband would have been foolish. His known track record was sufficient evidence of his toxic behavior. Giving him one last chance in the same environment would be insane.

She called her husband on the phone and told him of

her decision. Predictably, he went ballistic and threatened her life. He tried every trick in the book to push her buttons of insecurity, doubt, and fear. He threatened to take the kids and disappear. He went on and on. Francis was able to obtain a protective order which prevented him from any contact with her or the children. Eventually he was mandated by the court to take an anger management class and to go to weekly counseling. Supervised third party visits were permitted.

His toxic behaviors of criticism, coercion, and physical abuse had landed him in trouble with the law. Now the burden of change was upon his shoulders. He could no longer rely upon these behaviors to control his family. He was at a crossroads in his life. He would either learn healthy skills or he would not. He would never again be with his family if he continued his dysfunctional ways. He knew now that Francis could and would leave him.

The point of focus is whether or not toxic behaviors will be accepted. If you roll over and permit them to continue, you have consented to live in the "culture of abuse." It is always appropriate to draw a line in the sand and to take a stand against abuse to protect yourself and others. Separation or divorce should not be trifled with, but may be the final option.

All of these tools are designed to keep you in control of your life. They are only of value if you use them. These tools have worked and are working for those who choose to live with emotional porcupines. Armed with these skills and attitudes you are prepared to enter the habitat.

CHAPTER NINE

ENTERING THE PORCUPINE'S HABITAT

Most people are nervous and a little frightened about entering the environment of a potentially dangerous animal. Going through a display of reptiles and poisonous serpents in a zoo, you probably have noticed the cautious behavior of many. Even though they are protected from the snakes by the safety glass, they are wary. The same level of caution needs to be exercised when entering the dangerous habitat of an emotional porcupine. Even if you are fully protected, you need to be alert to potential danger.

Just as knights of old protected themselves with suits of armor, the emotionally healthy must go into the battle with protection. Make no mistake. It *is* a battle and you *will* be attacked by the toxic person. Some of the skills and attitudes you will need when you encounter an emotional porcupine have previously been discussed. Others will be explained in this chapter.

APPROPRIATE ARMOR

❑ Reaffirm your desire to become your healthiest and best self.

❑ Let go of the expectation to change the toxic person. Also let go of the expectation that they will give the acceptance, love, approval, or other things you desire.

❑ Change the focus from pleasing the toxic person to pleasing yourself and staying in control of self.

❑ Define your own standard of excellence in specific terms.

❑ Live to your own definition of "enough.".

❑ Ask yourself, "What would a good and loving person do?"

❑ Ask yourself, "How would I counsel my child in this exact circumstance?"

❑ Follow that counsel.

Four of the principles of being appropriately prepared to engage a toxic person are illustrated in the following story:

SHARON WANTED TO BE LOVED

Sharon wanted to be loved. She wanted her husband, Aaron, to be happy. One of her dearly held values was a peaceful home where everyone was kind and people "got along" with each other. To Sharon, this meant sacrificing what she wanted for the greater good. No matter how hard she tried, however, she was unable to accomplish her dream.

Aaron was constantly criticizing Sharon. She couldn't try hard enough. No matter what she did, it didn't quite measure up to his expectations. She was convinced that if she tried harder, her efforts would be enough for Aaron. She was a co-dependent who felt responsible to make him happy. She could not do it, but she kept going back. She just wanted affection, acceptance, and appreciation for trying and for accomplishing what she did. She wanted no more nor less. Sharon, however, kept coming for her approval to a "toxic source"—her unhappy and never-pleased, husband, Aaron.

When I talked to Sharon, we started immediately on a program where she accepted responsibility only for her *own* happiness and unhappiness.

I explained to her the following:

"You are not responsible for Aaron's happiness, nor his unhappiness. That is his choice. You are hereby released from trying to make him happy. If he is unhappy, that also is his choice.

"For the purpose of our discussion, I want you to think about a GOAL as something over which you have control. It depends solely upon you. A WISH is an expectation that depends upon others for its fulfillment. According to this definition, is making Aaron happy a goal or a wish?"

"It's a wish," she said.

"Is making yourself happy a goal or a wish?"

"It's a goal, because it depends upon me," she responded.

"Is getting acceptance, affection, appreciation, and love from Aaron a goal or a wish?"

"It's a wish," she said dejectedly.

"Sharon, it is your own expectations that are setting you up for failure. They are based on a false premise that if you are good enough you will receive acceptance. Remember that all frustration comes from unmet expectations. You are going to a dry well for water, and no matter how many trips you take to the well, your expectation for water is never going to be met. Aaron is a dry well. You have one hundred percent control over being a loving person. That's a worthy goal. You have no control of being loved by others. That's a wish.

"If you choose to stay in this relationship with Aaron, you will have to change the rules of engagement. You will need to establish a new set of goals which truly depend upon your doing what you can. It is up to you to take control of your happiness and commit to the objective of becoming your highest and best self. You have your own natural resources, your own gifts, talents, and abilities to accomplish this task. Your expectations must be reasonable and within your sphere of control. Do not depend upon Aaron for your acceptance.

"Let's go over some ground rules which will allow you to stay married to Aaron and to survive living with a toxic personality:

"BECOME EMOTIONALLY HEALTHY YOURSELF. This means you accept responsibility for being a happy person, and for controlling your own behavior. You own it. You do not need to make Aaron happy. You cannot, even if he were to agree. He alone is responsible for his happiness and unhappiness. It's his choice. As long as you act in such a way that gives him the impression that you have the power to make him happy or unhappy, why should he accept responsibility for his life? When things go wrong, he will blame you. It's your fault. 'You should have...,' or 'shouldn't have...,' 'you need to...,' or 'didn't need to...,' 'you ought to have...,' or 'ought not to have....' He will transfer to you the responsibility for his unhappiness if you let him. It's so easy for others to blame you for their lack of happiness. That is what toxic people do.

"It's your choice to take control of your life and to forgive yourself for your past. You must also make your own plan to become a higher and better self, independent of Aaron, or of anyone else. Regardless of the past, you can make positive choices in the present. Do not trade happiness for pity nor sympathy. It's a poor trade. Many do it every day. It is a cop out. Give yourself permission to be emotionally healthy.

"LET GO OF THE EXPECTATION THAT AARON IS GOING TO GIVE YOU THE ACCEPTANCE, LOVE, OR APPROVAL YOU DESIRE. Let go because the current interaction between the two of you isn't meeting your needs. Your relationship has been established on the premise that pleasing your husband is the objective. If you are successful, you may enjoy short term approval. However fundamental and basic your desire for acceptance, it may be like shifting sand in your relationship with Aaron.

Change your focus from pleasing Aaron to becoming an emotionally healthy person. This does not mean you are to become an island of self-centeredness. It means you are to focus on becoming your best self. This is the only way you can escape the treadmill you are on.

"DEFINE YOUR OWN STANDARD OF EXCELLENCE. In other words, define what is enough for you. Do not let anyone else set the parameters of what a good mother is, what a good wife is, or what a good person is. Let go of the expectation of measuring up to their definition, their wants, their needs, their expectations. The way to release yourself is to stop trying to *please* them in order to be loved by them. Co-dependents find it hard to let go of wanting to please others and frequently wind up pleasing no one.

145

"LIVE TO YOUR *OWN DEFINITION* OF ENOUGH. You can at least please yourself. If your expectation is 'pleasing others,' you have no control over doing so, because the toxic personality will keep redefining the standard in such a way that you can never measure up. The thing to keep in mind about a toxic person is that you are 'darned if you do' or 'darned if you don't.' They are going to be frustrated with you, regardless of your behavior. You cannot be governed by their frustration. Keep in mind that they use the frustrations of others as a tool to manipulate, control, and intimidate. They also have endless lists of expectations. Just as you get close to doing everything on the list, Aaron will change the list. He can never let you be enough.

"When you see the insanity of this treadmill, you will come to realize that toxic people are 'crazy makers.' They drive you crazy trying to please them. The crazier your life becomes, the more in control they become; and because you are going crazy, the focus can be on your aberrant behavior. *You* are the one out of your mind, and *they* are the ones who are justified. Most toxic people were raised that way in their families. They were never enough as individuals, as children, or as siblings, so, what's the big deal? Not measuring up, not being enough, trailing barbs, constant criticism, or blame-fixing is normal to them."

If Sharon chooses to stay in the relationship with her toxic husband, she will have ample opportunity to practice the "art of receiving his criticisms." She will need to set up her own goals for improvement wherein the judge and jury of her performance is herself. She already knows what the verdict will be for anything she does as judged by Aaron. It won't be enough for him! But it will be enough for her. At last, she can succeed. The rules of the game cannot be arbitrarily changed by him.

146

The boundaries cannot be shifted. There will be a greater chance for success if Sharon takes control of her own mental health and sets her own standards of excellence. The solution for Sharon is to commit to become her highest and best self and to embark upon a solo course to becoming emotionally healthy.

Sharon committed to apply the rules she learned for surviving a toxic personality. Armed with new determination and a "fresh writing pad," she was ready to deal with Aaron's complaints.

One of Aaron's main complaints was about Sharon's housekeeping. His standard of housekeeping as stated to the counselor was, "I'm reasonable. I just want a clean house." The unstated, unrealistic expectation by Aaron was, "Anything less than perfection will be criticized."

Sharon's standard of housekeeping was "I'm reasonable. The house is clean, but not clutter-free. I like to keep some of my projects out where I can see them. It reminds me of what I need and want to do with them."

She reviewed the criticism of Aaron and set her ego aside and determined it was not reasonable to have several projects out in the open all the time. After thinking about it and talking it over with one of her friends, she came up with a plan to obtain some orange boxes, label them, and place her different projects in them. She decided she would only keep one project out at a time. The other undertakings would have to be stored and rotated. This now became her personal standard of excellence.

Aaron's actual words when he found out about her plans to put her projects in orange boxes and store them were, "That's great. I'm really proud of you, but why don't you put all the projects in boxes and take out the one you want only while you are working on it, and then put it away also?" (Notice the "trailing barb." He could never just compliment Sharon. He had to add a suggestion for improvement.)

If Sharon's expectation was to please Aaron, she would have been disappointed by his response. In his mind, her solution was a step in the right direction, but it wasn't "quite good enough."

As a counselor I told her, "It will take time and practice to free yourself from feeling disappointed with his responses."

She asked me, "How am I supposed to respond to a trailing barb?"

"Why don't you smile when he gives you a trailing barb and say in your heart, 'That's Aaron.'"

"Your verbal reaction to him could choose to focus on the positive part of his statement. 'I'm glad you were proud of me. Frankly, I'm proud of myself and I feel good about it.'"

"Don't respond to the negative trailing barb. Ignore it. When you choose to comment on it, you are reinforcing its worth. If he won't let it go and continues to fuss and fume over the one project you have out at a time, acknowledge his frustration and continued criticism by saying, 'I'm sorry you're still frustrated over my one project being out, but it's just the price you pay for being married to a wonderful person like me!' Your resolve must be firm and consistent. If you waiver or give in, you will only encourage his criticism."

Another area of expectation for Aaron concerned her level of education. He had expressed, "I think Sharon needs to get a Bachelor's Degree. It will make her more marketable if something happens to me. Also, women who are college educated are more interesting to talk to."

Her response was, "I don't want to take the time to go back to college right now. I want to be a wife and a mother. I'd rather increase your insurance or look at some other options."

She reviewed Aaron's criticism and set her ego aside to evaluate his concern. "Education is important and it would make me a better self if I were to expand my mind. I have time to do something, but I don't have the time or the will to be a full-time student." Sharon pondered her options. She visited with some friends and family. She bounced some ideas off them to see if she was being reasonable. Finally she explored her proposal with Aaron, the toxic, who she knew in advance would not find her solution "good enough." This time it was not his acceptance she sought, but to inform him of the options she could support.

Sharon set her own standard, her own goal. She decided she would like to be a trained real estate agent and was committed to go to school to do so. This would give her a career which she could rely upon if needed. Also, she could work at her own pace.

Aaron's actual statement was, "You never do what I want you to do. Why can't you just once do it my way?"

The answer to his question was this, "Because you have unreasonable expectations. Even if I were to sacrifice my total identity to what you think I should, need, and ought to be, I would still not be enough. You would still be dissatisfied with me and both of us would be miserable. I can't be responsible for your happiness nor for your unhappiness, Aaron. I'm trying really hard to be accountable for my own happiness. *That's why I can't do it your way. I can only do what I can do."*

As long as Sharon was afraid to be honest with her feelings the relationship remained the same. Yes, there were risks. Aaron could have decided to leave. He could have escalated his anger. The issue, however, was what Sharon would do.

WHAT IS THE LOVING THING TO DO?

Loving includes polite, respectful, cordial, and considerate behaviors toward others. It doesn't mean you have to throw your arms around them. It does mean that you will treat them in a civil way. Toxic people need love too. You may not think they deserve your love based upon their conduct. However, being a civil person is not about them or their behavior. It is a choice you make to live life as a caring person. Living life as a good person must be an unconditional investment.

The loving thing to do with toxic people may be to stay as far away from them as you can. Your level of involvement will depend upon your ability to protect yourself from their toxic ways. It is a waste of time and energy to become angry with them or to hate them. It will not change them. Realize you cannot get from them what you want. They are a dry well from which you cannot draw water. They are what they are. You must let go of the expectation you possess for them to be different in order for you to be "okay." Once you accept this reality, you can make a choice to love them.

Being a loving person does not require you to be stupid or unguarded. It does not require that you trust those who have demonstrated they are not worthy of trust. You must evaluate the level of trust you can invest in each relationship. Remember, trust and love are two separate issues. Trust is the "fruit" of responsible behavior. Trust is a very conditional investment.

It is appropriate to mourn the loss of the relationship which "could have been." It is emotionally unhealthy to pretend the relationship is something it is not and may never become. Ultimately, you have to evaluate how much love and how much trust you are able to devote to each relationship.

150

A WAY TO EVALUATE

Sometimes, people are so close to the problem or are so emotionally involved they lose all sense of perspective. Here is where the tool of counseling your best friend or your own child plays an important role. Imagine you are counseling your own child who comes to you with the identical problem you face. Your child explains to you in precise detail the nature of his or her concerns, which mirrors exactly your circumstance. Next, your child asks, "What should I do? I will not hold you accountable because the decision is mine alone. I just want your honest opinion. Should I leave or should I stay and work on it?"

Knowing what you know, how would you counsel your own child? Experience tells me people will often counsel their children with greater objectivity and fairness than they would allow themselves in the same circumstances. Sometimes we tolerate an unbearable situation that we would never ask one of our children or our best friend to endure. If the counsel you would offer to your child or best friend is honest and heartfelt, you should have the courage to take your own counsel and follow your own advice. When you seek to become your highest and best self, you are indeed your *own* best friend.

As you read the following story, be thinking about which tools discussed in the previous chapter might assist Sandy in her relationship with her mother-in-law.

SANDY AND HER MOTHER-IN-LAW

Carol was a classic toxic mother-in-law who felt no one was good enough for her Jeff. She truly believed that Sandy seduced Jeff into marrying him and that Jeff married below his potential. Sandy never felt accepted by Carol. They would make small talk with each other, but they both felt a cautious reserve. Carol was openly critical behind Sandy's back about her skills as a wife and mother. Sandy tolerated her mother-in-law, but was deeply hurt by her statements which found their way back to Sandy's ears via a sister-in-law and other family and mutual friends.

Sandy hated going over to Carol's home because Carol spent the whole time doting on Jeff. She waited on him hand and foot. No wonder Jeff enjoyed going over to his mother's. She did the same with the grandchildren, but expected Sandy to work in the kitchen or join with her in waiting upon the rest of the family. Sandy complained all the way there and back in the car. While they were in Carol's home, Sandy bristled with quiet frustration. Jeff and the kids had a better time when she did not go along.

Jeff was aware of both his mother's disapproval and of Sandy's hostilities toward his mother. He felt constantly torn between them. He felt everything was a test of his loyalties between being a son and a husband. He was always hearing his mother dropping hints about how he should insist that Sandy do a better job. Sandy was equally open in telling Jeff about his mother's weaknesses of being critical, overbearing, and interfering. Sandy also expected Jeff to defend her by standing up to his mother and telling her to stay out of their lives.

Carol, the mother-in-law, was always buying gifts for Jeff and her grandchildren and for some of her favorite daughters-in-law who bowed to her wishes. Sandy felt she couldn't compete and purposely discouraged any relationship with Carol and her grandchildren as a form of punishment for Carol's inappropriate conduct.

I suggested the loving thing for Sandy to do was to go to Carol's home and have a good attitude, *but* if she could not, then to stay home and do something she would like to do.

I recommended as follows:

"Send them off to Carol's with a smile and receive them back with gladness. Don't sulk, pout, or play the role of a martyr. In this way you remain in control of your life and avoid setting up unnecessary competition with Carol.

"Focus on being your own person and meet your own standard of a good wife and mother and even a good daughter-in-law. This is the loving thing to do. All human relationships are composed of two people. You can only be one-half of any relationship to which you are a party. In a nontoxic relationship you can enjoy emotional closeness and both give and receive loving behavior. In a toxic relationship you can still be a loving person, but you must always protect yourself by drawing boundaries with which you are comfortable.

"Define for yourself a one-sided program where you are willing to gift unconditional acts of kindness. Do this, not because Carol 'deserves' it, but because you are a loving person. To act in this manner is consistent with the goal of becoming your healthiest and best self."

This is how Sandy chose to respond to her challenge:

Sandy decided she would invite Carol over for dinner once a month. She felt it would be a good idea to organize, with the other daughters-in-law, a surprise birthday party for Carol. She determined to treat her mother-in-law with respect and in a polite and civil manner. Sandy agreed to a number of activities that were reasonable, that did not involve going to the mother's house. She let go of any demands for her husband to choose between her and his mother. She did these things because she was a good person not because Carol deserved it or because she was looking for any approval from Carol. She imagined how she would counsel her own daughter in an identical situation and then followed her own counsel.

A LOVING PERSON

It is true that every person has the potential to love. The focus on being a loving person is defined by our loving behaviors. Affection, acceptance, and appreciation are all ways in which love can be expressed. Specific loving behaviors include holding hands, hugging, kissing, and appropriate touching. Kind and encouraging words, sincere praise, courteous expressions of thanks and appreciation are examples of loving behavior. Giving encouragement for even the slightest improvement reflects an emphasis on the positive. Thoughtful visible efforts and deeds communicate acceptance. Cards, flowers, an extra effort to clean a car, change the oil, make sure a task is finished, all become ways of expressing love. There is no substitute for the will to be a loving person. Phony behaviors will eventually discredit the insincere.

Remember: Do not do the loving behaviors with the expectation of being loved, appreciated or valued in return ! Do them because you are a loving person.

Accepting a definition of yourself as a loving person because you are able to love unconditionally allows you to deal with difficult personalities. The power of personal example cannot be denied. Patience must overcome anger. Respect must replace verbal abuse. Kindness and gentleness must win over harshness and insensitivity. Invitation, enticement, and persuasion must emerge in lieu of compulsion, intimidation, and domination. Only when we are focused on becoming our highest and best selves can we replace toxic responses with these positive ones. Unless and until we are committed to take control of our lives, we allow toxic people around us to dictate our happiness and sadness.

Trying to punish others by making ourselves unpleasant people is a poor choice. Withholding love as a punishment or as a sign of disapproval is an error. Whenever a person chooses not to be a loving individual it is a mistake. We have already discussed that trust and love are different. But why do people decide to withhold civil behavior even within reasonable limits? Do false pride, self-righteousness and holier-than-thou judgmentalism deprive you of a loving disposition? Yes! The point is you can be a loving, kind, or respectful person whether or not someone else is imperfect or flawed. What about an ex-spouse, a toxic in-law, or an estranged child? Do you abandon your loving efforts because of their inability to appreciate it?

"ALL MY EX'ES LIVE IN TEXAS"

Dealing with toxic ex-husbands, ex-wives, and ex-in-laws is never easy. Emotional wounds are often reopened by required contact with the ex'es. The reasons for the divorce are seldom resolved, and blame fixing continues to be the focus. In this hostile environment, children become the pawns on an emotional chessboard. They are coerced, emotionally pressured, and cajoled into empathizing with one parent or the other. The sad truth is there are no winners.

Because emotions run high, dealing with ex'es is especially difficult. But nothing defines an emotionally healthy person more clearly than how they decide to respond to the toxic. Assuming that trust is nonexistent, it is still possible to act and react in a healthy manner. It is important to behave in civil ways. Remember, respect says more about who *you* are than who *they* are. Proper decorum on the part of a healthy person sends a clear contrasting picture of the unhealthy spouse if one exists. Joining in dysfunctional behavior only destroys the credibility of all those involved. Who hit who first? Acting in a dignified and respectful manner preserves the integrity and credibility of the respect-giving person. Consider the difficult, yet loving choices made in the following story.

TO BE NICE OR NOT TO BE NICE

Every year the family held a reunion. It was a tradition involving five generations of living relatives. Dave, a son-in-law, had divorced Martha. It was a thirty-year marriage with five children. Four of their children were now married, and only a fifteen-year-old son was left at home. The big question on everyone's mind was whether or not to invite Dave to the family reunion since one of his grandchildren was to be honored at the reunion. Because it was Martha's side of the family that held the annual event, it was decided that Dave would not be invited.

Martha asked my professional opinion. It was obvious she was shocked by my answer. I recommended that the family be gracious and extend an invitation for Dave to attend the family reunion. I suggested the family treat him with respect and with kindness. Most of them had known Dave for thirty years and had a genuine caring for him in spite of the recent divorce.

Martha's sister called me on the phone and asked me if I were crazy for making such a suggestion. She was in charge of the reunion and the invitations. It was her opinion that if Dave were allowed to come it would be "showing approval" of his divorcing her sister. Even though Martha had come to feel all right about Dave going, not inviting Dave would show the family was united in their support of Martha.

I told Martha's sister that I had a prediction to make about the family reunion. I suggested that not inviting

Dave would force some of her nieces and nephews (Dave and Martha's married children) to take sides. Some of them wouldn't come because they would feel sympathy for their father. I predicted that hard feelings would ensue and the big happy family reunion would be less and less attended by Dave and Martha's married children.

Before I could finish the rest of my prediction she interrupted me and said, "Today one of the married children called me and cancelled."

I asked her if that were really the objective of the reunion, to create divisiveness. "Invite Dave and be gracious. He may or may not come, but if you treat him with respect, your nieces and nephews will be supportive of your activities. If not, you will lose more than Dave. It's your choice."

Many phone calls were made. A genuine effort was made for Dave to attend the reunion with Martha and the children. It turned out better than expected. The reunion was a well attended success. Awkward moments were quickly passed over in a sincere outpouring of love and friendship.

Dave and Martha have years of weddings and many significant events to attend in the lives of their children and grandchildren. It requires an emotional maturity possessed by few to accomplish this level of respect and civility.

The stories of hatred, hostile ex-spouses, and toxic ex-in-laws are legendary. The question is what kind of a person are *you?* Not what kind of a person is he? Do you let everyone else define who you are? Is your life lived only as a reaction to others? Why should you let anyone keep you from being a loving, kind, or respectful person? Your NOT LOVING them is not going to change them, and your LOVING them may not change them. But life will be better for you if you live it as a loving and not as a toxic person.

One observer has noted that grandparents get along better with their grandchildren than with their own children. They seem to be more loving and far less critical with their grandchildren. This has lead to a humorous saying: "Grandparents and grandchildren are natural allies *because they share a common enemy*!" Most grandparents focus on loving their grandchildren and not on changing them or criticizing them. The result is grandparents are more effective in creating an environment which is conducive to change in human behavior with their grandchildren than they were with their own children. One wise grandpa observed, "I just love 'em, I don't try to change 'em." What if more people adopted that attitude?

IT ISN'T TOO LATE

Everyone wants to love and be loved. It has already been established that being loved by others is a wish, a worthwhile wish, but out of your control. Being a loving person is a goal within your grasp. Loving depends upon you but *being* loved depends upon others. Putting your focus on being a loving person can provide you internal peace if you let go of the expectation of being externally rewarded.

PAIN IS INEVITABLE; MISERY IS A CHOICE

Each individual will face toxic personalities in this life. It is emotionally painful when this person is a loved one. More than painful, it is soul-wrenching. However, dealing with a toxic personality is also an opportunity. It is certainly an unwanted one; nevertheless, the wonderful truth is *life is choosing*. Life is a choice of how to act and how to react. This brings the discussion full circle. It is not about being a victim. It is about living! It is about finding joy in the process of becoming your highest and best self. It's all about living in a hostile world, but not being a part of that world. It is *not* "an eye for an eye" and "a tooth for a tooth." It's about living in the real world and applying the principles of happiness and self-control. It's about calling upon the power we have to choose. It's finding out there is greater peace and joy in being self-defined than in being defined by others.

CHAPTER TEN

WHAT IF I'M A PORCUPINE?

After every lecture on "Dealing With The Toxic Personality," I have people come up to the lectern. Most have comments or specific questions about a toxic loved one. However, there are always a few who say, "You have described me perfectly. I'm a toxic person, but I don't want to be. I don't want to be an emotional porcupine. What can I do to change?" My response to them is straightforward.

SO YOU WANT TO CHANGE?

Change is a process and you are the only one who can do it. It begins with recognizing there is a problem The next step is wanting to change. This is called motivation. Only you can provide the momentum necessary for lasting change. Replacing toxic behaviors with healthy ones takes time and patience. This is the acquisition of new skills and attitudes. The final step is application. This is "walking the walk" and not just "talking the talk." This is where theory becomes practice.

FOUR STEPS TO CHANGE

I.   RECOGNITION . . . . . Becoming aware of toxic behavior in yourself

II.   MOTIVATION . . . . . . Possessing a sincere desire to change

III. ACQUISITION . . . . . Acquiring replacement skills in order to replace toxic behaviors with positive ones

IV. APPLICATION . . . . . The cessation of toxic behaviors and interacting with others in non toxic ways

Fortunately, habits can be changed. Nearly all behaviors are learned. Toxic behaviors are among those which are learned. They can be replaced with a new set of responses. You must be willing to learn replacement skills and then apply them. If you truly do not want to be an emotional porcupine, pursue the following process of change:

I. RECOGNITION "AIN'T EASY"

Recognition of detrimental behavior and getting out of denial "ain't easy." Replacing life-long bad habits is difficult, but possible. Bringing yourself to the point of recognition of toxic behavior is also difficult when you are defensive. That is why when people come up after a lecture and identify themselves as toxic and have a desire to change, half or more than half, of the battle is won. They are on their way.

II. MOTIVATION

The desire to change is the foundation of motivation. Remember motivation for changing toxic behaviors must come from your own heart. It's a fool's dream to believe that toxic behaviors will just disappear. They have to be replaced. This requires that you be motivated sufficiently to learn new ways of responding to your frustration and new ways of communicating your expectations.

III. ACQUIRING POSITIVE COMMUNICATION SKILLS

If you are like most toxic personalities you may not know that toxic behaviors are ineffective. You may not know *how* to act differently. You may honestly be doing what you think is best. You are probably aware of the hostility and resentment others have toward you. However, you may not know why they feel as they do or what to do about it. What do you do with a bad idea? The answer is to replace it with a better idea. How do you change a poor communication pattern? The answer is to replace it with a positive communication pattern.

UNDERSTANDING HOW WE COMMUNICATE:
THE THREE MESSAGE SYSTEMS

In interpersonal communication there are three primary message systems. The first is "facial expression and body language." As much as 55% of meaning is derived from looking at a person's countenance, posture, and demeanor. This means the interpretation is visual. It is centered in the eyes. The second message system is the "tone of voice." About 37% of how we interpret meaning comes to us from our ears. The tone and intensity of volume we hear helps us to understand the central idea that is being communicated. The third message system is the choice of words. Only 8% of meaning is attributed to the actual words we use.

Ironically, we do our clearest communicating when we are negative. In other words, when we are upset, our facial expressions, body language, tone of voice, and words are consistent. All three message systems are sending the same signals. This, of course, makes it easy to understand and interpret the message. However clear our message, if it is toxic it will be poorly received.

We do our worst communicating in the positive. Because we are not as animated when sending neutral or positive messages, it is more difficult to discern intent. When someone is yelling and screaming, their eyes are bugging out of their heads, and they are waving their arms up and down, it is safe to assume this person is upset, angry, and negative. However, when someone pays us a compliment and they are calm, serene, and smiling, many of us question the sincerity of their words. Meaning becomes more difficult to interpret.

MIXED MESSAGES

A "mixed message" is one where the three message systems are not congruent. The facial expression and body language are negative, the tone of voice is negative, but the words are positive. For example,

> John asked Bonnie if she would like to go to a late movie. Bonnie frowned, let out a large sigh, and said, "Yes, I would."

This was a mixed message. It creates all kinds of difficulty in interpreting meaning because the three message systems (body language, tone of voice, and words) were not congruent.

Another example of a mixed message is the interaction between David and Nicole:

David showed up at dinner time and smelled the hot bread baking in the oven.

"That sure smells good," he said.

Nicole responded, "Would you like to have a slice of fresh, hot bread?"

"Oh, no thank you," replied David, "I don't want to impose."

In this case the facial expression and body language were positive, the tone of voice was positive, but the words sent a different message.

THREE MESSAGES:
POSITIVE, NEGATIVE, AND MIXED

There are only three kinds of messages we can send, i.e. positive, negative, or mixed. Our self-worth may be enhanced or damaged by how we interpret meaning. Low self-worth may be the result of believing the mixed and negative messages over the positive ones. If a child or spouse is subjected to an overwhelming barrage of mixed and negative messages, they will begin to believe them.

IV. APPLICATION IS "WALKING THE WALK"

Most people are aware that their chances for increased health begin immediately when they stop smoking. Their health doesn't change when they just think about not smoking anymore. It doesn't change when they just make a commitment to stop smoking. Their health only improves when they *actually stop* smoking and sustain their commitment. So it is with toxic behaviors. It is easy to feel good about wanting to stop. It is easy to feel good about making a commitment to stop. Relationships will not improve because we make a commitment for them to improve. Only when we replace toxic behaviors with positive ones will the relationship improve. There is a huge gap between commitment and application.

It is generally not a good idea to announce that you are going to change a behavior. You are setting yourself up for failure. By raising the expectation for change in the eyes of others, there is greater frustration and disappointment that will follow the failed attempts to perform to the stated objective. Promises of change are meaningless: "I'll stop drinking, I promise, if you will only come back." "I'll stop smoking." "I'll stop yelling." "I'll lose weight." "I'll stop improperly criticizing…," and so on. Since credibility is already a problem, it makes no sense to set yourself up by announcing behavioral changes that have not yet occurred. A better way is to let action speak for itself. Behavioral change will be noticed, especially if there is consistency in the new behavior. After a new pattern of positive interaction has replaced the toxic behaviors, your words will have more credibility.

Here are four common ways in which toxicity manifests itself. In your quest to become a more loving person you will need to replace these toxic behaviors:

1. Feeling the need to control others by threat, intimidation, abandonment, etc.
2. Being a perfectionist
3. Being a highly critical person
4. Being judgmental

When several of these characteristics are assembled into a consistent pattern of interaction, one may come to the sudden awareness that he or she has a toxic personality. It is time for you to face a moment of truth. Honestly answer the following questions and get a measure of where you are in relation to toxic behaviors:

AM I TOXIC TO OTHERS?

HAVE OTHERS SAID OF YOU...

	TRUE	FALSE
1. You're a perfectionist!		
2. You're a controlling person!		
3. You're a highly critical person.		
4. No one is ever good enough for you!		
5. You hold a grudge a long time.		
6. You are stingy with compliments.		
7. You're often blaming others.		
8. You're impossible to please!		
9. You withhold love as a punishment.		
10. You can never give a compliment without a "but..." following.		
11. You are judgmental.		
12. You are easily offended.		
13. You often contradict others.		

	TRUE	FALSE
14. You frequently complain about what *isn't* being done.	_____	_____
15. You frequently interrupt and correct others.	_____	_____
16. You parent equals by telling them what they "should, need, and ought" to do.	_____	_____
17. You are mad, upset, or angry much of the time.	_____	_____
18. You react to others *not* doing what you want them to do by yelling, screaming, swearing, or name calling.	_____	_____
19. You make threats of divorce or abandonment.	_____	_____
20. You are rude, insensitive, curt, abrupt, and do not respect the opinions of others.	_____	_____
21. You see yourself as more hard working, or more responsible, or more capable, or more intelligent than others.	_____	_____

TOTAL "TRUE" ANSWERS   _____

EXPLANATION FOR NUMBER OF "TRUE" ANSWERS:

0 - 3	Normal, but not necessarily healthy
4 - 7	Critical and hard to live with
8 - 12	Highly critical and nonaccepting of others
13 - 16	Definitely toxic and dangerous to the self-worth of all
17 - 19	I foresee divorce, rebellion, rejection, and conflicted relationships
20 - 21	You are best suited for living alone on an island

After taking the foregoing test if you find that you are "best suited for living alone on an island," you will have a great deal of work ahead of you in replacing toxic behaviors with positive ones. Those of you who score seven and above may face the skepticism of your loved ones that you will be able to change . You may even have your own self-doubts about your ability to change. It is of paramount importance that you learn to communicate love.

WHAT DO YOU MEAN WHEN YOU SAY YOU LOVE ME?

It is amazing how nebulous, elusive, and difficult it is for people to define "love." To some, love is an unidentifiable feeling. To others, it is a romantic ideal. For still others it is working hard to provide food, clothing, and shelter. How complex can love really be? On radio and TV we are constantly bombarded with "love stories." Music, poetry, and the movies portray love in such an abstract way that people are left to wonder "what is love?" If love is that hard to define, how will we recognize it? What if I love a spouse or child and they don't know it? What if the negative messages I'm sending overshadow the fact that I love this person?

LOVE DEFINED

For the purposes of this book, let's define true love as any thought, word, or deed that is supportive of the "loved one" becoming his or her healthiest and best self. Behaviorally, "true love" considers the means, the way, and the "how" we treat our loved ones. In other words, "how" we say it or show it is as important as "what" we say.

169

Love is affection, acceptance, and appreciation. It almost always involves service to others. Most of us need to improve in being congruent with our positive love messages. Our facial expression and body language, our tone of voice and our words need to be consistent. Positive messages, born of sincere concerns, are not that hard to communicate. If I were a toxic communicator and I wanted to change, I would learn to give sincere praise, recognition, or approval as an end in itself. Positive statements would stand alone. There would be no "buts" added to the compliment.

"I LOVE YOU" PROGRAMS

As previously discussed, "I Love You" programs come in all sizes and shapes. The one thing any successful relationship has is shared time by common consent. Another factor in developing an "I Love You" program is age appropriate activities. Frequently adults try to bring children into an adult world instead of the adult entering the world of the child. Granddaddy learned this lesson the hard way.

GRANDDADDY AND THE GRANDSON

Granddaddy wanted to show his grandson that he loved him. He decided to take his grandson to a football game. The Grandmother asked the Grandfather if he was sure he wanted to take a four-year-old to a football game. "He will get bored, he won't understand, and he will be going to the bathroom all the time," she said.

The Grandmother could not have been more right. It was a terrible experience for both of them. Granddaddy had purchased root beer and popcorn for the little guy. He spilled all the popcorn on the people just below them at the game. However, he did drink the pop. Granddaddy had to leave the game at exciting times to take his grandson to the bathroom.

Upon their return the Grandmother didn't need to ask how it went. She could see it upon their countenances. Granddaddy was frustrated because he tried to bring a four-year-old into an adult world activity. The grandmother suggested the grandson would have been happy just to go to the park and play on the swings. The next time they went into the world of the four-year-old. It was wonderful. Grandmother winked at her husband and said, "If you want to build a relationship with a four-year-old, you have to think like a four-year-old." Granddaddy said the way his memory was slipping he would catch up with their grandson in no time at all. They laughed.

Age-appropriate activities for teenagers may range from working on a car, going to a recital, or an activity which involves fun, friends, and freedom.

FOLLOWING THROUGH WITH AN "I LOVE YOU" PROGRAM

Carrying out an "I Love You" program requires acts of unconditional love independent of the poor judgment decisions of others.

Professed love absent of loving behaviors will never convince anyone he or she is loved.

If the majority of our interaction involves criticism, punishment, and reproof and if most of the attention we give is negative, the words "I love you," fall on deaf ears. There must be credibility in the loving behavior of the reforming toxic person. One detrimental behavior to overcome is the withdrawal of promised rewards.

171

CHARITI AND HER FATHER

Chariti was a fourteen-year-old girl with a passion for animals. Horses and dogs seemed to be her obsession. Since they lived in a suburban area on a quarter acre lot, owning a horse was out, but a dog was a possibility. Chariti spent weeks going to the library and reading about every breed of dog. Finally, Chariti decided she wanted a Schipperke. She had pictures on her walls of this little, black dog without a tail. It looked very much like a black fox and about that size. Every Saturday Chariti and her father would drive around looking at pet stores and checking out the newspaper ads as part of the father's "I Love You" program.

Then Chariti broke one of the family rules. It was not a difficult rule to remember. The rule was if the children's plans changed while they were with their friends, they must contact either parent in person or over the phone. If the parents could not be reached, the answer was "No!" The penalty was two weeks of being grounded from all activities except school and church. Chariti knew the rules. One Friday night she and a girlfriend were planning on going to the movies. At the last minute her girlfriend canceled so Chariti called another girlfriend and spent the night at her house without informing her parents. Chariti had been in a fight with this particular girlfriend, but had made amends that night.

When the mother and father came home at midnight, they did a bed check. They found the other seven children sound asleep in their beds. Chariti was gone. The mother called up the first girl friend's parents and was informed that the plans had been canceled. The mother began to imagine the worst. Maybe Chariti was dead. Maybe she had been hit by a car and was in the hospital.

All of Chariti's friends were called except the one where she happened to be. The police were contacted, the

172

hospitals were checked and the mother began searching for her daughter by driving around the neighborhood in the car. It was 4:00 a.m. when the mother and father commended her spirit to God and went to bed.

Ironically, Chariti had spent the night less than one-half block from her home with Jeannie. About 9:00 a.m. on Saturday, Chariti came bounding through the front door all smiles and cheerful. After the gravity of her insensitivity was explained to her, she was grounded for two weeks.

Chariti cried. Through her tears she said to her father, "Does this mean we are not going to look for a dog today?"

The father replied, "We are still going to look for a dog today. It is not because you have been good. It is because I'm good and I love you. You are still grounded for breaking the rules, but this is a different thing."

Looking for a dog was part of the father's "I Love You" program. It was independent from the "I Trust You" program. It was part of the father's unconditional love. Every week the father would hold a sharing time with each child. It was a time to talk or play games. In Chariti's case, the time had been allocated to looking for a dog. This was an unconditional act of love. It was not a time to be withdrawn as a punishment or taken away because of an infraction on the part of the child. There were other consequences that could be used for breaking the family rules.

In the foregoing story the father was acting out of love. The message is not to use love as a punishment. When people withhold loving behaviors as a punishment they become emotionally unsafe.

Additionally, when parents withhold promised rewards, they lose credibility and trust. One father promised $500 for a report card of straight "A"s. However, because the teenager broke one of the family rules, the father withheld the $500. In doing so, he destroyed his credibility as a man of his word. He also destroyed the adolescent's belief that his father could be trusted to do what he said he would do.

THE REFORMING TOXIC:
CHOOSING TO LOVE OR TO WITHHOLD LOVE

Toxic people withhold love, friendship, or association for many reasons. Peer or family disapproval may keep one from establishing a loving relationship or being a loving person. Obviously, anyone would have reason to be concerned about a drug-abusing axe murderer or an obvious-to-everyone else dysfunctional person. Toxic people in the process of reforming have a difficult time loving those who are less than perfect. Without tolerating the intolerable, without assuming that loving them is approving of everything they stand for, what about loving them because you are a good person, not because they are perfect? Do you have to focus on the flaw? Do you really feel that your job is to be constantly correcting others? Why do you persist in seeing only what loved ones are not, rather than seeing the good that is in them?

What is it that keeps you from loving? Is it fear of being hurt or rejected? Yes, that has to be a part of it. Is being a loving person always having to be held hostage to the fear of rejection? No, not always. If your desire to be a loving and a healthy person is greater than the fear of rejection, then it is possible to be a loving person.

With a history of being toxic your motives may be questioned. You may only be able to send a greeting card on a birthday or special occasion until you have earned the trust of your loved ones. Acting in a positive way could include a phone call or civil behavior. When dealing with an "emotionally safe person," a sincere hug or an enthusiastic smile would be appropriate.

BALANCING THE POSITIVE AND NEGATIVE

A pitfall on the road to becoming a loving person is the danger of focusing on the negative. Spouses can easily fall into this trap. When you find someone is withdrawing from you, stop and evaluate your approach.

The essence of a good relationship in a family is to love. It is to help others become their highest and best selves. This is not "psycho-babble" or some socially acceptable thing to do. It is not about being politically correct. It is about loving. A solid "I Love You" program complete with weekly shared time and experience is necessary. Treating a loved one with respect enhances the possibility of not being perceived as an enemy. The kindness of a "thank you" and "please" engenders respect. If one is treated consistently with respect, the credibility of the critic increases. Balance is important. There is a need for *at least* as many positive things to be stated as negative. The problem is negativity breeds negativity and then all the critic can see is the bad. The toxic who is unwilling to develop an "I Love You" program and acknowledge the good as well as establish an "I Trust You" program will almost certainly be viewed as an enemy.

This is not just about avoiding becoming a porcupine. It is about loving and being loved. It's all about eliminating a self-defeating behavior and empowering love. It's about letting the feeling of love get through an aura of negativism. It's about being an emotionally safe person. It's about being a more effective communicator. It's about helping loved ones

175

become their highest and best selves. It's about better relationships at work and at home.

THE REFORMING TOXIC'S CHALLENGE

The most difficult challenge reforming toxics face is the skepticism of those who were victims of their toxicity. Even if those who are reforming cease their negative messages and begin to communicate sincere acceptance, others may not believe the change is real. People who are familiar with the reforming toxic's past history of criticism and sarcasm will find it difficult to trust them. Also those who have been exposed to years of nonacceptance messages may not believe the person can change. I have seen people whose efforts to change were mocked and scorned as too little, too late. Now the reforming toxic has to deal with other people who won't forgive.

AL AND HIS TOXIC FATHER

Toxic Dad had spent a life-time being critical of his son, Al. The father was always telling Al to do better. The problem was the father's approach. Sarcasm and ridicule were the only communications Al remembers from his father. When Al was twenty-seven and his father fifty-two, his father underwent a quadruple heart bypass surgery. It changed the father's life. After the operation, the father wanted a close relationship with his children, but Al was leery of his father's attempts at reconciliation. Al had given up years ago on trying to please his father. Resentment and distance replaced any desire Al had for his father's acceptance and love.

Even after his father apologized, Al felt unsafe and "waited for the other shoe to drop." Al was so used to anything positive being followed by a negative statement that he was disbelieving, skeptical, and untrusting. He rejected his father's attempts and discounted any of his father's positive statements.

I explained to the father that he was dealing with an issue of trust and credibility. Only time, consistency, and building a positive history could establish trust. Discouragement would be the father's greatest test as he patiently persisted in his quest for a closer relationship with his son.

There was an element of pay back and retribution in Al that the father had to overcome. Al had craved his father's approval for many years. Not receiving it was replaced by resentment and hurt. Al's father could do no more than ask for forgiveness and endure with a positive attitude. Six months before the father's death, Al and his father made their peace. This reconciliation would not have happened if Al's father had not been willing to persevere in the application of positive communication skills.

Reforming critiholics, perfectionists, and controlling people need to be at least as patient with others as others have been with them.

SHEDDING THE QUILLS OF TOXIC BEHAVIORS

Stopping the toxic negative behaviors begins by recognizing them. Contrast and comparison is a good way to see the differences:

TOXIC BEHAVIORS CONTRASTED WITH POSITIVE REPLACEMENT BEHAVIORS

1. Constant criticism, fault finding, inappropriate and improperly given criticism

   Learn the "art" of appropriate criticism; rarely use criticism

177

TOXIC BEHAVIORS CONTRASTED WITH POSITIVE REPLACEMENT BEHAVIORS

Toxic Behaviors	Positive Replacement Behaviors
2. Perfectionism, unrealistic and unreasonable expectations of self or others	Realize your expectations of others need to be age, time, and circumstance appropriate; have reasonable expectations of self and others
3. Ridicule and rejection	Appreciation and acceptance
4. Being judgmental	Positive silence; Eliminate judgmentalism
5. An inclination to reject solutions without adequately evaluating them	Be open to alternatives and honestly evaluate them. Think before you speak
6. Failure to respect the personal space of others (standing too close, opening doors without knocking, borrowing things without asking)	Respect the personal space of others Stand at least an arm's length away; knock before entering; ask before taking something, say "please" and "thank you"
7. Mocking, scorning, and belittling others	Positive silence; eliminate these behaviors
8. Attacking the worth of another by name calling, i.e. "dumb" or "stupid," etc.	Focus comments on issues or behaviors, not on the person
9. Embarrassing others in front of friends, family, co-workers, or strangers	Be alone with the person before delivering criticisms or comments that will be interpreted as negative
10. Messages of incompetence or inadequacy	Acknowledge competence and project confidence in their ability to succeed
11. Constant direction giving	After initial instructions, wait for request for information from the other person or give written instructions

TOXIC BEHAVIORS CONTRASTED WITH POSITIVE REPLACEMENT BEHAVIORS

12. Ceaseless preaching

Ask for permission to share your opinion; keep it brief

13. An unwillingness to acknowledge the legitimate progress of others

Acknowledge the legitimate progress of others

14. An inability to show understanding empathy, or compassion for other people's feelings and views

Develop active listening skills; Give sincere understanding

15. Giving "Trailing Barbs" which means when acknowledging accomplishments of another adding "but..." to the end of the compliment

Let compliments stand alone without a "but..." or a detracting statement

16. Not seeing or recognizing what has been accomplished, only what remains undone.

Comment on what has been accomplished in positive terms

17. Habitually playing the "Devils Advocate" and defending the opposite

Positive silence; active listening

18. Easily offended by others

A thicker skin, allowing others to hold differing opinions.

19. Making others feel obligated by guilt

Ask sincerely for what you want

20. An unwillingness to negotiate

Negotiate, bargain, trade

21. An inability or unwillingness to truly be grateful

Being truly grateful

22. Hypersensitivity to being criticized

Learn the "art" of receiving criticism

TOXIC BEHAVIORS CONTRASTED WITH POSITIVE REPLACEMENT BEHAVIORS

23. An inability to send messages of adequacy

Send messages of adequacy, such as "Good job!" "That's great!"

24. Incessantly contradicting and correcting others

Positive silence, allow others a different opinion without comment

25. Constantly interrupting and correcting the conversations or stories of others

Positive silence or allow others to be responsible for their own words; Do not "parent" or correct them

26. Being argumentative and opposite

Positive silence is better

27. Nonacceptance messages

Positive silence or set a time to discuss sincere concerns at a mutually agreeable time and place; set a "Red Hour" (or ten minutes) each day to discuss negative concerns and leave the rest of the time to be "emotionally safe" time

28. Constant complaining

Positive silence or set up a specific time to deal with concerns (limit to once a day for ten minutes)

29. Frequent references to past failures of others

Positive silence; forgive and forget or remember that you forgave

30. Regretting, focusing on lost opportunities in the past

Focus on the present and what can be done

31. Martyr

Appreciate any positive efforts of others

32. Consistently pointing out the "unfairness" of life

Positive silence or look for the positive

TOXIC BEHAVIORS CONTRASTED WITH POSITIVE REPLACEMENT BEHAVIORS

33. Mad, angry, upset most of the time	Reduce expectations and you will reduce your frustration; examine expectations to see if they are "realistic"; be appreciative for the good; smile! Or use positive silence
34. Being rude, insensitive, curt, and abrupt	Sincerely ask for what you need; be pleasant; give courteous answers
35. Sarcasm	Positive silence or sincere statements
36. "Parenting" your equals	Use language of respect and request with equals
37. Blatant disrespect for the opinions and attitudes of others	Allow others their own opinions or use positive silence
38. Controlling	Ask for what you need, but do not try to control how others do it
39. Hurting others' feelings	Express appreciation, acceptance, and affection for the good in others
40. Withholding love, acceptance, affection, or appreciation	Express love; develop an "I Love You" program separate from an "I Trust You" program
41. Fomenting a crisis	Create a spirit of peace
42. Unwillingness to forgive	Honestly forgive self and others; do not bring up the past
43. Being negative	Limit negative expressions of others to agreed upon times and places; positive silence
44. Yelling, screaming, swearing cursing, and verbal abuse	Calmly ask in a sincere and polite manner for what you want

TOXIC BEHAVIORS CONTRASTED WITH POSITIVE REPLACEMENT BEHAVIORS

45. Physical abuse	Zero tolerance; anger management required
46. Sexual abuse	Zero tolerance; counseling required
47. Threatening divorce or abandonment	Assurance of "We will find a way to make it work."
48. Threatening to kill yourself	Express confidence in healthy solutions
49. Preoccupied with evil, wrong, and negative behaviors	Limit exposure to negative friends, TV, movies etc.; engage in positive interactions
50. False praise	Sincere praise
51. Self-righteous, holier than thou attitude	Recognize contributions of others
52. Others are always worried about hurting your feelings	Honestly evaluate the comments of others without getting upset
53. Others are always "walking on pins and needles" around you	Relax and help others feel comfortable around you
54. Codependency	Define a healthy self; live to your own standard of goodness

IF YOU CAN'T IMPROVE
UPON SILENCE, DON'T TRY

Notice how many times in the foregoing list "positive silence" was given as the healthy alternative to the toxic behavior. Positive silence is not only a good replacement skill, it is an absolutely essential one. It means controlling your natural impulse to comment verbally or to project a negative countenance. In addition to your words, your body language and your facial expression need to be neutral or pleasant. Positive silence is having your body language and your facial expressions in positive congruence. They are noncritical and nonthreatening. It may require the biting of your tongue or counting from fifty backwards. It may even entail leaving the room until you can deal with others in a civilized manner.

MAKING OTHERS FEEL COMFORTABLE

Another positive replacement skill is the ability of helping people feel comfortable around you. This is called being gracious. Being "others" centered and not "self" centered is a key to being gracious. Most toxic people lack the empathy and perspective to be gracious. There is a certain self-centeredness about them that puts them in the middle of their own narcissistic universe. Empathy is the ability to feel the needs of others. Focusing on being appreciative of others and showing forth sincere approval for the smallest gestures of kindness is a way you can truly be gracious and empathetic. Your ability to focus on the positive will help other people feel comfortable around you.

The cessation of negative behaviors is a tremendous accomplishment. It ought to be rewarded by genuine and sincere appreciation. However, it probably won't be. Reforming individuals should not expect external validation. If it comes, wonderful; if not, "bummer deal." Remember you need to build a history of trust in order to establish your credibility. Time and patient application of positive behaviors are your greatest allies.

Some relationships may never be salvaged. Remember, "you are only one-half of any relationship to which you belong." Each relationship will stand or fall on its own merits and according to the willingness of each member to contribute to its success. As a reforming toxic, you can set a goal to become more positive. Others will have to choose their actions in relationship to you. But you should not remain unhealthy just because other people are having a hard time accepting the new you. Go ahead and shed the quills of your toxic behaviors and remain available for healthy interactions with those who are willing to have a relationship with you.

Replacing toxic behaviors with positive ones requires the courage to be vulnerable, awkward, and exposed. As with any new set of skills, they require practice and repetition. The learning curve will vary from person to person. Some reforming toxics will find that their meager efforts are responded to almost immediately by acceptance-starved loved ones. Children are frequently quick to forgive and forget. They are eager for positive interaction. Spouses and adult children are more skeptical and wary. Nevertheless, practice, practice, and more practice brings confidence to reforming toxics in their newly acquired positive behaviors.

CLAIRE, THE REFORMING CRITIHOLIC

The hardest thing for Claire was not adding a trailing barb to a compliment. She would find herself saying, "but" after every compliment she tried to give. She had no logical basis for her feelings. (Feelings are seldom logical.) She simply felt compelled to say something instructive.

"Thanks for doing the dishes tonight, but could you remember to wipe out the sink so it doesn't have water spots?"

"I'm so grateful you brought the car home on time, but I hope you left enough gas for me to run my errands."

Claire wanted to ask for help from her family. I warned her she was possibly setting herself up for failure. However, if she could handle the pressure, I recommended that she announce to the family her intentions to stop giving trailing barbs and that she would pay fifty cents to anyone who received a trailing barb. I suggested she increase it to a dollar the second week, five dollars the third week, ten dollars the fourth week, and twenty dollars the fifth week. If she really wanted to break the habit she could go to fifty dollars the sixth week and one hundred on the seventh week and back to twenty dollars for every week thereafter. It cost Claire about $115.00 before she finally stopped during the fifth week. Most habits take about twenty-one days of consistent and conscious choice to change them.

Claire reported the following humorous story. Her sixteen-year-old son came home five minutes before his curfew on a school night.

Claire said to him "Thank you for being home on time, but…"

Her son, anxious for $20.00 during the fifth week said, "But what, Mom?"

She didn't know what to say. She was going to say, "but you are cutting it pretty close aren't you?" Instead she said, "but, but nothing. Thank you for coming home on time and now I will get my 'but' out of here."

AM I TOXIC TO MYSELF?

There are two directions in which one's toxic nature manifests itself, i.e. inward and outward. The set of negative behaviors directed inward are sometimes referred to as self-defeating behaviors. In this case, one is "toxic to himself."

Many who are self-depreciating, who are always putting

themselves down, see it as as virtue. It is not. It is a false humility. True humility is free from selfish motives. True humility is modest and unpretentious. The inability to accept a compliment is selfish. It lacks graciousness and is an insult to the giver of the compliment. What appears as modesty is really a guise for negative self-focus. The inability to accept a compliment is a slam on the giver because it challenges the truthfulness and sincerity of their message. Making someone feel badly about saying something nice is a toxic behavior. Not being able to receive something nice that is said in sincerity on the part of another is a self-defeating behavior.

IF I'M TOXIC TO MYSELF:

		TRUE	False
1.	I am always putting myself down.	_____	_____
2.	I have a difficult time accepting compliments.	_____	_____
3.	I am a perfectionist.	_____	_____
4.	I blame myself for the failings of my loved ones.	_____	_____
5.	I have said that others would be better off without me.	_____	_____
6.	I want to hurt myself or cease to exist.	_____	_____
7.	I feel manipulated by guilt, ridicule, or rejection.	_____	_____
8.	I seldom feel that I am good enough.	_____	_____
9.	The good times are few and far between.	_____	_____

		TRUE	FALSE
10.	I have a negative, pessimistic attitude toward life that I call being "realistic."	_____	_____
11.	I seem to be consistently disappointed in myself.	_____	_____
12.	I'm depressed or discouraged much of the time.	_____	_____
13.	I frequently (weekly) lose my temper and yell, swear, or use derogatory names.	_____	_____
14.	I have threatened suicide.	_____	_____
15.	I diminish my accomplishments.	_____	_____

TOTAL "TRUE" ANSWERS   _____

EXPLANATION FOR NUMBER OF "TRUE" ANSWERS:

0 - 4	Normal, but not necessarily healthy
5 - 9	Needs Counseling
10 - 11	Serious need for professional help
12 - 15	Major self-worth makeover required; medication may be needed during transition time under a doctor's supervision.

BUILDING SELF-WORTH

Self-worth is a combination of the positive and negative messages we received while growing up and the conclusions we draw from all those messages. When children are constantly criticized, and consistently given nonacceptance messages, they become convinced they are of little worth. Acceptance, approval, recognition, and self-actualization are basic human needs. When a person is denied these needs, the need for validation is at war with the nonacceptance and nonapproval messages. The conflict translates into a resentment for those sending the toxic messages and the belief that maybe the nonacceptance messages are warranted. Believing you are capable is replaced by doubt, fear, and believing that you are incapable. Doubt and fear of adequacy, worth, value, or desirability of association creates an inward focus. Tolerance for any criticism is eliminated. Even when justified, necessary, and appropriate, there is a hypersensitivity to any criticism.

Frequently criticism is responded to with rage or anger. These are the behaviors of those whose self-image has been so damaged they finally join in by adding their own negativity with self-defeating behaviors.

Remember, recognition of your toxicity and getting out of denial is the first step. Having the motivation or desire to change your ways is the second step. The third step involves acquiring new positive behaviors. The last step involves applying skills. The next chapters will help with identifying and eliminating self-defeating behaviors and replacing them with healthier ones.

The miracle of change is made possible by the choice to do so. Every person is capable of improvement, of going from where he is to a better place. It all begins by believing it is possible.

CHAPTER ELEVEN

CRITICISM:
THE GREATEST QUILL
OF THEM ALL

For those who don't want to be an emotional porcupine, and for those who have to live with them, the following information is crucial. The "culture of abuse" is sustained by uncontrolled and improperly given criticism. If a relationship is to survive intact and healthy, we must learn how to deal with negative feedback in healthy ways. If we do not learn how to properly give and receive criticism, instead of a mutual improvement association, the relationship will become a mutually abusive depreciation society.

All porcupines are defined by their quills. A porcupine without quills is not a porcupine. Most toxic personalities have as their greatest challenge the overcoming of inappropriate criticism. Indeed, CRITICISM IS THE GREATEST QUILL OF THEM ALL!

CRITICISM DEFINED

To criticize is to censure, to find fault, or to focus on a weakness or a shortcoming. It is to reflect disapproval, denunciation, and/or nonacceptance. Inherent in most criticism is blame-fixing and condemnation. Criticism implies failure to act appropriately and communicates a sense of inadequacy. It is reproof. It is a negative reaction to an issue or behavior created by self or another. Frequently it is born out of frustration because of expectations for better performance. The objective of those who give criticism is to change the one being criticized. Often the critic is hopeful of a change of heart or an improved behavior. *Criticism is extremely toxic to the human spirit. It is more likely to kill the desire for change than it is to inspire it.* This is especially true of criticism which is uninvited, unauthorized, or inappropriate. Even when criticism is invited, required, and appropriate, the damage to the self-worth can be irreparable. It needs to be given with the greatest care and sensitivity.

The art of giving and receiving criticism in an appropriate way is a skill almost all can develop. It has more to do with having a positive attitude than being a perfect person. Criticizing in an appropriate way requires self-control, patience, and focusing on the best way to approach another. When these ingredients are present, the focus can remain on the issue or behavior in question and not the worth of the individual being criticized or the packaging of the one who is the giver of criticism. If not carefully and thoughtfully approached, both parties to the criticism become toxic.

Change is hard. Habits are difficult to break. However, becoming identified as an emotionally safe person makes it worth the effort. Inappropriate criticism has no chance of success because the content of the message is lost in the presentation, i.e., the body language, the tone of voice, etc. If being healthy is the objective, uninvited, unauthorized, and inappropriately given criticism will not make another person healthy. If we are not possessed of self-control, patience, and a healthy approach to criticism, the giving and receiving of criticism will be counterproductive. When criticism is given or received by someone who is emotionally out of control, impatient, or resentful, poor reactions are predictable. So are the hostile outcomes. Even appropriate criticism runs the risk of rejection. The difference between acceptance or rejection of a critical message may be the demeanor of the message bearer.

There are more effective ways to change behavior. They are to invite, entice, encourage, inspire, reward and affirm. Uninvited, unauthorized, and improper criticism will place the focus on the critic, not on the critic's message. Criticism is only effective to the level of the receiver's willingness to listen. The teacher is limited by the pupil's willingness to be instructed.

On occasion being critical is justified. The qualification is that the critic is prompted by the best interest of the other and remains in emotional control. When genuine concern dwells in the heart of the critic and he or she is in emotional control, the greatest opportunity exists to be heard and not discounted.

Someone once observed that the real art of giving criticism was the ability to tell people they were going to hell in such a way that they look forward to the journey. There always seems to be a little bit of truth in these homey expressions.

It is instructive to note how Noah Webster's 1828 Dictionary defined the words "Criticise [sic]," and its synonyms "Reproof," and "Sharpness":

- CRITICISE   [sic]: To notice the beauties and blemishes
- CRITICISED [sic]: Examined and judged with regard to beauties and faults
- CRITICISM: The art of judging with propriety of the beauties and faults
- REPROOF: Blame expressed to the face; censure for a fault, reprehension
- SHARPNESS: Keenness of an edge; Acuteness of intellect; quickness of understanding

Two hundred years ago a "critic" was one who could see the beauty as well as the blemish. Reproof had to be spoken to the face of the person being criticized and not behind his back. "Sharpness" meant to be acute of intellect and to demonstrate "niceness" when discerning another. To "reprove with sharpness" was to censure another directly to their face at a proper time. It meant to be precise and exact in focusing on the behavior or issue being discussed. It involved empathy and understanding.

There are times when criticism is necessary. There are circumstances which require the courage to be appropriately critical. There are issues that demand attention. There are instances when criticism may be the forerunner for true change and improvement. However, in general most people criticize out of frustration. Giving and receiving criticism with the best interest of the other in mind is difficult for both the giver and the receiver. It is hard for the giver of criticism not to be overcome with negative emotion, to become angry, to yell, or to package the criticism in such a way that the focus is on the messenger and not on the message. It is equally hard for the receiver of criticism to focus on the content of what is being said whether or not the critic is out of control emotionally. The receiver of criticism is easily sidetracked by defensive reactions. The manner in which the critic is inappropriate with their timing, tone of voice, or demeanor will be the focus, and not the validity of the criticism.

The more centered in the issue or behavior the critic is, the easier it is to give and receive criticism, reproof, and chastisement. The more we are "ego" involved and "self" focused, the more difficult it is to give or receive criticism without making pride the issue. Because it is difficult does not excuse the sincerely concerned from giving and receiving criticism in an appropriate way.

Criticism is not given as an end in itself, but as information which is to help the individual become a better self. Helping the person to improve is the objective of criticism. That objective will be lost in a sea of words, defensiveness, and negative emotions unless the approach to criticism is appropriate. *How* the criticism is packaged will largely determine whether it will be honestly evaluated or rejected. This means a great responsibility is placed upon the shoulders of the critic.

One of the challenges faced by the critic is the fact that many people will only be honest if they are angry. Anger gives them permission to criticize. It is a dysfunctional behavior learned in the family of origin. It is ineffective as a means of changing behavior. Some people feel that their anger is an exclamation point to the message. They maintain that anger adds emphasis and lets the one being criticized know how important the message is. The truth is anger places the entire focus on the messenger and not on the message. What is remembered is not the message, but only the anger. The truth of the message is lost in the negative emotion of the critic. In order to be an effective communicator, the focus needs to remain on the message. Anything that detracts from the message is counterproductive. Why would any rational person want to be ineffective? The answer is rational people don't.

THERE IS NO SUCH THING
AS CONSTRUCTIVE CRITICISM

There is no such thing as "Constructive Criticism." To construct is to build, to edify, or to put together. To criticize, according to the currently accepted use of the word, is to tear down, to find fault, or to condemn. These two words describe two separate and opposite processes. One word takes away all the meaning from the other. They are antonyms. The thought of criticism being constructive is absurd. In certain literary circles this coupling of two words with opposite meanings, such as "constructive criticism," is referred to as an "oxymoron." It makes as much sense as saying someone is a "wise fool."

BLOODLETTING

Knowledge doesn't seem to interfere with human tradition, however. When people have been taught something loud enough or long enough they tend to believe it even in the face of overwhelming fact and evidence to the contrary. For years the medical profession practiced "bleeding" their patients. By strong oral and religious tradition, it was believed that all sickness was in the blood. An educated person could not be disabused of the idea. After all it was taught at Harvard, Oxford and the Sorbonne. It seemed perfectly logical to the doctors and professors that if the impure blood of a person were the cause of sickness, then one should drain off as much as one could to give the patient more opportunity to survive.

While the scientific world was breaking away from false tradition and all educated men scoffed at blood sacrifice, they nevertheless continued to practice medical bloodletting until the 1800's for scientific healing. Who knows the untold millions who died of bloodletting? The justifications for the deaths were, "Oh well, maybe if a little more blood had been let, the patient might have lived." In like manner, who knows the untold millions whose self-worth has been sacrificed because of the critical "bloodletting" of well-meaning others? "Oh well, maybe with a little more criticism their self-worth will improve and their behavior change."

Imagine living in a society when most of the educated doctors, teachers, rulers, and the mass populous believed in bloodletting and you discovered they were in error. What happens to people who make statements that run counter to popular folk belief? History records that *all* of their blood was "let." How well was Copernicus received when he announced that the earth revolved around the sun and not the sun around the earth? He feared for his life. It doesn't matter that he was correct. He went against tradition, religion, and "God." Traditions die hard. For hundreds of years there was a Flat Earth Society. How could there be a Flat Earth Society even after the earth was proven to be round? Most people would chuckle at this. How could any sane, rational, intelligent human being continue to maintain some obviously ludicrous notion in the light of all the evidence to the contrary?

So it is with "constructive criticism." In the current societal structure the educated, the rulers, and the masses all believe and practice "constructive criticism." It approximates a religious tenet of faith. It is as difficult in our time to convince someone that there is no such thing as "constructive criticism," as it was to convince former societies that the earth was not flat and that bloodletting was ineffective.

Criticism in and of itself never builds anything. It never has and it never will. The process of construction is separate from the process of demolition. There are companies that deal exclusively with demolition of buildings. Other companies specialize in building construction. Imagine what would happen to the building if the demolition contractor arrived. What part of construction would take place? There are also companies that do remodeling. Two different processes are involved in a remodeling project. It is a tricky business. The remodeler must insure that the basic integrity of the structure remains intact. The part to be remodeled is carefully dismantled. The wrecking crew is cautious to demolish only that part of the building which is to be replaced. The tearing down requires a different approach than does the construction phase. We are either tearing down or building up. The fallacy is we can do both at the same time. How do we build anything while we are tearing it down? In the field of construction a demolition crew who tore down an existing structure which was scheduled only to be remodeled would wind up in a law suit. When a well meaning person shares "constructive criticism," he is sending in the demolition crew.

That most people misuse the phrase "constructive criticism" in their vocabulary is evidence of their misunderstanding of the two processes involved. It is also a witness to the difficulty of changing firmly entrenched traditions. Except for its redundancy, "*destructive* criticism" is a more accurate phrase to describe the tearing down process. The constructive process is an edifying one. Positive reinforcement best describes the construction process. Criticism does not reinforce a positive behavior. It describes a negative one. "Constructive criticism" is a not only a misnomer; it is a myth.

Those who emphatically defend criticism as "constructive" tend to idealize it. They see it as a "right," a moral imperative, a positive trait, and a responsible behavior. Their legacy is a trail of devastation to self-concept. If only they could step back and view the consequences of their acts of destruction. If only they would objectively measure the practical effects of criticism. They would conclude that the cure was worse than

196

the illness. The real tragedy is the damage done in ignorance to the self-worth of a loved one. Before doctors washed and sterilized their hands, many people died of infections carried by the doctor from patient to patient. As well meaning as they might have been, as compassionate and self-sacrificing their efforts, the consequences were deadly. Well meaning people continue to kill self-worth believing they are doing a good thing. They have failed to understand there is no such thing as "constructive criticism."

CRITICISM IS TOXIC

There is, however, a time and a place for criticism. There are issues and behaviors which need to be corrected. The demolition process involves the use of appropriate criticism. If criticism is so toxic, how could its use ever be appropriate? Think of criticism as a tiny vial of smallpox vaccine. Applied in a small dose to a specific area it will immunize the person. If too great an amount is administered, it will inflict the very illness it was intended to prevent. Therefore, toxic substances are controlled and frequently carry warning labels. They are carefully regulated and restricted to specific uses.

Criticism is like an herbicide which kills all plant life that comes into contact with it. Even diluted, it can be devastating.

THE WELL-MEANING FARMER

There was a farmer in Idaho who sued his well meaning neighbor for the misuse of a deadly chemical herbicide. It seemed that the well-intended neighbor had sprayed both sides of a long private road common to both farms with an herbicide to kill all of the weeds growing there. In his desire to destroy the weeds, he failed to consider the side effects of the wind. As a result, thousands and thousands of dollars' worth of damage was done to the cash crops growing in the fields. The wind had carried the deadly herbicide far beyond its intended application. So it is with criticism. The judge disregarded the "good" intentions and focused on the consequences of destruction. The well meaning neighbor paid a great price for his ignorance. The judge, although sympathetic, held the well-meaning farmer accountable for the effects of his behavior.

Well-intended critics need to be very cautious. Criticism intended for a specific application has side effects that frequently outweigh the assumed benefits. In human relationships the attempts to remove the weeds may result in the destruction of the surrounding growth of creativity, motivation, and a positive outlook on life.

People tend to justify the general use of criticism when only its specific use is appropriate. There are those who will argue that a sword, although a weapon of war, could be used for varied purposes such as harvesting grain, chopping wood, or defending ourselves. Like the sword, criticism is used for emotional war. It maims, injures and destroys emotional bonding even in the closest of family relationships. A surgeon would be stopped at once if he came to the operating room with a sword instead of a scalpel. Criticism is often used as a sword, when it ought to be used as a scalpel. Exactness and great care are required by qualified hands if the operation is to be successful.

Criticism is so much a part of current society that it is considered normal. Cannibalism is also accepted as normal in certain headhunting societies in Borneo. As repulsive as cannibalism may be to others, it is quite natural to them. Just because something is accepted as normal does not make it right. Criticism is emotional cannibalism. It kills self-worth and devours confidence.

CRITICISM IS A CANCER

Imagine being called into the doctor's office and then being told that a malignant tumor is growing in your body. The x-rays show that it is the size of an orange. The doctor suggests immediate surgery, tomorrow.

"Don't eat anything for twelve hours before," he says, "I've scheduled emergency surgery for 10 a.m. tomorrow morning." He continues to talk and to say words and you can see his lips moving and hear his voice in the background. They are words of hope. His voice fades in and out. Is this a sick joke? Like some out-of-body experience, you find yourself dispassionately watching this entire scene. It is as if the mind left the body and you are standing in the corner of the room watching yourself sitting there listening to the doctor.

"The lab report came back positive," he pauses. "It is cancer."

Late payments on a note co-signed with a son seemed important on the way to the doctor's office. Also, the annual performance review with the boss is coming up. There is a busy calendar scheduled for this week. This is a bad time to have cancer. A lot of people are expecting things. There isn't time for cancer. Disbelief sweeps over you. Something inside cries out, "It's a lie, it's not true!" Something deeper inside just cries and wants to be held.

"I don't want to frighten you, it is just routine common sense to check with a lawyer and make sure your affairs are in order, just in case some unforeseen circumstances prevail." If there were ever a polite way to say death, he just did: "unforeseen circumstances prevail."

"Read the pamphlet, it will tell you all we know about cancer."

Numb and void of feeling, your eyes stare at the words. "Cancer is a change in the normal growth of cells, but the causes have not yet been fully determined. A great many cancers can be cured with surgery and radiation treatment." It all sounds so sterile, so impersonal. "But it must be treated properly before the cancerous cells have begun to spread or colonize in other parts of the body." Carcinoma, sarcoma, leukemia, ad nauseam..."

"Dear Lord, if there is anything I can do, any change I could make, I'll do it. Let this be a bad dream, let me wake up in a cold sweat to find out like Ebenezer Scrooge in Dickens', *A Christmas Carol*, that it is not too late for me." *Criticism is a cancer, Wake up!*

IT MAY NOT BE TOO LATE

It may not be too late if you act now. A normal relationship infected with the cancer of criticism will begin to consume itself. Has the cancer of criticism consumed so much of your language that you are past the point of a cure? Has the disease robbed your relationships of the ability to survive it or the power to resist it? Criticism gnaws at the sinews of any relationship with its dour and destructive effects until it leaves the relationship lifeless. It creates deep wounds and makes enemies of one-time friends, co-workers, and family.

Many have lived so long with intense criticism they cannot imagine a relationship without it. It is likely they were seriously

200

criticized as children. Why would marriage be any different? Why should their own parenting be any different? Why should any relationship with friend, co-worker, or family be free of what has become a way of life? After all, isn't that what life is all about, speaking our mind at will? Is there a danger in wanting to help so desperately that we kill the very thing we profess to love?

SYMBIOSIS OR PARASITISM

Relationships, like the human body, have a life of their own, and they can die. They can also be wonderfully healthy. A relationship is an association between two people. As you have learned, the best relationships are those where each helps the other become their highest and best self. It is helpful if we think of a relationship as having a shared existence, a mini-ecosystem of its own. It is instructive to understand that symbiosis is a term used in Biology to refer to the association of two living organisms which exist for the benefit of the other. Symbiosis is the opposite of "parasitism." A parasite is one organism that feeds on the body of the other. A true parasite lives on or in another creature from which it gets its food, always selfishly, at the expense of the host. It may or may not kill the host, but usually parasites are unable to survive independently. Lice and tapeworms are parasites as is mistletoe whose host is the oak tree.

Some human relationships are composed of one and sometimes two parasites who stay together for all the wrong reasons. Many do so because they do not believe they can survive alone. Where both are parasites, they consume one another. The opposite is true of a symbiotic relationship. Most lichens, which are composed of an alga and a fungus, are examples of symbiosis; the alga provides the food, and the fungus provides the water and protection. In this association or relationship, neither is harmed and both benefit. It is truly a mutual improvement association.

Relationships, whether husband-wife, parent-child, employer-employee, brother-sister, or friend to friend, have a life of their own. The relationship will never be greater than the part that each contributes to make it successful. When both parties are committed to a mutual benefit that helps each to become their highest and very best, a symbiotic relationship exists. This is the ideal. This is the only defensible position a loving person can take to help loved ones become their best. Anything less will ultimately turn one or the other into a critical parasite.

Criticism is the most common choice of behavior when someone is angry, disappointed, or even concerned. It is also the *least* effective in changing behavior. When critical people are asked why they are criticizing, they frequently respond, "I wanted to correct their behavior, answer, issue, or statement." However, a truer answer is people usually criticize because someone is not measuring up to expectations and they are frustrated. The truth is most criticism is based on frustration.

FRUSTRATION COMES
FROM UNMET EXPECTATIONS

Nowhere is this axiom more applicable than with criticism:

"All frustration comes from unmet expectations.
There is no such thing as a frustration that is not tied
to an expectation."

Sometimes the relationship between an expectation and a frustration is obvious. One was expecting a raise in pay at work and didn't receive it. Frustration is a first response to an unmet expectation. It is normal and natural to feel frustration. Some people set themselves up for frustration by possessing unrealistic or unreasonable expectations. For example, "If you really love me, you will be able to read my mind and know how I am feeling." This is both unrealistic and unreasonable. However, because the expectation wasn't met, the party became frustrated. The issue is what happens to the frustration?

UNDERSTANDING FRUSTRATION

Frustration is a reaction. There is an entire range of human emotions we can choose from when reacting to frustration: i.e., resentment, hate, anger, disappointment, resignation, silence, despair, depression, determination, meditation, humor, love.

Frustration is a first reaction. Choosing an emotional or mental response is a second reaction. Choosing a behavior is a third reaction. Often the time it takes to go from frustration to behavior is a millisecond. Reacting to frustration is a learned behavior. It was learned in the home. Each family developed their unique system of dealing with frustration.

THE JONES FAMILY

In the Jones Family "silence" meant trouble. When everyone was silent it meant feelings had been hurt and someone was very frustrated. The air was thick and relationships were strained. The body language was closed and defensive. No one knew for sure what it was that caused the "silence," but either Mom or Dad was offended or hurt and not talking to the other. The children grew up and watched this pattern unfold day after day and year after year.

As the children interacted with each other they likewise reacted to hurt by shunning, silence, and withdrawal. The silence would last for days. Problems were seldom talked about. One day the wounded person would begin to carry on normal conversations. This was the signal the person was now approachable. In most other ways the Jones Family functioned quite normally.

THE BLAKE FAMILY

In the Blake Family, people don't talk, they yell. If a Blake couldn't be heard in his or her normal tone of voice, they just kept elevating the volume. One person didn't stop talking just because someone else was talking. To outsiders it seemed like utter chaos. The Blakes were used to several conversations going on at once. The family members became very animated when they talked. The body language was exaggerated. Arms were flailing, fingers were pointed, and facial expressions were intense. Everyone seemed to have very strong opinions about everything. None of the Blakes hesitated to let the others know what they thought or how they felt about matters of little consequence. In the Blake Family a person yelled if he or she were frustrated. Ranting and raving were used to make the point.

A JONES GIRL MARRIES A BLAKE BOY

The outcome of a Jones/Blake marriage is predictable. During the courtship, the Jone's girl's silence was tolerated, but not understood. The Blake boy's yelling was ignored and excused as stress related. The marriage was a train wreck waiting to happen because of the different family patterns of dealing with frustration.

The Jones' dealt with frustration by giving the "Silent Treatment" to the offending party. The Blakes dealt with frustration by yelling. These patterned behaviors had a long history. Practice, tradition, and habit had entrenched these reactions to frustration. Replacing these learned reactions to frustration with healthier responses would not be easy. It would require the willingness of both parties to retrain their brains. Replacement behaviors would have to be agreed upon, then practiced, and practiced some more until they became the norm for their mutual interaction.

BRINGING PEACE TO THE "HATFIELDS AND THE McCOYS"

When I met with the Jones Girl and the Blake Boy, they were already emotionally divorced and a step away from physical divorce. They were both in the counselor's office to give the marriage one last chance "for the children's sake." As noble a reason as it was for staying in the relationship, it wasn't the healthiest example to give to their children. It would be in the children's best interest to see their parents work through their problems in a civil and reasonable manner.

I gave them a worksheet on frustration and asked them to fill it out.

HOW DO YOU DEAL WITH FRUSTRATION?

All frustration comes from unmet expectations. What are your most frequent frustrations in this relationship?

THE FIRST REACTION TO UNMET EXPECTATIONS IS **FRUSTRATION**

I am frustrated because I expected_____
a. (Example) ...him to pick up after himself and clean up his own messes.
b. _____
c. _____

THE SECOND REACTION TO UNMET EXPECTATIONS IS EITHER AN **EMOTIONAL OR MENTAL REACTION**

EXAMPLES OF **EMOTIONAL** REACTIONS :

Resentment, hate, anger, disappointment, despair resignation, depression, anxiety, nervousness, worry, fear withdrawal, silence, revenge, crying, yelling

a.   (Example) I choose anger and resentment
b.   _____
c.   _____

EXAMPLES OF **MENTAL** REACTIONS:

Positive or negative silence, denial, ignore the person, no immediate comment, meditate, ponder, think about a productive response

a.   (Example) I choose silence and ignoring the person
b.   _____
c.   _____

THE THIRD REACTION TO UNMET EXPECTATIONS IS YOUR **CHOICE OF BEHAVIOR**

CHOICES OF BEHAVIORS:

Positive or negative silence, improper criticism, withdrawal, crying, rage, yelling, parenting, panic attacks, laughing, working harder, singing, smiling, avoidance

a.   (Example) I choose to criticize and yell
b.   _____
c.   _____

206

When they returned the worksheets to me, I asked them if they had thought about the fact that "Reactions" are "Choices." They both confessed that up to now they hadn't thought about reactions being choices. With great effort and a lot of practice they chose a new set of emotional reactions and a different set of behaviors.

The Jones girl chose to verbalize her need to take a "time out." She also agreed to re-engage in positive communication within an hour of having been offended. This emotional and behavioral reaction went totally against the Jones' family tradition. The Blake boy agreed to take a "time out" followed by writing out his concerns if he could not control the tone of his voice and logically explain his position.

People want other people to do what *they* want them to do. Therefore, when others are not performing to expectations, they lash out, nag, gripe, complain, murmur, cry, swear, and verbally attack them. Another response to unmet expectations is to sulk, pout, withdraw, and give them the silent treatment. Neither of these reactions to unmet expectations is as healthy as criticism properly given while being in emotional control and logically explaining our frustrations at a mutually agreeable time and place with the other person.

Ironically, while our lips are dripping with verbal venom, our hearts are hoping that someone will love us, care for us, respect us, accept us, appreciate us, and want to be with us, and even overlook our weaknesses. There are more productive ways of communicating frustration, and they work. Criticism doesn't remove frustration, it describes it. Frequently, criticism feeds its own fire, and what started out to be a contained fire, becomes a massive forest fire burning out of control. Criticism is a description, not a cure. Does describing a fire put it out? Would it matter how outrageous and emotionally charged the person was who was describing the fire?

If the critical person does not find appropriate ways of communicating his frustration, he will eventually and invariably increase his critical nature and destroy his own effectiveness as a communicator. Being less effective, his frustration increases until he explodes into anger or tears of resentment. He may implode into sulky silent oblivion, where despair dwells and all travelers nearby give him a wide berth. It need not be. There is a way to properly express our frustrations and to do so in such a manner that both the giver and receiver are edified. However, there is another myth about criticism we will explore.

DOES IMPROPER CRITICISM CHANGE BEHAVIOR?

No! Even properly given criticism does not change behavior. The change comes when the one being criticized accepts the message as valuable and changes himself or herself. If the sheer act of criticism worked in changing behavior, there would already exist a perfect utopian society. The irony of ironies is that many people criticize in order to change behavior. They truly believe that a verbal description of unacceptable behavior will make it go away. Criticism which is uninvited, unauthorized, and improper antagonizes, alienates, and creates deep hostility toward the giver of criticism. Many self-righteous givers of criticism feel divinely appointed and comfort themselves by assuming they and God are on the same side. So they tilt at the windmill as if this critical quest were some holy mission and they must expect rejection from others as the price they must pay for being "right" as the emissary of truth. Tragically, these people live in self-delusion. There are things that change human behavior. However, describing behavior in critical terms, or rejecting behavior through critical words and deeds does not change it.

Nonverbal criticism such as a frown does not change the behavior. At best, a verbal or non-verbal critical message only describes the behavior in question. Whether the message of rejection comes verbally or nonverbally, the person being criticized will most often reject the one who is doing the criticizing instead of rejecting the unacceptable behavior. Change occurs when the motivation for change comes from within. Criticism comes most often from the outside. Criticism is a lousy motivator.

Coaches who exert the most profound positive effects upon their athletes are the ones who believe in their players, who genuinely care about them and accept them, and who inspire them to greatness. Most of the outstanding coaches recognize that relationships are like bank accounts. We have to make deposits if we expect to make withdrawals. Those coaches who use fear, intimidation, ridicule, criticism, sarcasm, and other belittling ploys, seldom inspire anything but resentment, hostility, and poor self-image. Sincere praise and acceptance inspire behavioral change because the motivation for change is coming from the inside.

Criticism is an outside force that may achieve a degree of control, but control is not change. Continued criticism will result in a double standard wherein the criticized party abides a controlled standard in the presence of the critic and lives his own standard when away or on his own.

Criticism is not only ineffective, additionally it may well be counter-productive because it weakens a person's self-worth as well as his confidence. The net effect of criticism is that some people change in spite of it, not because of it. Criticism, invited or not, lessens the probability for real change. One of the true dangers of listening to criticism day in and day out is that those so treated come to believe they are not worthwhile, they can do nothing right, and they may become self-critical. Soon, there won't be a need for anyone else to criticize them, for they will do it themselves. Self-criticism becomes self-fulfilling prophecy and all of the evidence of being criticized by others now is joined by all the evidence they amass against themselves. In the jury of their minds there can be only one verdict with so much negative internal and external evidence, i.e. guilty as charged of not being truly worthwhile.

For centuries, tyrants have controlled the masses through fear, threats and criticism. What they also created was an underground movement against themselves, adversaries instead of partners working in a common cause for the good of each. There will always be opposition, even to a kind or benevolent king. But should a man's enemies be those of his own house and heart? Enemies from the outside may come, but why would anyone want to create enemies of their friends, family or co-workers by being one who alienates others through constant criticism? Forced conformity is a shallow victory and a poor substitute for cheerful cooperation rendered from a willing heart.

CHAPTER TWELVE

BEWARE OF
THE OTHER QUILLS

Blatant criticism is obvious and easy to identify. There are other forms of criticism which are slightly more subtle, yet still inappropriate. There are many sophisticated ways to send harmful messages of inadequacy, incompetence, and failure to measure up to the critic's expectations.

RECOGNIZING COMMON FORMS
OF INAPPROPRIATE CRITICISM

SARCASM:

Sarcasm is the act of making fun of a person in a clever way. It is an ironical taunt in the guise of humor. The word originally came from the Greek [sarkazein] meaning literally to strip the flesh. Yet sarcasm cleverly becomes justified. Because it is couched in humor or truth, the critic feels vindicated. Ironically, most people who use sarcasm feel as though their message is less toxic because it rides piggy-back on humor. The one being sarcastic can always claim humor as his objective, while removing a strip of flesh from the one lashed by the tongue of the critic.

Sarcasm, I now see to be, in general, the language of the Devil (Thomas Carlyle,1846).

For example "I like your hair, dear. I wonder how it would look if you combed it." It's a funny line. Everyone laughs. Even the one who is the brunt of the joke may laugh, but inside, where self-worth abides, they bleed a little and feel less worthy as a human being.

TRAILING BARBS:

Trailing barbs are a form of criticism. Often, even when giving a compliment, there is some holding back of full acceptance. A "trailing barb" is a statement added to a compliment which expresses that a "better job could have been done." The critic's creed is "Do more for less and a better job," because what you have done is not good enough.

EXAMPLES OF TRAILING BARBS

"That's so nice your boy, Gary, got a B+ in math. Did you know his cousin, Darrell, got an A?"

"Dinner was great tonight. If we could have had a dessert, it would have been perfect!"

"The lawn looks really nice. Thanks for mowing it. We need to do a little better job on the trim, however."

ANALYSIS, APPRAISAL, EVALUATION:

Because these terms are primarily logical and not emotionally based, they frequently seem justified. Things can be evaluated and ideas can be and ought to be subjected to the scientific method. Performance can be measured. Productivity can be appraised. But when analysis, appraisal, and evaluation become subtle forms of masking criticism, they are no less devastating to the one being judged. Because the criticism has been intellectualized, it appears more "constructive," more palatable, and less toxic. Not so.

> *"This egg was boiled for four minutes, instead of three, wasn't it?"*

> *"The pie seemed to have more cinnamon in it."*

> *"Sales seem to be down in your area."*

> *"You look worn out and tired."*

People are human beings with basic emotional needs of acceptance, love, belonging, and appreciation. Even the most self-actualized person on earth, subjected to a consistent diet of criticism, will eventually retreat to a fantasy world of books, TV, or sports, or become a hermit, or even fall apart emotionally.

A key to giving criticism in job performance or life performance is to separate "the ego," or sense of self-worth, from the behavior or issue to be criticized. This will be discussed in greater detail later. For now, the focus is to more fully understand the destructive and damaging nature of all criticism. Many fail to recognize how much criticism impacts upon their daily lives. They are unaware of its many forms and its effects.

QUESTIONS:

Many people feel that if their criticism is given in the form of a question, it is not really criticism, it's only a question. But the "didn't you," "haven't you," "aren't you" questions have an implied criticism, and the assumption is they "should have." Does this mean that you can never ask a question? No. It means be aware that many questions are implied criticisms and therefore "destructive." Some questions are calculated to appear innocent, but are subtle forms of criticism. This blind spot qualifies the giver of criticism as emotionally unsafe and toxic to the self-worth of others.

The issue here is quite simple. Are you concerned about building the self-worth of a loved one, an employee, or a friend? If the answer is no, then proceed full-speed ahead. "Damn the torpedoes" and let the emotional chips fall where they may. However, do not sit in a rest home a bitter and lonely old person, wondering why no one comes to visit you. Don't expect to be loved for being toxic in the here and now. If you are such a realist, then follow this pragmatic counsel: develop the art and skill of giving and receiving appropriate criticism. These skills will make you more effective, not just well-liked.

Frequently, people in positions of authority, such as a CEO, production manager, or quality control expert, say, "I don't have time to worry about 'feelings.' I'm responsible for bottom line, production goals, and quality product." It's as if all employees are to be devoid of feelings. They are not. Job satisfaction, approval, appreciation, and validation, are work related self-worth issues. To ignore them is to fail to consider all elements of a problem you are trying to solve. So, does one need to consider if the questions asked are implied criticisms? Yes, unless an employer wants to spend his time dealing with employee turnover, retraining costs, and personnel problems above and beyond the normal headaches of management.

THE "ENTRAPMENT" QUESTION:

This is any question which is designed to elicit a comment which is then immediately refuted by the critic.

"Did you see that movie?" asked Craig.

"Yes, I loved it," said Donna.

"It was so violent and sexual, we left early," retorted Craig.

Craig's morally superior stance is intended to build up Craig and put down Donna. When dealing with "entrappers" it is a good idea to answer a question with another question which throws the responsibility back upon their shoulders. For example, "What did you think about it, Craig?"

After a few encounters with entrapment-type questioners, it is wise not to dignify their question with a direct response. What they are looking for is a forum to express their personal opinion.

DIRECTION GIVING:

"I wasn't being critical, I was just giving them directions." When someone is always giving directions to a loved one or an employee, especially uninvited opinions or uninvited directions, it is interpreted as a lack of confidence by the one who is receiving the directions. "Do this, do that, don't do it that way, watch out for that car, turn left, pick that up, put that down...," ad nauseam. Be aware that direction giving can be a form of criticism because it assumes the receiver is not capable of performing to an acceptable level without the superior suggestions of the critic.

People like to please. Children want to impress their parents with their new-found knowledge and skills. Employees like to impress a boss with new-found ways of improving production performance. Excessive direction giving stifles creativity. It sends a message of incompetence to the receiver. The real problem may be an over-inflated sense of ego on the part of the giver of directions. Some psychologists suggest those who are always giving directions are themselves quite insecure. The constant giver of directions may want to feel needed.

> *"I declare, I just don't know what goes on here when I'm not around to keep this place together. I don't think you could find your head if it weren't attached to your neck."*

In giving directions, the same principle of respect applies when invading the space of any person or relationship. First, ask for permission and do not proceed unless it is given. Genuinely petition. For example, a small child is just learning how to tie his shoes. "No, no, you are doing it all wrong. Do it this way!" The tone of voice is critical and the directions are saying, "You are incompetent." They may lack the skill, the practice, and knowledge, but are they really incompetent? Do they deserve the impatient, critical tone of voice? What is the objective? If the objective is to assist in the development of an independent personality, then ask for permission before you give directions. It may be a trial of patience to watch a child or an adult struggle with a task that may appear simple to the observer. However, it will not be as frustrating as dealing with the low self-worth of a child or adult who lacks self-confidence.

> *"Honey, would you like me to show you how to tie that shoe? I remember how frustrated I used to get when I was your age when my fingers didn't do what my brain wanted them to do."*
>
> *"No, I want to do it myself."*
>
> *"OK, but just in case you need some help, let me know."*

If the direction-givers are not careful, they will develop dependency-centered children or employees. The recipients will feel incapable of doing anything. Also, they will fear that whatever they do will be wrong to the direction-giver. Therefore, they show no initiative, no creative efforts. Now the direction-giver has created his own nightmare. More and more of the decisions have to be made by him. People are always coming to him to have him tie their shoes, since he is the only one who really knows how to do it right. Now the direction-giver can complain that nothing gets done unless he is there to tell everybody what to do. Usually, the direction-giver rises to the level of his incompetence and ends up feeling over-burdened with the work of ten.

If you are in this pickle and want to get out of it, stop giving uninvited directions. It would be more confidence building to say, "I'm sure you can figure it out, and by the way, whatever you come up with will be fine."

If it's really not fine, then don't offer it, but begin to let go and foster independent behavior such as saying, "Come up with a couple of options, Dave, and bring them back to me."

Another reaction engendered by direction giving, is deep animosity. Most people resent the direction giver as being condescending. They feel patronized and put down as if they were thought of as not being capable of thinking or knowing the directions by themselves. It may be better to let them learn by their mistakes than to be resented as a hovering and overprotective direction giver.

BEING CONTRARY:

There is a blind spot for some called "being contrary." It is sometimes called contrariness. It is the practice of correcting facts as perceived by the critic. Typically, one person will be telling a story, making a statement, or relating an incident. The one "being contrary" will jump in uninvited to tell the truth of what happened, to correct an error, or to set things straight. It is intimidation, a kind of emotional arm-twisting. Being contrary is a compulsion. It is also rude, insensitive, and a violation of the space and relationship of the speaking person. The contrary person feels justified in displaying this lack of respect, because they are *right*. They are *being honest*, or they are *telling the truth*. This empowers them in their own mind to butt in. Contrariness is the act of interfering in an ongoing conversation in order to correct a perceived misstatement. It is the act of interruption. It is a form of criticism. It is presumptuous and acts without the permission of the speaking party. It is argumentative, frequently arrogant, imprudent, and distracting.

SALLY, MARY, AND JOHN

Sally and Mary are having a conversation about a recent trip to the zoo that Sally and John had taken with their two children. Sally says to Mary, "We really had fun and the kids loved it."

John, who is in the room, but not invited into the conversation, interjects, "No, they didn't. The animals scared them to death. They didn't have fun at all."

"Well, I thought they had fun in spite of being frightened by the bears. Anyway," Sally proceeds talking to Mary, "the kids were so cute when we got them cotton candy."

John interrupts, "They weren't cute, they made a mess and got it all over their hair. It was terrible."

Sally persists, "As I was saying, Mary, I wish I had a camera and could have taken their picture; it was a precious moment."

"You hate cameras," insists John.

Not only is this kind of behavior rude and insensitive, it is also condescending. Most people are uncomfortable being around those who are contrary.

MIKE AND JANE

Mike and Jane are talking to each other. Mike is remembering his first impressions of how they originally met. Mike is experiencing feelings of warmth and loving toward Jane.

"I remember when I first saw you after graduating from High School."

"No," said Jane, "you first met me at a dance in High School."

"Anyway," said Mike, "the first time I saw you that summer, you were sitting on the fender of my best friend's car. I thought how lucky he was to have such a pretty girl sitting…"

"It wasn't your best friend's car, it belonged to his dad, and I wasn't sitting on the fender, I was in the front seat."

Whatever good feelings Mike had for Jane are now gone. He is angry with her. She, on the other hand, feels totally justified, and wonders why he can't be honest in telling the story. She is blinded by *contrariness*. After all, she was only setting the record straight by telling the truth. He shouldn't be so sensitive. He is only angry because she caught him in a lie. "I wish he would not exaggerate. It is so embarrassing when he tells these stories and gets all the facts mixed up." So goes the reasoning of Jane. However, contrariness is contradiction and an invasion of the right of the speaking party to relate his or her own first person experience. Both John and Jane should have asked for permission to criticize.

Most of the time, it is unwise and inappropriate to be contrary. It is especially rude to interfere between two others involved in an ongoing dialogue. It is rude even if you are a part of the conversation. Contrariness is counter-productive to a healthy verbal interaction. Most people afflicted with contrariness have a "debate mentality" and see themselves as being intellectually honest, open, and forthright. In other words, they see it as a strength and are often puzzled as to why others are offended.

Another form of contrariness is taking the opposite view or the opposing side. They see themselves as defending the underdog or bringing balance to an issue. It is a way of thinking and an extremely difficult bad habit to break.

TOM AND KATHY

Tom is expressing his frustration at his work and how unappreciative his boss is, when Kathy begins to defend Tom's boss by pointing out the pressure he must feel by having all the responsibility. Kathy is being contrary. She is trying to make the situation better by arguing with Tom about his feelings. "You should be grateful you have a job," says Kathy. "It's worth not being appreciated and maybe he was just having a bad day."

Contrary people defend and try to explain an opposite view when the real issue is the right of someone to express their frustration. The situation of Tom complaining to Kathy calls for understanding and not for solution.

Ideally, contrary thoughts are best written down. They are best shared at another time, or reserved for a later, private moment. Permission to express the contrary thought should be sought for first. Next, an appropriate time and place should be agreed upon. Disregard for this counsel will lead the person who is afflicted with contrariness to stumble blindly through life. They will feel as though they are wonderful communicators. In reality, they are passed over and over for advancements or promotions because they are perceived as brash and lacking in sensitivity. Many contrary people are gifted, talented, bright, capable, and superior in performance. Therefore, contrariness becomes a liability, not an asset. Although they may be right, and certainly are in their own eyes, they are not as useful to the company, organization, or relationship as they might have been. Instead of abandoning the behavior, they abandon the job or relationship. They move on with the same self-defeating behavior to inflict it upon the next job or relationship. Once recognized, then acknowledged, and then controlled, the contrary person can again be perceived as emotionally safe and function as a productive partner in a relationship.

ONE UPMANSHIP:

His high school is the best high school, his choice of cars is the best. His home state is the best state. There is an old song which says,

"Anything you can do, I can do better, I can do anything better than you."

In this kind of relationship, the toxic "one up" person acts as if he is in competition with you. Even if you don't want to be in competition with him, everything you do is compared to someone else who does it bigger and better.

TRUTH AS CRITICISM:

"I'm not being critical. I'm only *telling the truth*. I'm just being honest," are statements used to justify criticism. There are many who are most unkind and lack judgment. In the name of *truth* they brutalize others. Smugly, the critic hides behind the truth regardless of its consequences. Some people feel that because something is true, they are justified in saying it, or printing it in the newspapers. There is a higher and nobler principle than truth: it is TO EDIFY.

A person could yell "fire" in a crowded theater, when there might only be a fire in a waste basket. But, it is true, isn't it? A young person could be exposed to every detail of sexual perversion known. *It may be true information, but it is not edifying.* Truth-seekers should not be kept from their quest, but wisdom dictates that truth be tempered with consideration for the ability of the recipient to handle it. Announcing the death of a mother or father to a child is a truth which requires consideration of the time, place, and circumstances of the child to bear it.

Criticism is a toxic, destructive substance injected from the outside. It needs to be controlled in its administration or the effects of the cure are worse than the original illness. It is well established that overcoming weaknesses, bad habits, and inappropriate behavior are best accomplished by building up the self-worth and self-confidence of the individual. Sincere praise for productive effort and positive reinforcement are the basis of modifying behavior. Blasting someone with their faults, even though true, is non-productive and certainly not edifying. It is true that people say truthful things in order to hurt or make another feel bad, and they are said in the heat of anger or frustration. Wisdom and common sense require that criticism be used sparingly. We should criticize so seldom that when we do we will be heard. The frequently critical person is tuned out before the message is delivered. Nor is it justified to criticize in the name of being honest. The so-called "open" relationship, where both members feel free to express their concerns, often provides a forum for the more critical partner. Maybe the fundamental question that ought to be asked is not, "Is it honest?" but rather, "Is it edifying?" Will it ultimately be uplifting? Will it be good for the individual and the relationship?" If a criticism does not qualify under the latter, it should not be spoken at all.

SELF-CRITICISM

Many people are their own worst critics. Their self-worth is so low they have a difficult time receiving love from others. Frequently they lack a certain kind of graciousness which causes them to reject sincere complements from others. When we cannot find self-acceptance it is very hard to believe an acceptance message from outside. On the other hand, some people enjoy fishing for compliments by being self-critical. The hope is others will come to their emotional rescue. This type of self-effacing is a ploy to receive acceptance.

> *"Did you make that dress?" or "Did you make that coffee table?"*
> *"Oh, yes, but it's just something I threw together. It's not very good at all."*
> *"No, no, I really like it. I think it's beautiful. I wish I were that creative."*

Most self-criticism is self-defeating, and a bad habit. Many times it is an effort to protect ourselves before someone else has a chance to tear us down. All of these behaviors are emotionally unhealthy. There is appropriate self-criticism which has as its goal to become one's highest and best self. But it is a false humility to deface ourselves in front of others.

223

Personal, private soul searching and reflection to become a better self is the kind of self-evaluation which may lead to improvement. In a safe environment, confessing our faults may be appropriate. However, making comments like, "I'm so dumb," "I never do anything right," "I can't believe how stupid I am," are not productive. Likewise, an inability to receive a compliment shows disdain for the giver of the compliment. It is very rude and also lacks graciousness. If someone gives a compliment, an appropriate response is, "Thank you."

Usually at this point in our seminar people begin to feel they can't say or do anything. They imagine they have done just about everything wrong. They feel there is no hope for them. They are convinced they have made a mess out of everything. Many would just as soon take another assignment other than Mother, Father, Boss, Friend, Brother, Sister, etc. It is a bit overwhelming. It is easy to get discouraged and even depressed. However, there is hope.

CHAPTER THIRTEEN

THE TWENTY-FOUR HOUR CHALLENGE

For everyone who wants to escape the addiction of criticism, the twenty-four challenge is the place to begin. For a period of twenty-four consecutive hours, refrain from criticizing anything, anyone, or even one's self. It isn't as easy as it sounds, but it is not impossible. When one "slips" he must start his or her twenty-four hours over again. One man moaned, "It will be forever before I get this assignment right."

Unless it is a life or death situation, abstain from all forms of criticism. This includes sarcasm, uninvited opinions, analysis, appraisals, evaluations, insights, questions, direction giving, or contrariness. There are a few people whose employment requires them to be critical, for example, building inspectors, supervisors, quality control, et. al. These special cases are exempt as long as they are on the job; the criticism must relate directly to the work. Lastly, even if the criticism is justified, ask for and receive permission to criticize.

All others will be required to abstain from all criticism for twenty-four hours. The majority of people do not succeed in their first attempt. Do not be too discouraged if you have to start over again thirty or forty times. But the moment you slip and criticize, the twenty-four hours starts over again. Do not criticize self, spouse, children, parents, co-workers, the boss, the government, or dumb drivers.

Warning! There are some traditionally hard times at which we are prone to criticize. These include being tired, hungry, driving, or when we are under a time pressure. Getting the kids to bed may push parents over the line. Notice most of this criticism is frustration driven.

WHAT ABOUT NONVERBAL CRITICISM?

If I think it, but don't say it, does it count against the twenty-four hours?

If a critical thought enters your mind and you get rid of the thought in a moment, then it does not count and you do not have to start your twenty-four hours over. If, on the other hand, you let that critical thought stay in you mind and develop it into a full production with quadraphonic sound and vista vision, then you must start over again.

"IT'S HARDER THAN I THOUGHT"

One lady who was invited to accept the twenty-four hour challenge looked puzzled for a moment. She glanced up at her husband who was standing by her side, and said, "Okay, I'll try to go for twenty-four hours without criticizing or dwelling upon a critical thought." Then, pointing to her husband, she said, "But he will never make it!" There was a pause. "Oh dear," she said, "I will have to start my twenty-four hours over again, won't I?"

Her husband did not verbally respond. However, he frowned at her and a slight sneer formed at the edge of his mouth. He also pointed his finger at her in a mocking manner. This, of course, was nonverbal criticism. It was pointed out to him that nonverbal criticism was also a reason for him to start his twenty-four hours over again.

The two of them walked off muttering, "This is going to be harder than we thought."

"Yes," I said, "Overcoming a lifelong habit is hard."

In one study involving more than eight hundred people, after three days only twenty people had been able to go for a period of twenty-four hours without criticizing. They were permitted to count sleeping time as a part of the twenty-four hours! The responses from those who made it were interesting.

THOSE WHO MADE IT

"It was easy," said one woman. "My husband and son were out of town."

Another woman said she used a technique from a seminar she had attended where everyone wore a rubber band around their wrist and each time they broke the rules of the seminar they snapped the rubber band.

One man in the group observed, "I was so criticized as a child that I decided I would not be a critical adult."

Another man suggested that we form an organization called "C.A." or Critiholics Anonymous and hold weekly support meetings.

One mother reported that after she had gone twenty-four hours, her teenage daughter, who was unaware of her mother's efforts, asked if she were feeling okay.

Because of the culture and accepted mode of communication, it is difficult to refrain from criticizing. Most have been raised in a critical environment. Many have been taught to be critical, analytical, and to subject people and things to the scientific method. Some have difficulty speaking a single sentence without criticizing. You shouldn't be too hard on yourself if you don't succeed in a week. This is a difficult assignment.There are, however, some very good reasons for trying.

WHY SHOULD I TRY?

There are several answers to the question, "Why should I try to stop criticizing?" Here are some of the more important ones:

- To lay the foundation for love instead of rejection
- To be able to increase the number of positive interactions
- To be more emotionally safe as a person
- To be more effective in communicating
- To reduce unnecessary conflict
- To experience greater peace and harmony in all relationships
- TO AVOID BECOMING A TOXIC PERSON

These are the results we should experience by abstaining from criticism:

- To be able to go twenty-four hours without criticizing
- To increase our awareness of the critical nature of society
- To become aware of our own compulsion to criticize
- To experience the power of self-mastery

WHERE DO I BEGIN?

You begin by taking the twenty-four hour challenge of not criticizing seriously. You begin by understanding the futility of criticism and accept what reality has taught you, "criticism doesn't change behavior." You begin by understanding that being critical and being loving are two different things.

WHEN I COULDN'T CRITICIZE, I HAD NOTHING TO SAY

Treena was a mother of five. She grew up under a constant barrage of criticism. After fifteen years of marriage her husband, Robert, left her and sued for custody of the children. Because Robert had tape recorded his wife yelling unmercifully at the children, the judge awarded all five children to the father. There was a ninety day waiting period for the divorce to be final. The wife came to the realization that she was going to be out in the street without a husband and without her five children. She pleaded and importuned her husband to go to a marriage and family counselor. He agreed.

When Robert and Treena showed up in my office, the woman was desperate and in a state of panic. I spent twenty minutes just calming her down. Finally, the story unfolded. She had been molested as a child. Her mother was toxic. Her father was a workaholic and never available to the family. The dysfunctions seemed endless and all too familiar. After she finished what was, in essence, a justification for her screaming tantrums, I asked her if she wanted understanding or solutions.

"Treena, you are about to lose your husband and your five children. Do you believe in the power of the human spirit to change? Do you believe that an individual has the ability to overcome a terrible background and choose to live a better life?"

"I want to believe that," she said, "and I am willing to do anything to save my family."

"Treena, I want you to stop criticizing this very moment. For one whole week I want you to *not* say one critical thing, not one word. If you are unwilling to follow my counsel or if you fail, I will not continue to be your counselor."

"Robert, if this marriage relationship fails you are going to have sole custody of these children and your wife will only be allowed to have third party visitation."

"That is my understanding from what the Judge said," replied Robert.

"My point is that you are going to have the full responsibility of correcting and guiding these five children. I would like you to begin now with this new assignment. In other words, if there is anything to be said in a corrective or disciplinarian type way, I want you to do it. I want Treena released from all expectations of criticizing, changing, or disciplining the children—zero expectations of criticizing."

"Treena, do you really understand what is required of you? I am asking you to quit cold-turkey, 100 percent, zero tolerance. If you fail even once, it's over. Do you understand, Treena? In less than ninety days that is going to be your role anyway. You have nothing to lose and a family to gain."

She wept and began to go into a pity party and degrade herself. I stopped her abruptly. "Treena, you can't criticize yourself either. Don't go there. Stop it this very minute. I don't want you to criticize anymore. Don't criticize yourself, your husband, your children, not one word. Do you understand?"

She quickly dried her tears and said, "Yes, yes, I understand."

"Please," I said, "repeat the assignment."

Treena repeated, "I am not to criticize myself, my children, nor my husband, not even one word."

"Yes, yes," I said, "that is the first part of your assignment. The second part of your assignment is to go home and love your children. Spend a few minutes each day with each child and do a loving, bonding thing with each one. If that is too overwhelming, then take one child a day and focus on doing a loving thing with that child."

They left the office with an appointment to come back in a week and report on the progress. A week later, when they returned, they came into my office and before Treena could sit down she burst into tears. These were soul-rending sobs. I was fearful that she had failed in her attempts at not criticizing and that this would indeed be our last meeting. I asked Robert if she had failed in her assignment of not criticizing. He looked as surprised as I was. "No," he said. "She was great. We had a wonderful week. It was the best week of our married life for me and for the children. We all got along great. I handled all the problems and she was a miracle. I didn't believe when we left your office last week that she could do it, but she did."

Treena was still crying. After a time she gained sufficient composer to cry out, "You don't understand! You don't understand!"

"What is it, Treena, that I don't understand?"

Between her sobs she blurted, "I DON'T KNOW HOW TO LOVE! I DON'T KNOW HOW TO LOVE!"

Treena thought that being a mother was criticizing and direction giving. She was only repeating what she saw in her home. To Treena that was the job description. She believed that criticizing was a loving behavior. Seeing that the children did what she thought they ought to do was her understanding of loving. When Treena couldn't criticize she didn't know what to say. She didn't know how to express love. She lacked the most basic skills in communicating acceptance, affection, and appreciation. She was right. She didn't know how to love. The next several weeks were spent in teaching Treena how to love, how to communicate acceptance, affection, and appreciation.

That was seven years ago. Treena and Robert and the five children have stayed together and are very, very functional and quite happy with life. On one occasion, after not having seen them in over four years, I asked Treena if she was ready to learn an appropriate way to communicate criticism. She became very serious and said, "I'm never going back there again, not ever." Since both she and Robert were happy and their relationship was doing well, I decided to drop it. Her words stayed with me, "I'm never going back there again, not ever."

The importance of eradicating inappropriate and improper criticism from our lives cannot be overstated. The twenty-four hour challenge is the place to begin. One woman decided to abstain from chocolate until she had abstained from criticism for twenty-four consecutive hours. It took her five weeks. Whatever it takes to control the tongue will be worth it.

There is an appropriate way to communicate negative feedback. Learning how to express proper criticism will not only improve your communication skills, it will make you an emotionally safe person to others.

CHAPTER FOURTEEN

THE ART OF GIVING
APPROPRIATE CRITICISM

When criticism is truly necessary, how do we share it and not become toxic in the process? Few enjoy a trip to the dentist's office even for necessary repairs. For most people receiving criticism is like going to the dentist. Skilled dentists guide their patients through the experience with as little discomfort as possible. Always the focus is on the patient's survival and good health.

Some will argue that physical pain, as bad as it is, is not as difficult to live with as emotional pain. The ability to share emotionally painful information in appropriate ways is an art. Minimizing the effects of negative feedback requires the skill of a dentist, the compassion of a Mother Teresa, and a sincere desire to help the one being criticize become his or her highest and best self.

People who have been hypercriticized may have no ability to receive even the best given criticism. This does not release us from the responsibility of improving our communication skills.

DR. LUND'S
QUICK CHECK GUIDE TO
THE ART OF GIVING APPROPRIATE CRITICISM

STEP ONE: THINK BEFORE YOU SPEAK

BEFORE YOU SPEAK ASK YOURSELF TWO QUESTIONS:

1. Is the criticism a part of my stewardship or business?
2. Is the criticism not only true, but is it necessary?
   If the answer to *either* of the foregoing questions is "No," then BACK OFF!
   If the answer to *both* of the questions is "Yes," then proceed with the following:

STEP TWO: THE PROCESS

1. Ask for, and receive, permission to criticize.
2. Be alone with the one being criticized at a mutually agreeable time and place.
3. Be in emotional control and logically explain your concerns. No yelling, crying, swearing, threats, physical, or emotional intimidation.
4. Stay focused on the issue or behavior in question. DO NOT ATTACK SELF-WORTH! Separate the issue from EGO. Protect self-worth.

STEP THREE: AFFIRM WORTH

1. Convey acceptance
2. Give affection
3. Show appreciation

READY, FIRE, AIM!

Before you open your mouth with "you should, you need, you ought," consider the consequences of your words. The uncontrolled critic destroys his own credibility and effectiveness. Some refer to this as the "Ready-Fire-Aim" approach. They are always READY to criticize with no regard for the feelings of the one being criticized. They FIRE their mouth off without thinking of the time, place, circumstance, nor the ability of the one being criticized to receive it. The consequences are usually disastrous and create unnecessary fallout. In the process of justifying their criticism they now try to AIM their comments to some productive purpose. Egocentric and insecure people refuse to admit that their approach was insensitive, ineffective, and poorly handled. They persist in putting the blame on others. They deny that toxic behavior is emotionally unsafe and damaging.

Respect is not earned. It is gifted as a reflection of your goodness. Appropriate criticism will always respect the time, space, and ability of the recipient of criticism to manage it. Before you speak, it would be wise to walk through the experience mentally and anticipate the reaction and desired outcome.

Dr Lund's Quick Check Guide To The Art Of Giving Appropriate Criticism is designed to be a ready reference. We will now consider each step in more detail.

STEP ONE:
BEFORE YOU SPEAK ASK YOURSELF TWO QUESTIONS:

1. IS THE CRITICISM ANY OF MY BUSINESS?

2. IS THE CRITICISM NECESSARY?

If the answer to *either* of the above questions is "NO," then butt out! Allow others their right to fail. If your concerns are serious enough to warrant outside intervention, then report the information to one who has the appropriate authority and BACK OFF!

QUESTION NUMBER ONE:
IS THE CRITICISM ANY OF MY BUSINESS?

In a family of eight children the youngest child frequently grows up thinking he has nine parents. They include Mom and Dad, and seven brothers and sisters. In spite of having two real parents, his brothers and sisters feel authorized to tell the youngest what he should, needs, and ought to do. The siblings give themselves permission to criticize because they are older. Some assume the right because they are bigger, faster, smarter, or stronger than the younger brother. There are those who feel they have a right to criticize absolutely anything that any family member may do which might negatively reflect upon them. Therefore, they are constantly correcting others and interjecting what "should," "need," and "ought" to be done by them. When we assume a responsibility we do not have, it is wrong.

The concept of individual stewardship is an important one. Each person is entitled to his own space and the right to manage his life within that space. This includes the right to succeed and the right to fail. There is much to be learned by both success and failure. Remember, there are only three major ways of learning. They are observation, instruction, and bumping into boundaries, i.e., experiencing consequences. It is important to allow reasonable consequences to perform their function.

It is a toxic behavior "to put your nose where it doesn't

236

belong." In regard to interpersonal communication it is always important to allow people their own lousy (or excellent) relationships. However, any form of abuse is unacceptable and will require third party intervention. The standard cannot be perfection. It must be a reasonable standard which allows for hurt feelings and disagreements. It cannot be a pattern of self-worth "assassination."

QUESTION NUMBER TWO:
IS THE CRITICISM NECESSARY?

The criticism may be true, but is it edifying and in another's best interest to hear it? Just because something is true does not mean that everyone needs to know it. An aging mother does not need to hear about all of the sins of her children when they were teenagers. In the same way, it is foolishness for parents to confess all of their transgressions to their children in the name of truth. Many of these facts only become "brain clutter."

Wisdom would dictate that the sharing of truth be appropriate to the ability of the receiver to appreciate it. There are many truths which should never be spoken. Just because they are true, does not justify their publication. This is not a justification for lying. The real issue here is a higher law than, "Is it true?" The higher law asks, "Is it edifying?"

TRUE OR EDIFYING?

A neighbor girl went away to have a child out of wedlock. She then decided to have the child adopted to a caring couple. She later returned, desiring with all of her heart to start her life over.

The girl is now doing well and the truth is only known by a small circle of family and medical personnel. Quite by accident her neighbor stumbled across the fact by being in the other town and encountering the couple who adopted the child. Putting the information they casually gave with some knowledge about the neighbor girl, the neighbor concluded the truth. A little investigation confirmed it.

Now the neighbor is involved in a conversation with someone who asks what she thinks about the girl. If she were to tell all she knows it would not be a lie. It is, after all, "only the truth." She would only be relating what she knows. It is gossip, however, and to spread the tale of what she knows could impact negatively on the young girl's future.

If our standard of judgment is, "Is it true?" then we could prattle away and tell all. If, however, our standard is a higher one, a standard that asks, "Is it edifying?" then our lips will be closed and we will not speak it. It is not necessary. It is not needed or called for; it is a truth which never needs to be spoken.

In conjunction with the question, "Is it edifying?" is the issue of whether or not it is in another's best interest to hear it. If the knowledge and criticism you have to share is truly in another's best interest to hear, then have the courage to share. If, however, no good thing can come of it, then exercise restraint and control the impulse to share it with *anyone*. A very important part of self-mastery is the ability to keep harmful knowledge from being said. People are more respected for constraint than indulgence. You will possess greater self-respect and self-mastery when you speak only the truth which edifies.

AN OLD LIE

Barbara and Doris have been best of friends since junior high school. Now, both are married and preparing to attend the same ten-year class reunion at the old high school. Barbara has found out that Doris didn't make the cheer leading squad in high school because of a false rumor. It's newsy, it's informational, and it is just plain interesting. It certainly is true that Doris suffered as a consequence of a false rumor. Is it edifying for Barbara to tell Doris? What earthly good could it do for Doris to know that now? Would it change the past? Will Doris feel better about herself just knowing she might have made the team had someone not spoken ill of her to the teacher? Will it impact on Doris' self-concept for good? Will it impact on Doris and her former teacher who acted on false information? Currently, Doris doesn't feel badly about the teacher, nor about the gossiping classmate whose lie kept her from the cheer leading squad. The teacher is the class advisor. Both Barbara and Doris will see her at the reunion. In addition, the girl who spread the false rumor is the class vice-president and she will be there also.

What do you think would happen if Barbara told Doris? Would the ten-year reunion be edifying for Doris? Would it be in Doris' best interest to hear this information about the past, and would it be wise for Barbara to disclose all she knows? The answer is if it would not edify, DON'T SAY IT. LET IT GO!! If it were a situation where the answer was "Yes, it is in my stewardship, and it is necessary," then proceed with Step Two.

STEP TWO: THE PROCESS

1. ASK FOR AND RECEIVE PERMISSION TO CRITICIZE

Asking for permission to criticize does not mean permission will always be given. It is as important to receive permission as it is to ask for it. If we proceed when denied permission, it demonstrates lack of respect for the boundaries of the person we criticize. If we criticize without permission, we are assuming a parent role over the other person. Authority does not include the right to disrespect another human being. No one has that right.

If we do not receive the permission to criticize verbally, we may ask for permission to communicate our criticisms in writing. The one being criticized could then read them and respond within a certain amount of time, perhaps twelve hours. This option gives the frustrated critic a place to take his criticism.

Writing down the criticism is important. It removes much of the intimidation factor and allows the one being criticized to focus on the content of the criticism. However, even in the written format criticism needs to focus on the issue and respect the reader. Otherwise, the packaging of the criticism and the delivery system supersede the message. Remember, people interpret meaning by looking at a person's facial expression and interpreting their body language. Tone of voice also distracts from the content of the message. Writing down the criticism provides focus for the critic and greater emotional safety for the one being criticized. It is a challenging art and skill to communicate verbally and keep the focus on the message and not on the messenger.

2. BE ALONE WITH THE ONE BEING CRITICIZED AT A MUTUALLY AGREEABLE TIME AND PLACE

Once permission to criticize has been verbally received, decide when and where the parties can be alone. The meeting should be at a mutually agreed upon time and place. For the disrespectful and the impatient, this is a waste of time. Most want to dump their criticisms in the here and now and move on to other matters. Criticizing anyone in front of others is a bad idea. The only exception is when the one being criticized requests a safe third party or truly agrees to it. People criticized in front of others suffer loss of face and humiliation. They feel belittled and are more concerned about other people who may be present than they are about the content of the criticism. This is especially true of children being criticized in front of their friends. If the critic is truly concerned about efficiency, he will be alone with the one being criticized at a mutually agreed time and place. For example, "Johnny, I would like to talk to you right after dinner, before your friends come to play," or "Mary, I can see this is a bad time, could we talk before you go to bed, about 9:00 p.m.?"

A parent, employer, or one who is in a position of authority may ask, "What if he or she refuses to give permission to criticize?" An appropriate response would be, "That is not an option. I was asking out of respect for you. Your options are to choose within the next twenty-four hours a time and a place that will be convenient for both of us."

It shows respect and restraint when we are willing to be alone at a mutually safe place. The opposite is also true. It shows disrespect and lack of restraint when the critic insists on the here and now. For those of us who want to enjoy a close relationship, being emotionally safe is enormously important. In addition to respect and restraint, the critic who is willing "not to criticize" in front of others is displaying loyalty to the relationship. It is hypocrisy to expect loyalty from others when loyalty is not given. A common complaint expressed by men and women is being criticized in front of their co-workers, friends, or children. The focus is not on the message but on the messenger's insensitivity. It is as if the critic had broken an unwritten rule by criticizing in front of others. He or she becomes emotionally unsafe and disloyal. Most people express feelings of resentment for the critic whose public displays of criticism are seen as violations of loyalty. Criticism in front of others is an emotionally unfaithful act. It is astounding to those being criticized that the critic could do so with such impunity.

There are consequences for humiliating someone in front of others. Emotional closeness will suffer. Respect will be replaced by resentment. Most critics are either unaware of these consequences or it simply doesn't matter to them. It is as though the critic felt justified for giving the ridicule or criticism in public. Therefore, the critic feels he has done nothing to deserve alienation. He expects that being "right" gives him permission. The critic assumes there will be no consequences for his self-justified behavior. His criticism was "deserved."

If "making the point" is his objective, if giving criticism in front of others represents a point of emphasis, then the rules for verbal warfare include public humiliation as a part of the escalation. Humiliation is an attempt to force a change in behavior. Those who agree to these rules of engagement should not expect to be loved for this counter-productive behavior, nor should they expect to be seen as emotionally safe. Disloyalty will breed disloyalty in return.

Behavior which says, "I am free to criticize anytime, anyplace, and in front of anyone I choose," is naive and could be amusing, except for its tragic consequences. Ironically, even when the critic is right, he is wrong in not sharing the criticism in private. To criticize in front of others and hope that social pressure will be on the side of the critic is foolish. The sympathy goes to the one being criticized.

Consider a classroom setting where a misbehaving boy is

truly guilty of rude and insensitive conduct. The teacher calls him by name and chastens him in front of the other students. In spite of the fact that the student is wrong and the teacher is right, the students will sympathize with the one being embarrassed in front of others. In this case the teacher is right in principle, but wrong in the time and place. The wisdom of being alone with the one being criticized is that the focus can stay on the message. Criticizing in public is a bad idea. Dealing with the emotional fallout and negative backlash often becomes a bigger problem than whatever the original issue was.

3. BE IN EMOTIONAL CONTROL AND LOGICALLY EXPLAIN YOUR CONCERNS. NO YELLING, CRYING, SWEARING, THREATS, PHYSICAL, OR EMOTIONAL INTIMIDATION

Facial expression and body language represent more than half of how communication is interpreted. It is vitally important to be in control of these bodily signals. When neck muscles are taut and the blood vessels at the temple are bulging, the focus is going to be on the messenger and not the message.

For some, it is more effective to write down what the consequences for misconduct will be. This removes all language and tone of voice and allows the one receiving the restrictions to focus on the content of the message. Writing it down also releases energy and serves to take it out of the body and mind and place it on the paper. In addition it requires some organization of thought.

When someone logically explains his concerns, it removes the element of emotionalism with its attendant distractions. Credibility is on the line when someone says they are being logical, although their behavior says otherwise. Criticism is difficult to receive under the best of circumstances. Adding emotionalism to the criticism only confuses the matter. The focus is the issue or behavior in question. It is best not to become angry, swear, or cry. Some feel this display of emotionalism adds emphasis to their point of view. However, the critic only succeeds in making himself the focus. Those who use physical or emotional intimidation as a part of their presentation, once again dilute the message and divert the focus to the messenger.

It is a dysfunctional and a self-defeating behavior to criticize anyone in the heat of emotionalism. If it is too sensitive an issue and tears cannot be restrained, it would be better to write it down. A third party professional or pastor can deliver the content in such a way the emphasis remains on the issue or behavior in question. Men feel manipulated when women cry. They resent it. They feel diverted from the true issue. Many women have this same response when men yell at them. Both yelling and crying shift the focus to the person and away from the issue. This is so frustrating that many men and women just give up. Breaking the nonproductive behavioral pattern of joining criticism and negative emotionalism is a difficult habit to modify. Nevertheless, appropriately explaining our concerns can be practiced and developed into a skill which will contribute to the process of better communication.

4. STAY FOCUSED ON THE ISSUE OR BEHAVIOR IN QUESTION. DO NOT ATTACK SELF-WORTH!

Part of the art of giving criticism relates to the ability to separate *ego* from *issue*. It is the aptitude of saying. "I care about you as a person, but I don't appreciate it when you leave your clothes on the floor."

EGO

Ego is not a bad word. Being egotistic, self-centered, or arrogant carries a negative connotation, but "ego" does not. Ego means the whole person, the self, the "I." It represents our personal identity. Ego is expressed as "my opinion" or "I feel this way." Self-worth or ego-worth is the value we place on our personal identity. It manifests itself by asking three questions:

- What is my worth?
- Is my input, effort, and time appreciated?
- Am I loved; am I lovable?

It has often been said that you are born into your greatest test in life, marry it, or give birth to it. Some have all three. Others struggle with the worth of their own lives. Self-worth is how people feel about themselves. Each relationship helps a person to evaluate his or her self-concept. The sum total of all the messages received from others assists in forming "self-perception." Job satisfaction, marital happiness, and self-acceptance are all impacted by "self-perception."

Our primary family is the greatest contributor to self-worth and self-perception. A child who is raised with a constant bombardment of "you are worthless," "you are no good to anybody," "you are dumb, stupid, and lazy" is going to have a problem with ego and with low self-worth. In a family where these messages are constantly sent, the child will seek for acceptance outside of the home. Even in a home where "positive ego strokes" are given, a child will look outside the home for validation to friends and acquaintances. The combination of friends, school, marriage or no marriage, work, church involvement, and feedback from society either reinforce the perception of self received from the home or negate it. One of the most important contributions a parent, a

245

family member, or a friend can make is to teach a child his or her worth. This important contribution is reinforced by treating the child, spouse, or friend with respect and love.

ATTACKING THE WORTH OF ANOTHER

It is never justified to belittle the worth of another. *Never!* It cannot be tolerated. We never have the right to attack the inherent value or self-worth of another, not in jest, not in the heat of anger, not out of frustration, not out of our own weakness, *Never! Never! Never!* This means no name calling, no swearing at someone, no belittling. It means no mental, physical, nor emotional abuse. This is not negotiable. When someone is called "dumb" or "stupid," it is an attack on their worth. To attack self-worth is presuming a right that the critic does not have.

It is a testimony to the futility of criticism when people lash out at one another and attack their worth as human beings in an attempt to deal with an issue or behavior. People in an emotional, irrational state of frustration, are seldom possessed with enough presence of mind to separate the real issues from the self-worth of the one being criticized. The struggle to learn love for self and others is the essence of life. Remember, love for others begins with appropriate love for self.

Appropriate criticism is that which separates self-worth from the unacceptable behaviors of the one being criticized. The difficulty of this task is enormous because so many have been programmed from their youth to equate their own worth with the criticism from others. He may be so hypersensitive to criticism that it would take a master in the Art of Giving Criticism to separate the issue from his sense of self-worth. It can be done. The "Art" of Giving and Receiving Criticism is the "art" of separating the self-worth from the behavior or issue to be criticized, and it is a task worthy of undertaking.

THE "ART" OF SEPARATING
SELF-WORTH (EGO) FROM THE ISSUE

This is a personal story which relates to my wife, Bonnie, who possesses a natural gift for loving independent from the obnoxious behaviors of others.

As a young married couple, there was considerable latitude given by both parties for each other's shortcomings. Nonetheless, I possessed a habit that truly made life difficult for Bonnie. We were both college students and took turns with cooking, housekeeping, and the washing. However, I was in the habit of taking my dirty stockings, rolling them together to form a ball, and then throwing them from wherever I was to the closet in the bedroom. Frequently, this would require a bank-shot off a wall. Just as frequently, the stockings would miss the closet and roll under the bed or down the hall or wherever their final destination would take them. Bonnie's newly-wed patience wore thin as days of this became weeks. Apparently, the final straw was a missed shot that wound up on top of the refrigerator. The stockings rested unnoticed on top of the refrigerator until the next day. Some of my wife's friends were sitting around the kitchen table, when my wife opened the refrigerator door, releasing the stockings and sending them on a downward flight, giving the appearance they had emerged from the refrigerator itself. This might be a difficult thing to explain to friends; i.e., why do you keep your husband's dirty stockings in the refrigerator?

I know not what Bonnie said. I do know that night, when I returned home from an evening class, there was something unusual about her countenance. I sat on the couch, removed my shoes and stockings and began to roll my stockings up into a ball. But Bonnie was standing in the pathway of the projectile. While I still had the germ-riddled stockings in my hand ready to fire, Bonnie asked permission to share a concern of hers. She said something like this, "Honey, there is something silly I would like to talk to you about. It really is a small thing, but it is something that would mean a lot to me."

"What is it?" I asked, totally unaware of the stockings in my hand.

"I bought a clothes hamper today and it would really, really mean a lot to me if you would throw your stockings in the hamper."

Somehow she had managed to separate my self-worth from an annoying habit of throwing stockings.

There are a number of unproductive ways to approach this same situation. She could have attacked me with criticism and said, "You have a disgusting habit of throwing your stockings all over the house. It's a sick behavior. Your mother never taught you anything. I'm not your slave, you know, I'm not here to pick up after you. How dumb are you anyway? Don't you know it's only common courtesy to pick up after yourself?" She could have, but she didn't. She spoke to me with respect. She was very much in control of her emotions. She had asked for and received permission to express herself. She logically explained her concern. We were alone at a mutually agreeable time and place. I felt no intimidation. She owned her expectation. The issue was indeed one that was a part of her business as well as mine. It was, after all, a shared stewardship. The criticism was not only true, but it was in my best interest to hear it. Eliminating the behavior in question was edifying to us both. There was no attack on my self-worth, because she had focused on the issue with great clarity. I almost felt like a hero for putting my stockings in the clothes hamper.

Learning how to separate "Ego from Issue" on the little issues prepares the way to deal with more serious matters.

JASON WAS IN THE HABIT OF LYING

Jason lied even when he didn't need to lie; and when he wasn't lying he was exaggerating. His friends were concerned because of this self-defeating behavior. Jason was being laughed at behind his back. Marion, his best friend, approached Jason and said, "Jason, you know, you are my best friend."

"Yes," he replied.

"I feel I need to talk to you about something that is serious," Marion said.

"Shoot," answered Jason.

"Not here where we can be interrupted. Let's go for a ride in my car." requested Marion.

Marion stopped the car and turned to face his friend. "I've been wrestling with this for days, Jason, and I've felt I just had to talk to you."

"What is it? Do I have bad breath?" retorted Jason.

Marion said, "It's more serious. I've chosen to overlook it, because I understand you and I'll always be your friend no matter what."

"What is it?" demanded Jason.

"People are laughing at you behind your back, because you have no credibility. You lie even when you don't need to. And you exaggerate all the time. Jason, you are really a neat guy. People like you just for you. It's not necessary, Jason, to lie. You are only hurting yourself. Well, there I said it. Will you still be my friend?"

Jason looked chagrined, "It's that bad?"

"Yes, Jason it is," responded Marion. "I've been thinking a lot about this, Jason, and I've come up with an idea. When I'm around you and I can see you're lying or exaggerating, I'll give you a key phrase and it will alert you."

Jason said, "I don't know if I can do it, but I'll try."

Is there an art and a skill to the giving of criticism? Yes, very definitely. It is time to practice. Remember, like bowling or golfing, or anything one does for the first time, it will feel awkward. And just like playing the piano or violin the first time, it sounds awkward. In spite of feeling clumsy and a little embarrassed, and ill at ease, do it! It is time to put it all together. It is time for a profound adventure into self-mastery.

When beginning to practice the "ART" of giving criticism, it is a good idea to say, "I'm very concerned about saying something that will hurt your feelings. I would like to be able to talk to you about an issue or behavior without your feeling I'm attacking your self-worth." "I love you," or "I care about you," or "I'm sincerely concerned and I just want to help you be an even better person than you already are. This is why I'm not yelling or crying. I am genuinely concerned."

STEP THREE:
AFFIRM THEIR WORTH:

Affirming worth is another way of saying that after you have criticized you need to show a genuine concern for the value of the person and the relationship.

How do you follow up a message of criticism with a message of acceptance? It is made more difficult by the fact that the one criticized may feel rejected, withdrawn, and alienated by the giver of criticism. Generally it is a good idea to separate the affirmation from the criticism by fifteen to twenty minutes. This gives the "receiver" of criticism time to settle down. It also demonstrates genuine concern on behalf of the critic to bring balance to the situation or behavior criticized. Warning! Do not use the occasion to review the criticism. The objective is to affirm their worth as illustrated in the following story:

"Bart, this morning when I criticized you about the Hansen Project, I was concerned that you might over react to the negative feedback. You are one of the hardest working employees I have. I want you to know that I have seen your sacrifices for the sake of the company and I genuinely appreciate all that you do for us. Please keep that in mind."

Human nature being what it is, inappropriately given criticism will add to the difficulty of showing forth an increase of love. The critic will often find that before he can show forth love, he has to apologize for the inappropriate way the criticism was given. He is not apologizing for the content but the delivery. If the critic allowed himself to be angry or to lose emotional control by yelling or by attacking the worth of the one being criticized, he has a self-imposed higher mountain to climb. First, he must undo the damage done by improper criticism. It may take an hour or so for the one criticized to be receptive. The very pattern of improper criticism destroys the credibility of the critic. Words of love mean little when loving behaviors are absent. To the one criticized, words of love seem hollow and empty, even hypocritical.

It is a very good idea to invite a friend or a loved one to practice the process together. It can be a very bonding experience to develop this art and skill with a spouse. Sometimes it is impossible because your friend or spouse is unwilling or unprepared to do so. Co-workers are a potential resource. A question that is often asked is, "What if I am the only one to do this?" This is a talent to be developed whether anyone else chooses to do so or not.

You may want to copy the guidelines for giving criticism onto a card and carry it in a pocket or a purse. Here they are, one more time:

- Think before you speak. Is the criticism within your stewardship and would it be in the best interest of the other person to hear it ? If not, don't say it. If it is then proceed.

- Ask for and receive permission before criticizing.

- Be alone with the person at a mutually agreeable time and place.

- Be in emotional control and logically explain your concern. No yelling, crying, swearing, physical, or emotional intimidation is allowed.

- Do not attack self-worth. Stay focused on the issue or behavior in question. Always be as specific as you can in separating the issue or behavior from EGO. Protect their self-worth.

- Affirm their worth to you.

RELATIONSHIPS

Remember, all relationships stand on their own merit. Any person is only one-half of any relationship to which he or she is a part. Younger children need to be protected from abusive older brothers and sisters. If not, an abusive "pecking order" will ensue. Abuse cannot be tolerated. It matters not whether that abuse is physical, sexual, verbal, emotional, or mental. It is the height of idiocy for parents to be abusive in stopping abuse. Parents are best served by being an example of the desired love and respect.

MOM AND BILLY

Billy was ten, the older sibling. The younger child, Micky, came into Billy's room and, without permission, took his remote control car and hid it. Billy confronted Micky, age five, and Micky lied about taking it. Angry and upset, Billy hit Micky then he came to his mother to make Micky give him back the expensive toy. Micky was crying, "Billy hit me, Billy hit me!"

The mother comforted Micky and then said to Billy, "Why did you hit him?"

Billy responded, "Because he stole my remote control car. Make him give it back, Mom, right now, or I will go into his room and break his toys!"

Mother sent Micky downstairs with these words, "I'll be down in a few minutes and we can talk about it."

Before Mother spoke, she thought about the desired outcome. Next she said to Billy, "I'm sorry that Micky took your car without permission. That was wrong. Your car will be returned. However, I need to talk to you about hitting Micky. Would now be a good time or would you like to wait ten minutes?"

Billy responded, "I just want my car back,"

"So would you prefer we talk about your hitting now or in ten minutes?" repeated Mom.

"In ten minutes," grumbled Billy.

"Fine, I'll set the timer on the stove for ten minutes. When it buzzes I expect you to be ready to talk to me," declared Mom.

The buzzer went off and Billy and Mom sat on the edge of Billy's bed. "Billy, I am sure you felt angry and upset to have your special car taken. What Micky did was wrong," said Mom, "but what you did in hitting him was also wrong. Two wrongs don't make a right."

"He deserved it, Mom, he is just a little thief. He's always taking my things," blurted out Billy.

"Right now, Billy, we are talking about your behavior. I love you son, and I know you will grow up to be a fine man. For now, I want you to know that it is never right to abuse someone. You must accept responsibility for what you did in spite of what Micky did. After I talk to Micky,

I want you to apologize to him for hitting him. Also I want you to take a time out for fifteen minutes for hitting your little brother. I meant what I said about loving you. I know a good boy like you will want to overcome a bad habit like hitting when you are angry. You go and set the timer on the stove for another fifteen minutes. Then sit at the kitchen table while I talk to Micky. When the buzzer rings, you turn it off and come and find me."

Billy was reluctant, but did it. Mom went to Micky and said, "Micky, may I talk to you now or in two minutes?"

Micky looked puzzled and said, "Now, I guess."

Mom responded, "Thank you, for letting me talk to you. Micky, right now there are only three people in the house, you, me, and Billy. I didn't take Billy's car. That means you had to take it. Don't lie to me because it will only make matters worse for you. I want you to go and get Billy's car right now and bring it to me." She was firm and looked him directly in the eyes. Micky returned with the car.

Mom continued, "It is wrong to take things that don't belong to you without asking. Do you know that, Micky?" Micky nodded his head, yes. "Would you like to get one for your own?" Micky again nodded, yes. "I will talk to you later about some work I need done and maybe you can earn some money and you can buy one. Micky, I love you. You will always be special to me because you are my little caboose. Nice boys don't take things that don't belong to them. You are a wonderful boy. A good boy like you doesn't want to do a bad thing like take someone else's toy without permission." Micky shook his head from side to side. "Here is the right thing to do. First, I want you to give the car back to Billy. Next, I want you to say you are sorry to Billy for taking his car. Afterwards, I want you to take a fifteen minute time out and think of something nice you could do for your big brother. Billy should not have hit you. That was wrong. Two wrongs don't make a right. He is going to apologize for hitting you. Right now he is taking a time out for fifteen minutes."

The buzzer sounds and Billy appears at the door. "Come in, Billy. Micky has something he wants to return to you."

Micky hands the remote control car to Billy and says, "I'm sorry, Billy."

Mom says, "I'm sorry I took your car without your permission." Micky repeats it.

"Billy, I want you to say 'Micky will you forgive me for hitting you?'" Billy said it.

"Now, Micky, I want you to say, I forgive you, Billy." Micky does so.

"All right, Billy, I want you to say, 'Micky, I forgive you for taking my car without permission.'" Billy repeats it.

"Ok," says Mom, "Now Micky is going to take a fifteen minute time out and think about what has happened here. Afterward I thought I would go for some ice cream. Would my sons like to go and get some ice cream with a mother who loves them both very much?"

In the preceding story all the elements of appropriate criticism were present:

- It was in the mother's stewardship and the criticism was necessary.
- She asked for and received permission to criticize them.
- She was alone with each one at an agreeable time and place.
- She was gentle and direct.
- She stayed in emotional control. There was no yelling, crying or abuse. She logically explained her concerns.

- She focused on the improper behavior and she separated the issue from the worth of each. She was fair and evenhanded.

- She confirmed their worth to her when she invited them for ice cream

What if the critic appropriately criticizes, shows forth sincere love, and is totally rejected on a consistent basis? Assume the one being criticized is not only hostile, but interprets loving behaviors as a mockery. Under these circumstances the appropriate giver of criticism must realize that he or she is dealing with a toxic person. This means you will not be able to say enough, be enough, or do enough to ever satisfy them.

DEALING WITH THE VERBALLY ABUSIVE

Harry is a verbally and emotionally abusing husband and father. He is always criticizing his wife and children. He is constantly calling them names like "stupid" and swearing at them. Wendy, his wife, has managed to deal with Harry, but fears the children will suffer irreparable damage. Every time Harry begins to criticize the children, Wendy jumps in to defend them. Then Wendy and Harry wind up in a fight. Harry is not justified in being verbally abusive. Wendy's issue is his verbal and emotional abuse. Harry has an issue with Wendy interfering with his relationships. He also feels she is parenting him by telling him what he should, needs, and ought to do. He sees Wendy as being disloyal to him in front of the children. Furthermore, he accuses her of choosing the children over him. Harry is right that Wendy has been mothering him. There is another way that Wendy could handle this situation that would take away all of Harry's complaints about her.

Unwittingly, Wendy, by mishandling her response,

gives Harry issues to argue, and thereby escape focusing on his abusive behavior. Because she parents him in front of the children, she is viewed by Harry as being the problem. This is typical of most arguments. Each party is arguing a point of view they can defend. Wendy wants to talk about Harry's abusive actions, while Harry wants to talk about Wendy's inappropriate reactions. What if Wendy would ask Harry for permission to criticize him? Maybe a letter or note could be written by Wendy asking for permission to meet with Harry to discuss a painful issue which threatens their relationship. It is not a good time to ask someone in the middle of an emotionally charged encounter if now would be a good time to discuss their inappropriate conduct.

When Harry and Wendy do meet alone, at a mutually agreed upon time and place, Wendy is nervous and maybe a little afraid, but she says to Harry, "I've asked to meet with you privately because I did not want to criticize you in front of the children. It's my way of respecting you. Also, I did not want you to think that I was choosing the children over you. Our relationship is worth working on and I love you. I know that the children are frustrating you and I want to help. I am troubled with the way you talk to the children. I'm concerned about their self-worth. Also, I know I'm not perfect myself, and I am willing to work on being better. I'm really looking for solutions, Harry. You love the children and you work hard to provide for us. I will try to help them be appreciative of what you do for all of us. I worry when I see either fear or despair in the children's eyes when you swear at them or call them names."

"This is the issue I have, Harry, and I honestly believe it's hurting your ability to have a good relationship with the kids. You are entitled to have a poor relationship if that is what you want, but not an abusive one. I fear for their self-worth when you call them names or swear at them. I love you and I love them, and I want to help if I can. What can I do to help? I have made several phone calls and I know where and when different anger management groups meet. I'll go with you if you would like. Think about it and we can talk later."

Some will say, "He will never let me complete the first sentence without interrupting me."

In such cases, write out the whole concern and the consequences in a letter. Obviously Harry is going to be defensive. However, Wendy has not compounded the problem with interfering, disloyalty, or causing Harry to lose face. If Harry is a good man, he will think about it and try to improve. Wendy needs to maintain her emotional composure. She needs to bring the same calm attitude to at least three such encounters. If he is a "bad" man then Wendy needs to confront him with an ultimatum to get "professional help" for anger management or leave for a specified period of time. Most do neither; instead they gripe and moan about what is, but make no attempts to positively effect change. What Wendy attempted to do falls under the category of seeking for common consent. By following this healthy approach, the focus is taken off of Wendy and placed directly in Harry's lap.

Earlier, it was pointed out that we can only share to the level of willingness of the other person. In the illustration, Wendy did what she could. She asked for and received permission from Harry before she criticized him. She made sure she and Harry were alone at a mutually agreeable time and place. She was in emotional control of herself and logically explained her concerns over Harry's abusive language and her fear of its impact on the children's self-worth.

Also, Wendy gave Harry a viable alternative. She prepared

a way for him to be successful. Wendy is only one-half of this relationship. She can only control her actions and her reactions. She can model proper behavior for Harry in interacting with the children. She can love Harry for the good he does in generally protecting and providing for the family. She may not feel she can trust Harry and his abusive relationship with the children, but Wendy can have an "I love Harry Program" and do an unconditional deed of love every day for him independent of Harry's language with the children. She will do this deed of unconditional love, not because Harry deserves it, but because Wendy is a good person. She wants to be a loving individual. By strengthening the overall relationship with Harry, Wendy creates a supportive environment conducive to change. Her phone calls showed effort to find a solution. However, all of her efforts could be defeated by Harry's lack of willingness.

Some might ask, "Isn't it a form if intimidation to threaten Harry with leaving if he does not change his abusive language?" Yes, and it depends on how serious Wendy is about the issue. This should not be a ploy. Wendy cannot threaten to leave over everything, or she is simply trying to emotionally blackmail Harry. Her saying that she will leave if Harry continues to verbally and emotionally abuse the children is a simple statement of fact, not an idle threat. Wendy may want to leave for a month or a week to underscore her words if Harry's behavior is not modified. This is setting boundaries to protect herself and the children.

For Wendy, this is a preferable and more appropriate overall response than to insert herself into every conversation that Harry has with the kids and wind up always arguing with Harry. Even if Wendy divorces Harry, he is still going to have some kind of relationship with the kids. This may include every other weekend, six weeks in the summer, and alternative holidays. In the end, Harry has to be responsible for his own lousy relationships. Wisdom would dictate that Wendy criticize sparingly so that when she does speak to Harry, her input will be considered, evaluated and weighed. Otherwise, Wendy will be perceived as a "nagging," "never-satisfied" person and the content of her messages will never be given sincere consideration. She dealt with Harry as a wife. She also dealt with Harry as the mother of their children. What she did not do was to constantly interfere directly with Harry's relationships. By acting the way she did, Wendy stayed within her stewardship.

HOW MUCH DO WE
HAVE TO SUFFER BEFORE CHANGE BEGINS?

How much unnecessary suffering is enough? How many tearful nights are enough? How much hurt, heartache, and sorrow are enough? When will they ever learn? At what point do we cry out, "It is enough!" "Uncle!" When will improper criticism stop? When will words of love be matched with loving behaviors?

The greatest thing the critic can do to convince the one reproved of their worth is to not repeat improperly given criticism. They need to show respect by restraint. If necessary, write the criticisms down on paper. Keep the verbal airways clear of criticism. Use the verbal channels for normal and positive communication. This extra effort may be required if the critic has a problem maintaining a civil tongue. Breaking the nonproductive behavioral pattern of joining negative emotionalism and criticism is a hard habit to break.

CHAPTER FIFTEEN

THE ART OF RECEIVING CRITICISM

The art of receiving criticism lies in our ability to honestly and objectively examine the negative feedback. Overcoming the natural response to be defensive and to truly listen to the criticism is a key. Writing the criticism down where it can be evaluated facilitates the examination process. With practice, a person will be able to deal with most criticism on the spot. However, when more time is required it is up to the one being criticized to set a time and place to meet with the critic. It is easier for the criticism to be evaluated away from the emotional intensity in which most criticism is given.

Evaluating the merits of the criticism is the next step. The evaluation is made in light of becoming our healthiest and best selves. If the recommended changes contribute to becoming our best selves, they should be adopted. If the analysis of the criticism is consistent with our time, energy, and will to change, it would be of benefit to us. After careful consideration of the criticism, honest disagreement is also an appropriate reaction. However, before we agree or disagree with the criticism it deserves to be honestly evaluated.

DR. LUND'S
QUICK CHECK GUIDE TO
RECEIVING CRITICISM

STEP ONE:

- STOP!   Immediately remove your EGO from the issue or behavior being criticized.

- LOOK   Look at the person.

- LISTEN   Do not defend, make an excuse, or apologize. Don't speak, LISTEN!

STEP TWO:

Write the criticism down where you can evaluate it.

STEP THREE

Feed it back without emotion.

STEP FOUR:

Excuse yourself from immediate response and set a time and place to respond.

STEP FIVE:

Evaluate the criticism and your resources for dealing with it, i.e., time, energy, will.

STEP SIX:

Respond at an appointed time and place. The response will fall into one of three categories:

- I will change.
- I disagree and this is why…
- I will not change because I am unwilling or unable to do so.

262

THE FIRST PART OF STEP ONE: STOP!

STAYING FOCUSED

Betty felt as though her husband was hypercritical. She felt his criticism was a blind spot. He was a good man in many ways, but he was emotionally unsafe. She wanted to know what she could do to fix him, because his pride would not allow him to come in to see a counselor. Ed, her husband, was a critiholic and negative about most things and people. I asked Betty if it were also true that she was hypersensitive to being criticized. She confessed she was, and admitted this compounded the difficulties in the marriage. I asked Betty if she would describe for me a typical evening with Ed.

"First, even before he sets foot in the house, he will be upset about bikes in the driveway or the yard, and comes into the house mumbling. I've gotten to the point where I feel sick to my stomach when I know he is coming home. He seldom has anything pleasant to say at all. Immediately he will begin to check to see if I did all the things he feels are important. It's like the Gestapo going over a checklist. He thinks we are talking, but I feel like it's an inquisition. If I fail to do one thing, I get a lecture. When I try to explain my schedule or my reasons, he gets angry and I cry. It's the same pattern day after day. If we make it through the checklist, we have some kind of dinner. I hate to cook anymore. He criticizes everything, and now he criticizes the fact that I don't cook as often. After dinner, he will go into his computer room until it's time for bed. If he ever comes out to watch a ball game on T.V., he yells and criticizes the entire time. Our intimacy is almost nonexistent. I don't want to be seen by him. I never feel like I perform to his expectations. I find myself making excuses to stay up until he has gone to bed, so I won't have to be with him. He knows something is wrong. He is always telling me I don't appreciate what he has provided for me and the family. He is a good provider and a hard worker. In his own way, I know that he loves me and the children. I'm getting to the point that if something doesn't change, I'm going to leave. I just can't take it anymore. That's why I am here."

"Betty, there are two things you can do immediately to improve your situation. First, protect yourself and second, learn how to live with a 'toxic personality.' Do you accept responsibility for protecting yourself against uninvited criticism or unwarranted criticism?"

"What do you mean?" she asked.

"You are choosing to be hurt. You are giving him a perfect target at which to shoot. What you have told me is that you have a whole series of expectations of how a loving person would treat you if he truly loved you. For example, if someone truly loved you, he would never criticize you, or your weight, or your efforts. You said it yourself, Ed does love you. It is also true that Ed is hypercritical. These are co-existing truths and they are not mutually exclusive. If you were to say, 'Ed doesn't love me because he criticizes me all the time,' I would say your conclusion is false. 'Ed loves you' and 'Ed criticizes you' are both true statements. Betty, I want you to focus on Ed loving you, and for now ignore any thought to the contrary. As much as anything, you object to how Ed packages his criticisms and their quantity.

"Let me teach you about criticism, about the art and skill of giving and receiving criticism. Giving criticism deals with the ego or self-worth of others, while receiving criticism relates to your own ego. Developing the art and skill of receiving criticism is more difficult than applying the principles involved in giving criticism. Those truly skilled in giving criticism have the ability to empathetically walk in the self-worth moccasins of others. Giving criticism properly has been defined as the 'art of telling someone he is going to hell in such a way he looks forward to the journey.' They possess the art of focusing on a negative issue or behavior in a way that preserves their sense of self-worth. This acquired talent of 'giving' criticism while respecting the value of the individual, happens because of being 'other centered.' The art and skill of 'receiving' criticism requires that we extend to ourselves that same respect for our self-worth. Appropriate self-respect means we do not empower others to devalue us.

"Your worth is not a topic for the toxic person to debate nor discuss. Those who want to do so are out of stewardship. It is not their right to pass judgement upon your worth. Your behavior on the other hand, may be inappropriate, improper, or unhealthy, and ought to be honestly evaluated by you. It has been said that no one can hit you over the head with an emotional club that you don't first put into his hand. A key to receiving criticism is the ability to separate an issue from your sense of worth as a human being. Being able to protect yourself from the negative effects of criticism is a part of the art and skill needed.

"There is a desire you must possess. It is the desire to become your highest and best self. Without that desire you will never be able to truly learn the art of receiving criticism. What if the criticism is valid? If you are not committed to become your highest and best self, you will not even evaluate the criticism on its merits. Instead you will be distracted by the way it was said. Your desire to defend your worth, and your ego will prevail.

"These two items are absolutely essential if you are to get past the messenger and focus on the message. First, no one has a right to comment upon your worth. If anyone does so, disregard it. He or she is only trying to manipulate you. The only power that another person has is the power you give by believing him. When Ed becomes abusive, excuse yourself from his presence. Say to him, 'When you are ready to focus on the issue I'll be back,' Do it. Don't let your fear and doubt rob you of dignity. Second, in order to handle criticism at any level you must possess a deep yearning to become your highest and best self.

"If you are going to be successful in receiving criticism from others, it will require that you live a higher law. The single greatest challenge to receiving criticism is the 'Ego.' Ego is not a bad word. It means your conscious self, your self-worth. Most people respond to criticism by immediately defending their ego. This is what you are doing when Ed criticizes you. The higher law you will be asked to live demands that you place your ego in a safe place—remove it as an issue. Protect yourself. Otherwise, every conversation with anyone about anything becomes an issue for ego validation, i.e., they must agree with you and you must be right, or you have no value. This means you become so emotionally involved in defending your ideas, behavior, and your 'Ego,' you cannot receive valid criticism. You wind up defending your sense of worth and you are not open to hear what the real issues are. Taking the focus off of your ego is a necessary step."

GOING ON A "MIND WALK"

"Let me tell you what I do. I have a very special box. When anyone criticizes me, I immediately take my ego, my sense of worth, and mentally put it in the box. It takes me a half second. Then I go in my mind to the bank and place the box in a safety deposit vault to protect it until I return. It works for me. However, each person has to find a way that works for himself or herself."

I asked Betty if she would like to know how some people

266

handle criticism by taking a "mind walk." A "mind walk" is a mental journey you take the moment someone begins to offer uninvited criticism. Imagine in your mind an alarm going off, just like those noisy irritating car alarms that go off when someone touches the car. Or think of your ego being in a bank vault, and when the alarm sounds, all the safe doors automatically close. Huge impenetrable solid steel doors, two feet thick, close off every window, door, or exit. Like the precious Mona Lisa, a treasure beyond price, your self-worth, is protected. It is safe. Now you can venture outside the bank, because your treasured self-worth is safe within the vault.

One man said his "mind walk" included a visual image of the critical person asking for the combination to the safe, and he would say, "I'm sorry, it's not available to you." He saw himself putting a package containing his self-worth into the safe and closing the door and spinning the dial.

A very inventive woman said she had a secret Personal Identification Number (pin #), like one finds at all automatic bank teller machines, that represented her ego and she didn't let anyone who was toxic know it.

Whatever the strategy, you must develop a system to protect your self-worth. There are numerous unproductive and relationship-defeating behaviors. Becoming confrontational, abusive and more toxic than the giver of criticism is one of them. On the other hand, becoming totally passive or becoming a doormat to be verbally abused, is equally unacceptable. The fight or flight alternatives are not as productive as a "mind walk."

Some simply choose to ignore any unauthorized criticism. In other words, don't sign for the critic's 'registered mail.' I have suggested to several people that they reward themselves twenty-five cents each time they were criticized. One woman said it wasn't enough. but a dollar would be! Each time she was criticized a dollar sign flashed in her eyes. Her ego was safe in the cash register. One man bought himself a new fly rod. At twenty-five cents a criticism, one young married wife bought a new pair of shoes in only a month.

"Let's assume that you develop an effective 'mind walk' that works for you. Your self-worth is safe. This means that you have removed self-worth as an issue, thereby avoiding any emotional melt-down. You are Spock on Star Trek. Professor McCoy comes ranting and screaming at you because you are not responding to his emotionalism. Although he calls you names like a pointed-eared, green-faced, half-human freak, it doesn't bother you. You look at him and say, 'Very interesting, but quite illogical.'

"Can you imagine how long a court reporter would last if he or she kept getting emotionally involved in each court case? If the court reporter cried and wept and asked the judge for a moment to compose himself or herself, that person would be fired. You are going to stay in control of your emotions whenever Ed's negative emotions flair up. You do so by ignoring his packaging. Disregard the 'how' and examine the 'what.' This takes practice and is a highly developed mental skill, to separate your worth from the criticisms of others. It can and must be done.

"Your objective with Ed is to focus on the content of his criticism. If the content of his criticism is an attack on your worth, you must protect yourself by leaving or ignoring it. You are Spock, the Court Reporter. Now, bring on the criticism, for 'sticks and stones can break your bones,' but words shall never harm you. You are going to pan for gold. You are going to separate the mud from the gold nuggets. The packaging of the criticism is the mud and the golden nugget is a truth covered in mud.

You are going to find gold among the quills of the porcupine. Accepting that truth may help you reach your objective of becoming your highest and best self. Yes, it is a lousy job of packaging. Yes, Ed said it poorly. However, by separating your worth and placing it in a safe place, you are prepared to logically evaluate the criticism and pan for gold. If there is no substance to the comments, they can be disregarded as having come from frustration, or a contentious spirit. If there is merit in the criticism, regardless of packaging, it can be evaluated for future benefit."

THE SECOND PART OF STEP ONE: LOOK!

"Remember, the art of receiving criticism is much more difficult than giving it. A concerted effort will be needed to separate your worth and your ego from the criticism. It will take practice and time and more practice and more time. However, the process does work.

"With practice you can separate your worth and put it in a safe place, then you are ready to focus on the message. Remember, you do not have to tolerate abuse. Walk away, go to another room, or just say, 'Excuse me please, I'll be back when you are ready to focus on the issue.' If Ed gets physically abusive, call the police. He is out of bounds. If you tolerate it, he will give himself permission to continue.

"Let's assume Ed is frustrated and criticizing you. Here is what you do. This is how to de-fang the tiger. You look him directly in the eye. If you look down it means you are letting his criticism impact on your self-worth. Even if his eyes are bugging out of his head and his neck muscles strained, look him sincerely in the eyes. Your objective is to focus on the issue or behavior about which he is being critical. You are in control of yourself. If you cave in to your emotions you will be rewarding him. You

269

have the power. There is a protective shield around you. This level of self-mastery and disassociation may even cause you to smile inside. His once effective techniques have no effect on you. It's almost an out of body experience. Betty, it is as if you are a third party watching. You are an actress on stage. Sincerely look into his eyes searching for the message."

THE THIRD PART OF STEP ONE: LISTEN!

"Truly listening and not reacting is difficult. There is a strong urge to want to explain, justify, or defend. Betty, this is where you 'zip your lip.' Don't apologize. Don't make excuses. Don't speak. Just gaze into his eyes and LISTEN.

"You are too young to remember the old style record players, but maybe you've seen one in an attic or a museum. They played records of different sizes. They would also play at different speeds, i.e., 45, 78, or 33⅓. The records of the same speed were placed in a stack on a metal center post. An automatic arm would extend from the side once the record was in place. A needle protruding from the arm fit perfectly into the record groves. At last! Music! It was quite primitive compared to the CDs of today. However, the old record players had an unusual characteristic. No matter where the record was playing, the beginning, the middle, or the end, if you bumped the record player, the automatic arm would stop and go all the way back to the beginning and start all over again. That is just like someone who is criticizing. If they are interrupted they go back all the way to the beginning and start over. Sometimes they increase the tone of their voice another octave because they believe you are not listening. So I want you to listen for the issue or behavior which is the object of his concern so he won't start all over again.

"Next, I'm going to ask you to write down his criticisms. This may sound like a contradiction. I've just asked you to look into his eyes and to listen to what Ed is saying."

"Won't writing it down distract me from looking and listening?"

"The answer is no. Look down to write and then look up into his eyes. Look at his eyes and the paper. It works and I'll explain why."

STEP TWO:
WRITE DOWN THE CRITICISMS
WHERE THEY CAN BE EVALUATED

"Years of experience have verified the importance of writing down criticisms. The difference between those who succeed in receiving criticism and learn from it and those who fail in this task is their willingness to follow this counsel. There are two important reasons why you should write down Ed's criticisms. The first reason is psychological. Writing down the criticisms will allow the them to enter your ears, flow through your brain, down your arm and hand on to the paper. Otherwise all the criticisms will stay in your brain. Maybe the greatest benefit is emotional. By writing down the criticism as an issue or behavior, you are protecting your worth, self-worth, and value. You are focusing on the issues or behaviors in question and not your ego. This is a totally legitimate process.

"The second important reason for writing down the criticism is to evaluate it at a later time. There are a myriad of secondary benefits:

- It alerts the critical person to just how often he is criticizing.

- It shows that you are willing to listen.

271

- It demonstrates a sincere attempt to improve.

- It increases your credibility.

- It helps you focus."

"What if Ed objects to my writing down the criticisms?"

"Most critics are suspicious of your motivation. They wonder if you are preparing for divorce. They are fearful you are building a case against them. They hate being reminded of how frequently they criticize. Most will object. They will also mock your efforts. This is especially true of the insecure. Be prepared for Ed to object to your writing down his criticisms. He doesn't want a record kept. 'Nevertheless', 'in spite of,' and 'regardless' of his objections, write down the criticisms.

"When he asks you, 'What are you writing down, Betty?' say to Ed, 'I'm writing down your criticism of my behaviors and issues so that I can honestly evaluate them.'

"Ed may say, 'Why do you have to write it down in order to remember it?'

"I want you to say in your own words something like this: 'Ed, if it is important enough for you to say, it is important enough for me to write it down. I'm sorry if it makes you uncomfortable, but this is my way of dealing with it.'

"Obviously, this will require courage on your part not to back down. If he fails to agree, offer him the alternative of writing you a letter expressing his criticisms where you can evaluate them. If Ed persists in being verbally critical, write it down.

"Now I am going to ask you to keep a writing pad and pencil within reach at all times. This may require writing pads in every room in your house especially the bathroom, bedroom, and glove box in the car. There will be at least two times when it will be difficult to do so. One is when you are in the shower or bath and the other is when you are driving. Even under these two conditions, I would like you to write down the criticisms on paper afterwards. Remember, from a psychological view, you are taking the criticisms from your mind and transporting them out of your body onto the paper."

Even as I spoke Betty was taking notes as rapidly as she could. "What you are now doing with me is what I want you to do with Ed. The difference is you feel safe here but not with Ed. But what you are doing now is perfect. You are looking, listening, and writing. Are you clear so far as to what to do? What are the first two steps in the art and skill of receiving criticism from Ed?"

"Protect my self-worth. Stop, look, and listen, and then write down the criticisms."

"That's right. No one has the right to physically, emotionally, verbally, or mentally abuse you. If you feel any of these are happening, excuse yourself. Simply announce, "I am leaving the room, not the relationship. Tell Ed you will be back when he is in emotional control (or when you are in control) and can logically focus on the concerns.

"Just because Ed is upset or frustrated does not mean you are being abused. However, you are the judge as to whether or not you are prepared to receive it. We will assume that Ed is on a critical binge, but it is not yet abusive. Let's review the steps so far. When verbally criticized do not defend yourself, do not make excuses, and do not justify your behavior. Just STOP, LOOK, LISTEN, AND WRITE. A defensive response, an excuse, or a justification is perceived as NOT HEARING, and usually results in the critical person repeating his verbal criticisms. Ed believes you are not focusing on the content of what he is saying to you. It's as if your ears fell off and he has to speak louder in order for you to properly get the message. Frequently, your excuses only upset him and add fuel to his fiery words.

"There is another benefit to listening and writing it down. When you choose not to combat, you help create an atmosphere which can allow you to focus on the issue or behavior in question. Also, not commenting can defuse the anger and take the wind out of their sails. If you choose to combat, the content will be lost in a war of words and the new issue that will emerge will be the self-worth of one or both of you. Soon a crisis of individual worth will be created and the focus of the original criticism will be lost.

"Adrenaline begets adrenaline, the heart beat speeds up, the body energy increases, and fatigue gives way to a new found power to combat. Not allowing the other person to get to you is the key. It is all about you staying in control of your responses. Writing down the criticism is a tool which allows you to stay in control."

STEP THREE:
FEED BACK THE CRITICISM WITHOUT EMOTION

"Betty, some people feel unless a person is emotional, he or she is not genuine. This is a characteristic learned in the family. Being emotional is equated with being honest. It's not only untrue, it is unhealthy. Imagine if you were only able to communicate while angry or crying. About half of all men feel manipulated when women cry. They feel it is a diversion from facing facts. Almost always when someone is crying or yelling it is a plea for understanding and acceptance. However, it is a diversion from the issue. Consciously or unconsciously, crying when criticized is a reaction to feeling rejected.

Sometimes, unless a person is emotional, he doesn't give himself or herself permission to express his or her thoughts. There are appropriate times for tears, but when someone is developing the 'art' of receiving criticism, it is a time to focus on the content of the critical message.

"Continue to write down Ed's expectations and frustrations. Be a court reporter. Eventually, he will finish. After he is through criticizing you, FEED IT BACK TO HIM WITHOUT EMOTION. Do it just as if you were reading a recipe from a cook book. For example, 'So what you are saying, Ed, is I spend too much time talking on the phone with my friends. If I spent less time on the phone, I would have more time to devote to cleaning the house and cooking.' This does not mean in any way that you agree with him or with his evaluation or criticism. It means you heard him. This acknowledges his concerns and gives him an opportunity to clarify or expand. It will have an end. Ed may launch into a repeat of the items. Just put a check mark by the criticism he has already mentioned."

Although Betty knew the things which were a source of frustration for Ed, she never let him fully express himself. Before he could complete a thought, they would be completely engaged in a verbal battle. Name-calling, swearing, yelling, and another night on the couch by one or the other ensued. The pattern was well-established. The next day, no one talked. Eventually small talk would cautiously give way to a guarded peace. Neither was emotionally safe for their mate. At the slightest hint of any criticism, Betty would go into a tirade and harangue Ed on his lack of appreciation, his insensitive nature, and attack his weaknesses. I asked Betty to hear him out, even if it involved repetition.

"Keep track of his criticisms. Which ones are recurring? After awhile, you will be able to number them."

Betty discovered that Ed was critical of five things:

1. She was overweight.
2. She allowed the kids to eat in the car.
3. She was a poor housekeeper.
4. She wasn't a good mother.
5. She was a poor money manager.

Betty wanted unconditional acceptance. She wanted Ed to overlook the fact that the doctors had told her she was borderline diabetic. However, weight loss would help her. I asked Betty if she remembered why she originally came to me. She said, "I was concerned about how to stop my husband from criticizing me. I really wanted you to fix him through me."

"I know you are reaching your wit's end. I sense you feel overwhelmed. What I am sharing with you is the answer to your question. You may not see it clearly, but by taking control of your ability to protect your ego, and committing to become your highest and best self, you are on the way to changing the interaction between you and Ed."

STEP FOUR:
EXCUSE YOURSELF FROM ANY
IMMEDIATE RESPONSE AND SET A
TIME AND PLACE TO GET BACK TOGETHER

"Avoid the very, very, very big temptation to verbally or emotionally respond at this time. This is not the time to cry, to become angry, or to stomp out of the room and slam a door. After this great exercise of patience, it would be a pity to lose all that effort. An immediate response shows no effort to honestly evaluate the content of the criticism. Ed may just want you to promise you will improve. However, when you do not keep your promise, he will use that to tear you down.

"This is what I want you to say to Ed. 'I've heard you,

Ed. It wasn't easy but believe me I have heard you. I'm not prepared to respond now. I need some time to think about these things. I want to evaluate my ability, willingness, and energy to make the changes you've suggested. I'm not capable of anything now but an emotional reaction. Give me three days to evaluate. I propose we meet on Wednesday night at 7 p.m. at the park. I will be prepared to talk to you then.'

"Do not allow him to draw you into a conflict. Excuse yourself and be civil and kind. This reaction will disarm him. He may not know how to respond except with a negative statement like 'Right! I'm sure you'll think about it and nothing will change.'"

STEP FIVE:
EVALUATE THE CRITICISM

"Betty, you do not have to live with Ed, nor with any one else. You do have to live with yourself, your life-long self. Self-improvement is *your* job. This is why you are committed to become your highest and best self.

"It's time to be honest with yourself. It's time to pan for gold. Maybe you have never given yourself permission to be honest. Is there any truth whatsoever to these criticisms? Until you honestly evaluate the situation, you will be an emotionally unhealthy person.

"I want to quickly review with you what an emotionally healthy person is.

- An emotionally healthy person accepts responsibility for her own happiness, unhappiness, and behavior. She realizes that life is a gift. It is her responsibility to improve her life. She escapes denial by facing reality.

- An emotionally healthy person is able to forgive herself and others.

277

- An emotionally healthy person will make a plan to take herself from the reality of where she is to a higher and better self.

"Betty, are you in agreement with these three basic characteristics of an emotionally, healthy person?"

"Yes," she said.

"Your willingness to accept personal accountability for your behavior and happiness, forgive self and Ed, and make a plan means you can now evaluate the criticism. For now we are not talking about Ed. It is not Ed's meanness, insensitivity, and improper criticism. Ed is not the focus. It is you, Betty. If you would like, I'll walk you through how to evaluate the criticism."

"Yes, I would like that. It's kind of scary. I'm not sure I'll like what I find."

"Do you remember where you put your self-worth?"

Betty and I met for six hours over the next two days. She was trying very hard to protect her self-worth around Ed. At the same time she worked on loving behaviors. Her mind-walk consisted of a fairy tale image of a woman whose aura was surrounded with a bright light that protected her from all harm. Her ego was safely guarded in the midst of the light. Like some powerful electronic field or bug-zapper, the criticisms would come toward her ego and be destroyed by the protective field. Betty was learning to evaluate Ed's frustrations.

Ed had managed to focus on five critical issues. Betty was overweight. Independent of Ed, she needed to lose thirty pounds because she was borderline diabetic. I asked Betty to evaluate her ability, her willingness, her time, and her energy for losing thirty pounds. It was obvious that she did not lack knowledge. What she lacked was commitment to the value of losing weight. She had the ability, the time, and the energy. What she lacked was

278

willingness.

"Betty, independent of Ed's criticism, would it be in your best interest to lose weight?"

"Yes," she said.

"Remember that an emotionally healthy person accepts responsibility for his or her behavior, happiness, and weight. They forgive self and they make a plan to become a better self. For our purposes a goal depends upon you and a wish is something that depends upon others."

I asked Betty to put together a realistic program wherein she could lose thirty pounds over the course of a year. "Make it a plan that does not depend upon Ed. It is your goal to eat more wisely and to lose one-half pound per week over the entire year. Are you willing to build or join a support group or weight management class and commit to stay with it for a year? This is not a commitment to me. This is a commitment to yourself to become your best self."

In like manner each of Ed's criticisms were evaluated. As Betty looked at "allowing the kids to eat in the car" she thought that what Ed really wanted was a clean car. She determined to ask Ed for a clarification. Regarding housekeeping she decided that she and Ed needed to agree on a common standard on what it meant to keep the house clean. She also decided to ask Ed for a clear definition of "what he considered a good mother to be." This did not mean that she would agree with Ed, but she was willing to consider his opinion.

Lastly she made a commitment to establish a realistic budget and to stay with it. She remembered the counsel not to verbally overcommit but to let her actions speak louder than her words. All of these decisions she believed would indeed help her to become a higher and better self, wife, mother, and friend.

STEP SIX:
RESPOND AT THE APPOINTED TIME AND PLACE

"Betty, when you meet tomorrow night with Ed at 7:00 p.m. in the park, stay in emotional control. This is a time of great defensiveness for the both of you. If he loses control, excuse yourself. If you feel you are going to go off the emotional deep end, excuse yourself. Set up another appointment. *Do not let this turn into an argument*. There is a tendency to let that happen.

"Do not overcommit. Remember actions speak louder than words. These last two days have been a good experience because you've changed your approach. Ed hasn't changed. He is reacting to you.

"Your responses will probably fall into one of these categories:

- I will change.
- I disagree and this is why...
- I need more specific information before I can make an intelligent evaluation.
- I am unwilling.
- I am unable.

"Go prepared. Write down in black and white what you are willing to do. Also have a specific list of questions that will clarify his definition of 'a clean house,' 'a good mother,' and 'a reasonable budget.'"

Ed could see some positive efforts on Betty's part as a result of counseling. Ed finally agreed to come and see me as a counselor. When I visited with Ed and Betty, I explained there are always three issues in any relationship. First, there is Ed with Ed. Second, there is Betty with Betty. Third, there is Ed and Betty. Each of them have issues separate from the person they married. Ed agreed. I asked Ed if he felt he was critical.

"No," he said, "I am just honest."

"Do others besides your wife perceive you as critical?"

He admitted they did.

"If you were killed in a traffic accident tomorrow, would all of Betty's challenges go away? Would she automatically lose weight? Would her skills as a mother and homemaker suddenly improve? If she were killed, would your ability to control your tongue go away as an issue?"

"I suppose not," admitted Ed.

"No. Your issues and hers are independent of each other. Ed, you have issues as a father whether or not Betty is around."

It was obvious that uninvited criticism had taken this relationship to an all-time low. Ground rules were established to which each agreed. Betty was to work on her issues, Ed would work on his issues, and the two of them together, with my guided help, would work on the relationship. Both agreed to follow the steps in the "Art of Giving and Receiving Criticism."

Giving respect took practice, as did asking for and receiving permission to criticize. After a few weeks, they were prepared to work on the art of receiving criticism. Betty was firmly entrenched in hypersensitivity. Ed was a "zealous" hyper-critic. It took great effort and considerable hard work, tears, and diligence before she was able to separate her self-worth from an issue or behavior. She learned to write down the criticism from her husband without comment.

The miracle that took place was that Ed became aware of his hyper-criticism. How? Every time Betty picked up a pad and pencil and began to write, he was reminded of who was criticizing and how often. This awareness alone had the effect of decreasing the sheer volume of his negative comments. The second miracle was his being able to complete his thoughts and fully express himself. The third miracle was his confession of how silly he felt listening to himself being out of control with body language and tone of voice, while his wife sat there writing it down. He became less intimidating and calmly related his concerns. Betty began to feel a sense of power in not letting his criticisms hurt her ego. She would feed back his criticism like a secretary reading the dictation of a letter to a boss. He would usually add a word or two and this part was over.

For example, Betty felt she was thirty pounds overweight, while her husband thought she was fifty pounds too heavy. For Betty, the kids eating in the car was a practical matter of feeding hungry children. For her husband, permitting the children to eat in the car was a sign of disrespect to him, and irresponsibility on her part. He wanted the car kept clean. He worked hard to provide for the family. Food on the floor or a greasy fingerprint on a window was considered an affront to his providership. He reasoned that if Betty cared, she could make the children wait until they were home, or go to a park to eat, but not allow them to eat in the car. For Betty, a budget was a guide; for her husband it was a divine decree. Clutter was acceptable to Betty; it represented a "pig pen" for her husband. Because she did not discipline the children the way her husband thought she should, he considered her a poor mother.

In Ed's eyes Betty was a fat, uncaring, overspending, poor housekeeper, and lousy mother who did not appreciate him. Because she felt her self-worth was under attack, Betty felt no motivation to change and had resigned herself to never being enough. Feeling totally unacceptable to him, she could not understand why he wanted to still be intimate with her. She hated him at times, and felt trapped in a marriage she could not escape. Without any professional or technical training, she was an economic prisoner. Each felt a love for the children and were looking for me to change their partner. The five issues remained the same, but gradually things began to change.

I suggested to Ed that what he was doing in criticizing Betty had not succeeded in changing her. I wanted him to let go of all five expectations. He wasn't sure he could. His moment of truth was about to happen. He was ready for the biggest "AHA" of his life.

"Is there any doubt, even the slightest, that your wife is unaware of your concerns about weight, the kids eating in the car, overspending the budget, her poor housekeeping skills, or her not being the kind of mother you would like her to be? Listen carefully to your own words."

"No. I know she knows. She just doesn't care."

"You are absolutely right, Ed. Betty does not lack knowledge of your concern. What she lacks is motivation to do anything about it. Betty is motivated by her dreams and her desire for acceptance, not by yours. She does not share your values. She is not convinced that your values should apply to her.

"Really think about it," I said, "of what value is your criticizing her? If she doesn't lack knowledge, why are you giving her knowledge? You ought to work on motivation and encourage her. Your criticisms of her are counter-productive. They only frustrate both of you and destroy any desire for her to want to change. She is filled with resentment for you."

"You mean I need to work on building her up and not on tearing her down?"

Aha! Shazam! I wasn't about to let him off the hook!

"Why?" I said.

"Because what I'm doing isn't working, and my trying to punish her and intimidate her by yelling only causes her to withdraw from me."

"What Betty lacks is a commitment to your values. She doesn't lack knowledge of what your values are. Currently, you are not her friend. You are not committed to help her become her highest and best self. Ed, do you even know what her values are, her hopes, her dreams? Remember all people are motivated by their goals, not by yours. Your agenda is to change her, to make her into your image of what you think she ought to be. The truth is, she is not acceptable to you and both of you know it. You, my friend, are at a crossroads. You can decide to focus on loving Betty as she is, or you can go on criticizing her. Eventually, one or the other of you will leave the relationship.

"If anything I have said makes any sense to you at all, then stop criticizing her today, and apologize to her for trying to make her into your image. Don't criticize her weight anymore. It is her body. It is her health. She has the responsibility to care for it. Negotiate with Betty on the budget. Be flexible, but also realistic. Let her see the true picture of your finances and give her the option of selling the house and moving to a less expensive one, where you will be able to spend more on other things, or enlist her support in making the sacrifices necessary to stay where you are.

"It's reasonable to expect hungry children to want to eat in the car. It's also reasonable to expect them to clean up after themselves. Give Betty some options. Prepare a way for her to be successful. For example, 'Betty, it would mean a lot to me if you would teach the kids to clean up after themselves. However, if they don't, would you please just do it yourself or hire a neighbor boy or girl to do it?'

"As far as the house cleaning is concerned, agree on a standard of cleaning that may be less than what you would wish and maybe a little more than Betty would want. If you are still not happy, then you need to either hire outside help to come in on a periodic basis and clean to your standard or do it yourself. After all, it is not her standard, it is yours. You must own it. If you want to spend time cleaning the house because you feel better about it, then do it with a good attitude and not attempt to put a guilt trip on her.

"Within the bounds of nonabuse, Betty is entitled to define for herself what kind of a mother she would like to be. She is also entitled to her own lousy relationship. She must also accept the consequences of her choices as they relate to the children and to you. She does not trust you. You are emotionally unsafe to her. It will take time and responsible behavior on your part. She can come to trust and love you again. My many years of experience have shown couples grow in and out of love several times in the same marriage."

I asked Ed if he would be willing to try. With quiet determination he nodded his head, yes. Next, I asked him to commit to treat Betty with respect by never criticizing her again without her permission. Also, I asked Ed to focus on the "Art of Giving Criticism." Again he nodded his head. This was a man who had been a "critiholic," all of his life, agreeing to reasonable behavior.

Betty, who was hypersensitive, was to specialize in the "Art of Receiving Criticism." What previously had been a weakness, was now becoming a strength. In order to finish her training in the art of receiving criticism, she was to evaluate the criticism. She was to see if doing or becoming whatever was criticized would help her in becoming her highest and best self. This was not according to her husband's standard, but according to her own. If losing weight was a healthy choice and consistent with being a better self, then she would have to accept the responsibility to join a support group or whatever was needed to make it happen. The next step in the "Art and Skill of Receiving Criticism" was to evaluate her resources. Did she have the time, the energy, or the will to accomplish the change? What choices could she make within the limits of her circumstances to make it happen?

Betty worked on her issue of hypersensitivity to criticism. Ed worked on his issue of being hypercritical. An amazing thing happened. Their relationship began to improve. As respect was gifted to each other, their mutually defensive attitudes were replaced with more loving dispositions. Each came to the awareness that true progress in a relationship is only made by common consent and by moving at a pace mutually agreeable to both. Everything isn't perfect in their relationship today, but they are emotionally bonded and walking a common path. Things are better than they have ever been and neither of them is willing to go back to the dysfunctional way it was before.

There are hundreds of relationships just like this one. The issues may vary, but the behaviors don't. Ironically, the solutions are also the same. People have to let go of their dysfunctional approaches and replace them with healthier ones. If the relationship is going to improve, then behaviors will have to improve.

Few have the courage or humility to face the truth of valid criticism. It is easier to pretend that all criticism is either a mistake or a misunderstanding. The ability to honestly evaluate negative feedback and to learn from it may be the difference between being average and being great. Individuals who develop this competence are not only an asset to themselves but to any organization or relationship that is fortunate enough to be associated with them.

CHAPTER SIXTEEN

FINDING TRUTH
AMONG THE QUILLS

For the reforming toxic and those who interact with them, learning from criticism is priceless. One of the most difficult skills to acquire in the entire range of human interaction is the ability to receive criticism and profit from it. So fragile is the human psyche that few can face the need to change without becoming defensive. It is very natural to respond to any attack by assuming a defensive posture. Nonetheless, being "natural" is a very poor excuse for limiting self-improvement.

Most people deal with the toxic by simply avoiding them altogether or by minimizing their contact. Another way is to profess you don't care about the approval of the toxic person. However, most people who say they have stopped caring, still hold feelings of hurt and resentment. They begrudge the nonacceptance of the toxic. Those who do run away wonder why they stayed so long in a difficult relationship. This is by far the most common reaction to toxic personalities.

There is a way to prepare yourself to live with a porcupine and to find golden nuggets of truth among the many quills of criticism. This way is so clever and intelligent as to border on genius, and it doesn't involve changing the toxic personality. However, it is not easy. Only those with a fixed determination and a firm resolve will be able to do it. It requires tremendous focus and mental energy. It is not a strategy for the timid or the frail.

What is the great secret? It is the ability to **separate your ego from the issue or behavior** being criticized. This is how you will find truth among the quills of the porcupine. It is the ability to focus on the truth of what is being said and not on the "WAY" it is packaged. There often exists in the unkind, hurtful, or even hostile words of a toxic personality gems of truth. These gems could assist you in becoming a better you. *Warning! Warning! Warning!* This approach of dealing with a difficult to love person is not for everyone. Like the warning label on dangerous products: *This could be hazardous to your emotional health.*

When does a toxin become harmful? Only when you take it into your system. If you do not introduce the poison into your body or mind it cannot hurt you. In laboratories one often finds a centrifuge. It is a rotary machine which spins at high speeds and separates items according to their different densities. Imagine having the mental and emotional skills of a centrifuge. What a fantastic accomplishment it is to have the ability to separate the truth from error regardless of the source, the delivery system, or the intent of the giver of criticism.

How valuable this trait would be to an employer. Imagine a work environment where the boss could sort through the complaints of the employees and find the nugget of truth that would improve the company and add to the bottom line. Instead of mere lip service and surrounding himself with "yes men," a boss who honestly evaluated the merits of a criticism would be a rare and precious find. Most employees are fearful of bringing legitimate criticisms to an employer for fear of being perceived as a complainer, incapable of problem solving on his own, or of being fired. There is plenty of historical evidence of the bearer of bad tidings being killed. The concern of job loss because of a fear of "Kill the Messenger" may account for the failure of many businesses. Untold millions of dollars in lost revenue can be attributed to the fear of employees to bring the truth to the boss.

What about an employee who had the ability to separate an issue from his ego? What if instead of complaining to the co-workers about what a jerk the boss is, defending himself to friends and family, or seeking refuge in a pity-party, the employee honestly evaluated the criticism from the boss and found a nugget of truth in it? What if the employee then acted upon the information for the best interest of the business. How valuable would that employee be to the corporation?

In interpersonal family relationships it is even more difficult to develop the skill of separating your ego from the issue. This is due to the value placed upon caring words in the family structure. Uncaring and critical words are harder to deal with when they come from loved ones.

How do we accomplish this incredibly difficult task of mentally and emotionally separating our ego from the issue or behavior? It requires a paradigm shift. It requires a new way of looking at things, a new mind set, and an uncompromising focus on two fundamental objectives.

MIND FOCUS NUMBER ONE:
I WILL SEEK UNDER ALL CIRCUMSTANCES
TO BECOME MY HEALTHIEST AND BEST SELF

When becoming our healthiest and best selves is the prime objective, it subordinates all other considerations. Pleasing others, being approved of, being well liked, wanting validation, or desiring appreciation are all examples of conflicting expectations. These aspirations may be appropriate for other occasions, but not while being criticized. While you are being criticized, the number one value, "I will seek, under all circumstances, to become my healthiest and best self," must dominate.

There may be a thin line between tolerating verbal abuse and seeking the truth amidst harsh and unkind words. No one is suggesting that anyone needs to tolerate the intolerable. However, most people are not capable or willing to listen to any criticism, no matter how valid it may be. Some interpret any and all criticism as abuse. That becomes a convenient way for them to avoid any responsibility for changing. By blaming the approach, they discount the truth of the message. When the focus is on the messenger and not the message, they successfully dodge the issue or behavior in question. The truth is held hostage to the imperfect delivery system. Now the fault is with "how" the message was given, not on the truth of the message. This common ploy is counterproductive to a person becoming their healthiest and best self.

KATIE'S OVERSPENDING

Kyle was frustrated with Katie's spending habits. She could never stay in line with the budget. Even though they had this conversation many times, she would still impulsively over-buy. It was not a matter of the budget being unrealistic. Kyle had increased his work efforts and increased the budget several times. He was discouraged and felt helpless. Any criticism of her spending habits were reacted to with tears, harsh words, and emotional separation that would last for days.

Kyle was being held hostage to Katie's inability to act in a responsible manner. There was no right way for him to handle it because she labeled every approach as unkind. The focus was always on his way of addressing the problem, not on the problem.

Only when she accepted responsibility for becoming her healthiest and best self could her spending behaviors be examined.

MIND FOCUS NUMBER TWO:
I WILL DO EVERYTHING IN MY POWER TO HELP THIS
RELATIONSHIP BECOME ITS HEALTHIEST AND BEST

Recognizing that a person is only one-half of any relationship is reality. Approaching the other half of a relationship with critical information designed to improve the relationship is an art. It is also a wish. If both parties to a relationship have as their shared common value "to do everything in their power to help the relationship become its healthiest and best," then criticism can be received. If not, self-worth will be the focus, not an improved relationship.

A KEY TO RECEIVING CRITICISM

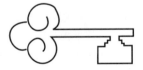

Once a person is committed to these two "mind focused" principles of self-improvement and changing self to improve the relationship, he or she is on their way to be able to find truth among the porcupine quills. A KEY TO RECEIVING CRITICISM IS TO TELL OTHERS *HOW* TO APPROACH YOU WITH A NEGATIVE MESSAGE, AND MEAN IT.

TIM AND JEANNE

When Tim and Jeanne first came to my office they were a frustrated couple. It was obvious they loved one another. Their ability to focus on loving behaviors had become lost in a war of words and defensive reactions. Both were "on guard" and ready to pounce on the other at the slightest hint of not being acceptable to the other.

I asked them what happened to the love that brought them together. The answer was all too familiar. It had been swallowed up in a sea of troubled words. Criticism of each other had created a distance. Defensive posturing replaced positive interaction. Fault finding, nit-picking, and sarcasm were the main content of their exchanges.

I told them there was a way love could be again enthroned as the governing principle in their relationship and asked if they would be willing to try. They responded in the affirmative. I asked them to focus on becoming their highest and best self and not on changing the other party. For one week they were to act in loving ways and eliminate all criticism from their vocabulary. Instead, they were to focus only on individual programs of self-improvement. They were to spend that first week on loving behaviors one toward another.

The assignment for the second week was to talk to three members of the family, in-laws, or friends (not the spouse) and tell them they were on a self-improvement program and they would like to know from them their honest views of what they could do to improve. They were to set up an appointment and show up with a writing pad and pen. They were not to comment on the remarks made about their needed improvement. After they were finished writing down the statements, they were to feed them back without emotion, thank the person for their input, and leave.

The next part of the assignment involved going to a

292

solitary place and honestly evaluating the criticism. They were to ask themselves, "Would making this change truly help me become my healthiest and best self?"

After they had evaluated each recommended change, they were to take a personal inventory of time, commitment, and resources necessary to make such a change. Did they possess the time, the will, or the energy to make the changes? After the inventory was reviewed, they were to make a plan complete with specific behavioral objectives. For example, all three people Tim talked to said he should lose some weight and exercise. Tim decided he would enroll in a weight-loss class and also begin a walking program three days a week. Jeanne was told by several people that her yelling and criticisms were areas of needed improvement. She cried at first because she knew it was true. They set up a regular time each day to review her frustrations and determined to practice "Dr Lund's Art of Giving Criticism."

They came to my office with their personal improvement programs and shared them with each other. I could not emphasize strongly enough the importance of their being supportive of the other without taking over a parent role. They were to be cheerleaders but not coaches. It was a relationship of equals. They were to give no criticism whatsoever to each other.

A very important part of this assignment happened during the third week. Each was to give the other person a way to approach them with negative information. In their quest to become their healthiest and best selves, it was their individual responsibility to provide the manual on "How To Approach Me." We explored several options.

In any serious self-improvement program we must accept the responsibility to let others know how to approach us.

HOW WOULD YOU LIKE ME TO
APPROACH YOU WITH CRITICISM?

1. Would you prefer a written note saying "I would like to talk to you about something critical?"
2. Would you prefer a phone call?
3. Would you prefer the direct verbal approach?

How do you want me to begin the actual criticism?

1. Should I tell you at least one positive thing about you first?
2. Should I bring one healthy option with each criticism?
3. Should I just say it directly?
4. Should I write it down?

Because it was distracting and difficult to deal with Jeanne's facial expression, body language, and verbal intensity, Tim decided he would like her to give him a note, identify the area of concern, and tell him whether it would be "painful or not." He also wanted to know how upset she was about it. They decided Jeanne would use the Richter Scale of 1–10 which is used to measure earthquakes. Painful was anything over 5. Then, he wanted time to prepare himself.

I asked Jeanne to give me an example of how she could now approach Tim with critical information. She wrote Tim the following note:

> Dear Tim,
>   I'm frustrated about the mess you left in the garage when you were fixing the lawn mower. Would you please clean it up? It's a "4" on the Richter Scale
>   Love, Jeanne

It was fairly easy for Tim to decide how he wanted to receive criticism, but Jeanne struggled with defining a way to be approached with the negative. Being blamed for anything was hard for Jeanne. In addition she was fearful of Tim's anger because it reminded her of her own toxic father. Finally, she decided that if Tim would be in emotional control and not be angry, she would prefer the direct verbal approach by saying, in a respectful way, "We need to talk."

This would clue her in and she agreed she would find time within fifteen minutes to let him express his concern. Tim would not have to bring a positive option or tell her one nice thing before the bad. He could just say it.

I asked Tim if he could give me an example of how he would approach Jeanne. He said, "Jeanne, honey, we need to talk."

Jeanne responded, "Now is okay."

Tim said, "I would really appreciate it if you would not contradict me in front of the children."

Jeanne's first response was to defend her statements. I explained that was inappropriate. The objective was to agree upon an approach to being criticized. The next goal was to make sure Jeanne understood the criticism.

"Before you respond, acknowledge his concern and ask him if he is prepared to discuss it."

During the fourth week they were to practice receiving criticism from each other by following "Dr. Lund's Quick Check Guide to the Art of Receiving Criticism." The entire fourth week they were to keep the focus on logically explaining their concerns. They were to avoid emotional outbursts.

The real test would come in the following month. They were to practice dealing with uninvited criticism from any source by writing it down and evaluating it without the traditional emotional reactions they were used to. When they returned, Tim was doing well and feeling better. Jeanne was somewhat depressed. She had come to realize that she had adopted so many negative attitudes she had become a toxic person. Originally, Tim was just as critical as she was because he bought into the negativity. Now, Tim was a new man. He wrote down all of Jeanne's criticisms and honestly evaluated them. Their relationship improved considerably because Tim was a healthier person. Jeanne was less negative and aware of her critical disposition. She yelled less, and criticized less because she recognized the behavior as dysfunctional. Old habits die hard. Jeanne's change was not as immediate as Tim's. She was emerging from a world long governed by negative emotion. It would take time to overcome.

There are many porcupines who are less harmful, but nonetheless highly critical and impossible to please. How do we find truth among the quills of these less toxic porcupines? This is where the Art of Receiving Criticism has it's greatest application. There are many relationships where it is not all bad or all good. The quality of these relationships would improve significantly if one, or both, could master the skill of finding golden nuggets of truth for self-improvement among the quills of criticism.

CHAPTER SEVENTEEN

RETHINKING THE DIRECTION OF OUR LIVES

Most of us are faced with several toxic people during the course of our lives. Sometimes we find that we have adopted toxic behaviors and have become noxious ourselves. For those of us who decide we don't want to be toxic anymore or for those of us who have to interact with toxic people, it is time to rethink the direction of our lives.

Reality has taught us there are only two constructive things we can do with the past. First, we can learn from it, and second, we can forgive ourselves and others and move on. We cannot change the past. However, we can take charge of our todays and our tomorrows.

I'VE GIVEN HIM ALL OF ME
HE IS EVER GOING TO HAVE

Every face tells a story. So it was with Carol's face. Only her's was the scarred face of a blind woman. How she became blind and scarred and how she overcame great adversity is a story of tragedy and true heroism.

Carol had been stalked for days by a rapist who had randomly picked her out of a crowd. One day, when Carol came out of a supermarket with her two little girls in a shopping basket and a bag of groceries, the man knocked her unconscious. He had parked his car next to hers. When she bent over to pick up one of the children he attacked. She was thrown in the back seat of his car. He drove off, leaving the two little girls crying for their mommy.

When Carol awoke in a motel room, her hands were tied and duct tape was over her mouth. Suffice it to say, she was raped and brutalized. Fearing she would identify him, the man stabbed her and left her for dead. Later that night he returned to dispose of the body. Carol wasn't dead, though she had lost a lot of blood and was wounded.

The rapist-murderer wrapped her in the shower curtain and as he began to move the body, she moaned. He realized that she was still alive and immediately put a gun to her head and fired. The bullet took out both of her eyes and the bridge of her nose. The sound of the gunshot brought a man from the next room. He struggled with the assailant but the rapist fled. He was caught and convicted. He served seven years and is out on the streets today. But what of Carol? She survived and is alive today. Her husband left her because he could not handle the responsibility. He was a coward, a quitter, and abandoned his family.

The road to recovery for Carol was a long and hard one. Today she shares her story of overcoming adversity and learning to forgive with others, many of whom are also victims of man's inhumanity to man. Invariably, she is asked how much time she spends thinking about him and the fact that he is free and she is blind. Her answer is amazingly insightful and profound:

> *"I've given him all of me that he is ever going to have. I'm certainly not going to give him my todays and my tomorrows."*

When she is asked how she deals with the injustice of it all, she responds,

"I've done the worst thing any person could ever do to a man like him. I've forgiven him and turned him over to God. I've taken charge of the life and the opportunities that are mine. I'm moving ahead with my life. God will deal with him."

Carol's story is one of true courage and inspiration. Each of us should pause and reflect on the importance of learning from the past and forgiving ourselves and others. After all, how many of our todays and of our tomorrows do we want to give our yesterdays? It is one thing to be victimized by another. It is quite another to victimize ourselves because we cannot learn from the past or forgive. Those who choose to live in the past, to live in the land of regret and complaint, do so at the sacrifice of their todays and their tomorrows.

Choosing to live life as a loving person is a choice few regret. It is much more common to regret our "nonloving" behaviors. We can, however, learn from our regrets. We can determine to be more loving and appreciative of all our existing relationships. This is what is meant by learning from the past.

MAY YOU ALWAYS WALK
WITH LOVE IN YOUR HEART

One of the great regrets of my life is not being able to go back and love my Native American grandmother. She was a perfect example of one who loved and never criticized. She ignored racial slurs. She simply didn't allow people to offend her. Her name was Emma. She was born on the Chehalis Indian Reservation in the State of Washington and spoke English with a broken accent.

I was eleven months old when Pearl Harbor was attacked on December 7, 1941. With many others, my father joined the Navy to redress the wrong of the "day that will live in infamy." My mother joined the work force, as many women did, to support the troops and to run the factories. She worked as a telephone operator throughout the war. There were many days she would work twelve hours.

As an only child I was cared for by my Indian grandmother. It was her golden brown, oval face I would see all day long until my mother came home. She called me "Jon-né." With myself, my father, and my grandfather named John, each was given a slightly different version of the name. I was "Jon-né" to her; the rest of the family called me "Lou." She would say, "Oh Jon-né, it good to see you." Her words were choppy; her love was not. She was always glad to see her grandson. I was her first.

The war finally came to a close. Hitler was dead and the Japanese signed an unconditional surrender on board the USS Missouri, the "Mighty Mo."

All during those war years I remember my mother and grandmother saying, "When the war is over, your father will come home." I was six when I remember seeing my father for the first time. He was dressed in his Navy Blues with bell bottom trousers and a collar with three white lines that went over his shoulders. He was wearing a white cap and spit-polished black shoes.

Because there was a shortage of houses for all the returning servicemen, my father, mother, and I lived in my Indian grandmother's house. It took my father a year to remodel our future home before I left my Grandma Em's place in Tumwater, Washington.

Something else happened at that time. I became aware that everyone didn't have an Indian Grandma. I became judgmental and unloving. People made fun of the way she talked. My schoolmates started to call me "Tonto." To top it off, my wild grandmother had divorced my grandfather and drank "firewater." (I told my children in later years that to be kissed by Grandma was an "intoxicating" experience.)

Notwithstanding her weaknesses, my Indian Grandmother really was a wonderful person. My mother said she never heard her speak ill or criticize anyone, not ever. Frequently my father would say, "Your grandmother misses you, Son, she asks for you all the time. Let's go over and see her." But, I was embarrassed by her. I judged her unworthy of my love. The five mile trips became fewer and fewer between our place in Lacey and Grandma's in Tumwater. I stayed away. I was always "too busy" with my friends. I made excuses and finally Dad stopped asking.

When I was nineteen, I was about to embark on a great adventure to Mexico. I remember my father saying something about Grandma Em's heart. Under duress, I went to see this loving and caring woman. When she saw me her whole countenance changed. "Oh, Jon-né, come, give hug."

After a forever hug and an "intoxicating kiss," we sat and talked about my life. "Before you go," she told me, "I give you a blessing."

She took hold of both my hands and looked deep into my soul. Then she said ten things which I should have written down, but didn't. I remember they all started with "May you always..." They had to do with the wind, the fire, the water and the earth. I only recall the first one:

"May you always walk with love in your heart."

I left for my great adventure and received word she had died of a heart attack a couple of weeks after I was in Mexico. After Mexico, I returned home, went to college, married, and became invested in education. After a Bachelor's Degree in Sociology, two Master's and a Doctorate in Interaction Analysis, I became profoundly interested in my heritage. It became an obsession. I was especially interested in the life of my Indian Grandmother. As a youth I had learned of a child born to her out of wedlock. The child was my Uncle Hank. Who was this woman who loved me and raised me as a child? Her life seemed to be less than exemplary. And yet I remembered the love she had for me.

By this time, my father had been killed in an auto accident. Grandma Em was survived only by her younger sister, Aunt Mildred. Everyone called her Millie. She was old and very wrinkled. Her eyes were bad. When she saw me, she thought I was my father who was called "Johnnie Jump Up" after a local flower. When I explained who I was, she said, "Oh Jon-né!" It was as if I heard the voice of my Grandmother again.

We talked for hours. Finally, I took both of her hands in mine, just like my grandmother did with me when I was nineteen. I said, "Millie, you have to tell me the truth about my Grandmother." She paused a long time and finally told me the whole story.

My Indian Grandmother had been violated on the reservation when she was fourteen years old. It was a traumatic experience in itself. She was rejected by the tribe, so she moved to Elma, Washington. Here too, a fourteen-year-old Indian girl with a white child was rejected. However, the consequences were overwhelming to a child-woman. It was more than a young girl could bear. She was rejected by both her people on the reservation and those who lived outside. She was very young, shunned, and alone. She kept the baby, and named him Hank. She started to drink after the rape and